T0258788

Project Management in Small and Medium-Sized Enterprises

The growing importance of projects in organizations, combined with difficulties in their implementation, is accompanied by the need for professional knowledge in the field of project management. It results from the complexity of project management problems and the difficulty of knowledge that must be applied. However, surprisingly little is known about this topic, especially in the context of European small and medium-sized enterprises (SMEs). **Project Management in Small and Medium-Sized Enterprises: A European Perspective** attempts to fill this specific research gap.

The book analyses the process of managing projects being implemented by small and medium-sized firms from Europe, identifies organizational processes, and verifies which elements of these processes require improvement. It concentrates on issues around the multifaceted characteristics of project management, with particular emphasis on the process of managing European small and medium enterprises.

The book is the result of many years of empirical research and consists of two main parts:

- A systematization of concepts, terminology, and thus knowledge in the field of project management, with particular emphasis on the phases of planning, organizing, as well as leading and controlling in the project, as well as small and medium-sized enterprises, with particular emphasis on their specificity and role in the modern European economy
- Verification and development of such model procedures in the management of projects so that the SME enterprises' functioning will be efficient and effective

There is a close relationship between the two parts. The theoretical part is the foundation on which practical considerations are later carried out. Integrating theoretical and practical issues, the book introduces new content to the literature and has the practical value of indicating how to manage projects in SMEs in the European Union. It also examines the decision-making processes related to project management in these organizations.

Anna Brzozowska is an associate professor of economics, in the discipline of management studies. Currently, she works in the Department of Logistics, Faculty of Management, at Częstochowa University of Technology, Częstochowa, Poland. She is the author of over 230 publications. She is also a scientific committee member of the *Economics, Management and Sustainability Scientific Journal*.

Wojciech Dyduch is currently the chairman of the College of Management and the head of the Department of Entrepreneurship at the University of Economics in Katowice, Poland. He is also a member of the Council of Scientific Excellence and the chairman of the Committee of Organization and Management Sciences.

Aleksander Pabian graduated from the Faculty of Management of the Częstochowa University of Technology in the field of Management and Marketing, as well as from the Academy of Young Diplomats with a specialization in Foreign Service. He holds the position of assistant professor at the Częstochowa University of Technology, Częstochowa, Poland.

Agnieszka Dziedzic is CEO of Eduexpert Spółka, Toruń, Poland. She holds a doctoral degree in management and quality sciences from the Częstochowa University of Technology, Częstochowa, Poland.

Project Management in Small and Medium-Sized Enterprises
A European Perspective

Anna Brzozowska
Wojciech Dyduch
Aleksander Pabian
Agnieszka Dziedzic

CRC Press
Taylor & Francis Group
Boca Raton London New York

CRC Press is an imprint of the
Taylor & Francis Group, an **informa** business
AN AUERBACH BOOK

First edition published 2024
by CRC Press
2385 Executive Center Drive, Suite 320, Boca Raton, FL 33431

and by CRC Press
4 Park Square, Milton Park, Abingdon, Oxon, OX14 4RN

CRC Press is an imprint of Taylor & Francis Group, LLC

© 2024 Taylor & Francis Group, LLC

ISBN: 978-1-032-31470-9 (hbk)
ISBN: 978-1-032-31471-6 (pbk)
ISBN: 978-1-003-30990-1 (ebk)

DOI: 10.1201/9781003309901

Typeset in Minion
by SPi Technologies India Pvt Ltd (Straive)

Contents

List of Figures

List of Tables

Introduction

The survival, and even more so, the success of each enterprise depends, among others, on the ability to obtain and ensure durable competitive advantage (Kachniewska, 2009, p. 7). Obtaining it was indicated at the beginning of the science of organization and management studies as a necessary condition for companies developing a strategy for their activities.

As a result of the search for sources of a stronger position in relation to competitors, new models of competitive advantage were created, and ensuring its durability was also considered. Attention was focused mainly to the position of the company in the sector, and it was argued that through proper product positioning[1] and/or achieving a dominant position in terms of costs, the company will be able to achieve greater added value than that achieved by the competition.

Over time, the so far leading concept of creating a competitive advantage by achieving a dominant position in the sector turned out to be insufficient in the new economic and managerial reality.

> The erosion of sector boundaries under the influence of innovation, internationalization and globalization of competition, and the fragmentation of markets (resulting from changes in the nature and structure of demand), meant that in the 1990s the position occupied by a company in the sector was no longer perceived as a source of its competitive advantage
>
> *(Szymura-Tyc, http://www.zti.com.pl/instytut/pp/referaty/ref4_full.html, reading: 12.10.2022)*

Attention was shifted to the resources at the disposal of the company (physical and those that do not have a tangible form) as the basis for building and maintaining an advantage (the so-called resource school).

> The fundamental premise of this school was that in order to understand the sources of an organization's success, one must understand the configuration of its unique resources and skills.
>
> *(Penc-Pietrzak, 1998, p. 17)*

The ability to acquire and use resources was considered in terms of key competences[2] characteristic of a given company, those that are difficult to copy or obtain by competitors. Researchers representing the Resource Based View, such as, among others, R. Barney, G. Hamel, C. K. Prahalad, T. Peters, or W. Ouchi, recognized competencies as decisive for the competitive advantage of an enterprise to a much greater extent than the position occupied by it within the sector.

At the same time, it was increasingly emphasized that the ultimate challenge to which companies' resources and competences must be subjected is their ability to generate additional value for potential customers (Szymura-Tyc, http://www.zti.com.pl/instytut/pp/referaty/ref4_full.html, reading: 25.10.2022). Increased pressure from the socio-economic environment (including the impact of stakeholders) and intensified competition, e.g. as a result of globalization, led to a change in the structure and hierarchy of the company's business goals, and above all to treating profit as the basic condition for their implementation, and not the superior goal.

The belief that it is necessary to take actions that will lead to offering the customer an excess of benefits[3] becomes universally applicable as a determinant of activities undertaken by theoreticians and practitioners of management. Over the years, researchers have come to the conclusion that the management process should in fact be subordinated to the interests of the groups in the environment.

As before, the need to satisfy the owners (shareholders), i.e. the group of stakeholders that invests in the enterprise, is primarily assumed. It is assumed that profit remains the subject of their interest, but it is possible to earn it only if the company has the ability to sell its products (Kachniewska, 2009, p. 12). At the same time, it is the customers who have the choice, and hence the only possibility of making a profit for the company is the ability to provide buyers with a greater sum of value than it would result from a simple calculation of individual values of the offer.

In management literature there are studies devoted to the issue of the relationship between the value for the customer and the company outcomes. This problem is being approached in a theoretical convention or through quantitative research. Certain paradigms are adopted in this perspective, for example, that value for the customer is created in the process of using the purchased product or service and that it is the basis for the perceived satisfaction in connection with the purchase and the usage of the product. It is also assumed that value for the customer is essentially a subjective assessment of benefits and costs perceived by the customer, made by them after the purchase and use of the product. The customer obtains it if the subjectively achieved benefits are greater than the subjectively perceived costs.[4]

Some researchers are of the opinion that the value for the customer can be written in the form of an equation. This value consists of quality indicator × quality indicator weight + price indicator × price indicator weight (Brilman, 2002, p. 95). However, this approach seems insufficient as it describes the value for the customer in terms of a specific relationship resulting from the reference to each other of only two basic categories of variables: price and quality. Meanwhile, it is often not possible to identify all the benefits and costs that make up the value for the customer. Achieving them is usually a long-term process. However, this is how a competitive advantage is built, the image of the company and its place on the market are created.

At the same time, it is a fact that contemporary enterprises, striving to provide customers with surplus value, undertake various types of projects. Projects are complex tools for shaping the future of enterprises. As consumer expectations are changing, quality and affordability, or even added value combined with customer service,[5] to-date are not sufficient factors these days.

We are currently observing a growing pressure on enterprises, which affects costs and firm performance. Customers demand more and more from companies, also from the small and medium-sized ones, and meeting these requirements is often not possible without proper, diligent and precise project implementation: "the success of the company is increasingly connected with the implementation of projects" (Cron et al., 2010, p. 15). Increasing customer requirements make companies try to improve their practices by implementing projects, whose goal is in facto one – to make the customer feel the surplus of value and, as a consequence, stay loyal with the company for longer. At the same time, the companies need to pay attention to their performance and competitive advantage. There is a certain tension growing between stakeholder needs (value for customers) and shareholder needs (value for organization).

The implementation of projects is a major challenge for most companies. Effective implementation of project, consisting in delivering the desired project result at a certain quality level, on time and within the assumed budget is a difficult task. The project is usually a very complex undertaking, which requires the use of an appropriate management methods, complementary resources, adequately designed structures, correlating technology, technical tools and knowledge, as well as people with necessary skills and competences. The task of contemporary management is to link all of these elements and use its contingency for a given project. Lack of proper combination leads to failures in the implementation of projects which is still a significant problem, e.g. resource-wise and deadline-wise. It remains a challenge for the future project management.

Practically, any project can fail. And that's what happens in many of the projects in small and medium-sized enterprises. Practically any project can fail. And that's what happens in most projects. For years, there has been a significant share of projects that are finishing with partial success or even failure If carrying out a project was a simple and predictable task, the project itself would probably become a process, and the project manager would no longer be needed. Meanwhile, over the last several years, the profession of project manager has been steadily gaining in importance, on a scale of individual countries (according to the research of the international personnel consulting company Manpower, the profession of project manager is one of the most sought-after professions in Poland, ahead of trade, engineering, financial and banking professions (Trocki, 2015, p. 10)), Europe, and the whole world. Forbes experts estimate that the project manager will be one of the top ten professions in the world in the forthcoming years.

The growing importance of projects in organizations, combined with challenges in their implementation, is accompanied by the need for professional knowledge in the field of comprehensive project management. It results from the complexity of projects, managerial skills sometimes lacking in times of uncertainty, unexpected problems, as well as the difficulty of know-how that must be applied. Meanwhile, many of the books on project management, which have been published so far are suggestive, interesting and inspiring. Some of them offer conceptual frameworks for project management. However, they usually consist of case studies deriving from business practice, or present universally accepted project management methodologies rather than results of exploratory research supported by a solid theoretical foundation. Increasing use of the term "projects" and reflecting on their management has created a sense of unity and progress in this area.

Although there are numerous and noteworthy publications in the subdiscipline of project management, still surprisingly little is known about this processes and mechanisms present in this area, especially in the European context. Hence, in terms of a specific research gap, one should consider the insufficient number of systematic literature reviews in this field and the absence of extensive analyses. A shortage of sources of knowledge on project management in European context may disturb many entrepreneurs, investors and institutions interested in this field. Some of the target audience can limit their intentions to a large extent on gut feeling, common sense, intuition, or sources that do not offer a comprehensive image of the project management in the European SMEs. The authors decided to try to somehow fill up the specific, identified gap by preparing this book. At the same time, they focus their attention on small and medium-sized enterprises (SMEs) since they undoubtedly play a very important role in the market economy of the European Union.

> Small and medium-sized enterprises (SMEs) play an important role in the economy of every country. One can say that they are the basis of all modern European economies. These enterprises stimulate economic growth by e.g. activating innovative processes and generating new jobs.
>
> *(Solinska, Iwaszczuk, 2008, p. 1)*

The perspectives presented in this book will allow us not only to analyse the process of managing projects being implemented by small and medium-sized firms in Europe but also to identify organizational processes and verify which elements of these processes require improvement. Therefore, the authors concentrate the topics presented in the book around the multifaceted characteristics of project management, with particular emphasis on the process of managing European small and medium enterprises. It seems that the subject of project management has not yet been widely considered in such a context by other authors dealing with the subject.

The book is the result of many years of empirical research, which the authors intensified between the years 2021 and 2022. The book consists of two main theoretical parts based on in-depth, systematic review of the literature. The first part of the book comprises the following:

- systematization of concepts, terminology, and thus knowledge in the field of project management, with particular emphasis on the phases of planning and organizing, as well as leading and controlling the project, as well as SMEs, with particular emphasis on their specificity and role in the modern European economy as well as empirical, presenting the results of our own research carried out in enterprises.

The second part includes verification and development of such the project management model procedures in the management of projects so that the SME enterprises' functioning will be efficient and effective) oriented towards higher firm performance of SMEs.

There is a close relationship between the two parts. The theoretical part takes a form of foundation on which practical considerations are later carried out. The structure of the work consists of nine parts that make up a coherent and uniform entirety: introduction, four chapters, conclusion, bibliography, and lists of tables and figures.

The order and content of the chapters correspond to the logic of the carried out research process, which was undertaken to lead to the hypotheses' proving. Among the most important features of this book, the following can be mentioned:

- it integrates theoretical and practical issues;
- it introduces new content to the literature on the subject;
- it discusses to-date publications, addressing some of their conclusions ;
- it has a practical value, indicates how to manage European Union (EU) projects in SMEs;
- it describes the views and beliefs of the authors, which are confirmed by the results of the conducted research;
- it helps to understand the dilemmas of decision-making processes in the aspect of project management in organizations; and
- it shows that the relevance of projects' management concept is open to exploration, conceptually and empirically in Europe.

Considering the aforementioned features, the list of recipients of this book is quite extensive. The primary audiences for the book are entrepreneurs of SMEs, scientists, decision-makers, European project contractors, managers in organizations, and expert bodies responsible for realizing and/or evaluating projects.

The book can also serve successfully as a textbook intended for masters students and PhD students in the following fields: management, entrepreneurship, and project management. This position will "enrich" the bibliographic portfolio, primarily of scientific but also academic items in the discipline of management science.

NOTES

1 It concerns the perception of the product by buyers. It consists in creating in the minds of the consumer the desired image of the product, distinguishing it from competing products (see more, Kąciak, 2011, p. 31; Falkowski, Tyszka, 2001, p. 86).
2 Competencies can be called assets or skills that allow the organization to operate, as well as the actions that the company can take with the appropriate use of its resources. Competences integrate capabilities, ensuring coordinated use of resources,

conditioning the achievement of goals set by the organization. A special type of them are key competences, defined as innovative combinations of knowledge, abilities (skills), and other resources, as a result of which a product of measurable value for the customer is delivered in accordance with his preferences and expectations (compare Flaszewska, Zakrzewska-Bielawska, 2013, p. 223).

3 The difference between the profit that he obtains after purchasing the product and the costs he incurs for its purchase (compare Smyczek, 2009, pp. 96–97).

4 Therefore, value for the customer is the excess of the benefits subjectively perceived by the customer over the subjectively perceived costs associated with the purchase and use of a given product (Szumilak 2007, p. 26).

5 The added value includes extra benefits for the customer related to, for example, having an additional function with which the product is equipped, its attractive design, packaging features (which can, for example, be further used for other purposes), and the possibility of gaining prestige, which relates to the fact of owning a product of a certain brand. On the cost side, this value may, in turn, be reduced by operating costs or non-financial outlays accompanying the possession of the product, e.g. irritation related to its use. In addition to the characteristics of the product, the way of perceiving the value is also influenced by service. Value extended by customer service is created primarily by those elements that precede, accompany, and immediately follow sales, i.e. consultancy, design, delivery, service, financial and commercial services. "Customer service accompanies a product (or service) throughout its entire lifecycle for the customer, providing a source of value by creating additional benefits for the customer and/or reducing the financial and non-financial costs associated with the purchase, use and disposal of the product" (compare Szumilak 2007, p. 27).

1

Projects in the Activities of European Enterprises

1.1 EXPLANATION OF THE CONCEPT AND THE ESSENCE OF THE PROJECT

The project is a collection of various partial works. It can be defined as a set of actions undertaken in order to achieve a specific goal and achieve a specific, measurable result. Often the result of the project is called the product of the project. Projects are tools for shaping the future. It is true that due to the implementation of them, progress in civilization has been made: both material (including the development of economic facilities, public goods, infrastructure, new products, etc.) and intangible – including new social and political concepts, new organizational solutions, services, cultural goods, etc. (Trocki, Wyrozębski, 2015, p. 7).

Although the very idea of a project has been known since the earliest times (the construction of Egyptian pyramids or the Chinese wall were, for example, projects), this concept cannot be still treated in terms of a uniform and strictly defined in economics and in the discipline of management sciences (Pietras & Szmit, 2003, p. 7).[1] This fact results mainly from the interdisciplinary nature of research on this issue (Sławińska, 2015, p. 158).

On the one hand, interdisciplinarity is still declaratively mentioned as one of the essential features of the modern way of doing science. On the other hand, however, such an approach is a source of specific problems, including, for example, those related to the unambiguous definition of the concepts introduced by the argument which assumes demarcation of science.

Scholars, however, agree on the etymology of the term "project". Etymology is the study of the history of words, their origins, and how their

DOI: 10.1201/9781003309901-1

form and meaning have changed over time (Braha, 2022, p. 2). Research on the history of words leads to remarkable insights about language and also, more generally, about the history of human civilization (de Melo, 2014, p. 1148). The origin of the term "project" can be traced back to the Medieval Latin word *projectum*, meaning: "something prominent". It is the noun use of the neuter of the Latin word *proiectus*, past participle of *proicere*, which means "stretch out or throw forth" (Figure 1.1).

Languages evolve and words undergo changes. In fact, it is nearly impossible to find a word in language that hasn't undergone any changes at all. Nowadays, the concept of project has evolved towards such definitions as the one proposed by the Project Management Institute (PMI). It says that a project in its fundamental sense should be viewed in terms of a temporary endeavour, undertaken in order to create a unique product or service (Cox, 2009, p. 5).

Expanding this definition a little, it can be said that a project is a sequence of defined in-time activities having a clear beginning and end, structured in terms of available resources and expected results. Such a set of activities or works is separated from the course of daily routine activities, carried out in parallel with it or with the entire delegation of the team to the project implementation (Łada, 2007, p. 37). It can be naturally concluded that activities defined in such a way are a part of the routine activities of almost every organization. However, there is also a very large group of organizations that implement their core operational activities through projects.

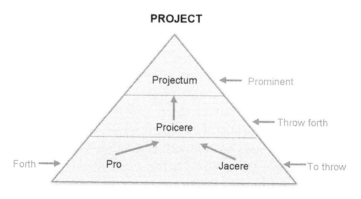

FIGURE 1.1
Etymology of the word "project".

Source: Own elaboration.

A slightly expanded definition of the term: project is provided by M. Bonikowska. According to the researcher, a project is an organized and timed sequence of many tasks aimed at achieving a measurable result, addressed to selected groups of recipients, requiring the involvement of limited human, material, and financial resources (Bonikowska, 2006, p. 52). Similarly, a project is an effort that involves a series of activities and resources, aimed to achieve a certain output, considering constraints like time, quality, and cost and which often introduces a change (Bahadur, https://www.researchgate.net/publication/340544935_Project_definition_Lifecycle_and_role_of_Project_Managers, reading: 15.05.2022).

J. R. Turner defined project as an endeavour "in which human (or machine), material and financial resources are organised in a novel way, to undertake a unique scope of work, or given specification, within constraints of cost and time, so as to deliver beneficial change by quantitative and qualitative objectives" (Rodney, 1998). In turn, according to the European Union's (EU) guidelines, a project is the definition of a logical set of activities leading to the achievement of a specific, measurable goal in a given time; defining a management structure with a clear division of responsibilities; planning a schedule and cost estimate; and monitoring and evaluation rules relating to the achievement of planned results (Jaruzalski, 2009, p. 55).

In the aforementioned definitions, the duration of the project is emphasized (defined and limited), as well as the fact that it has a precisely defined goal that serves as the assumed result. "Each project must have a measurable goal, for which a time frame can be defined and for which a specific person is responsible" (Figure 1.2; Ward, 1997, p. 86). The condition for the measurability of the goal is to include it in the quantitative category (e.g. sell several thousand watches in a limited package) or in the type category: yes or no (e.g. we have satisfied the customer/have not met his expectations).

FIGURE 1.2
Project as a means to achieve a goal.

Source: Elaboration based on Samset, 2003.

The definitions also indicate the group of beneficiaries – recipients of the project. The resources that must be allocated to its implementation are also mentioned. Other features of the project include (Marcinek, 2006, p. 16):

- the fact of being realized through human effort;
- singular, individual, and unique character, being a temporary arrangement, and also because the undertaking is more or less unique, uncertainty is often greater than in permanent ventures;
- dissimilarity, i.e. lack of connections with the traditional, routine activity of the enterprise;
- being carried out on a specific schedule and through activities interconnected with each other;
- the need to involve various types of resources; and
- the fact of being burdened with a high degree of difficulty and risk.

These features are an indispensable part of every project, but the presence of people as a group of participants in a specific project is equally important:

[T]he achievement by an organization of any goal is associated with team-work, not because there is no room for individualists, but because the complexity of most endeavours is often beyond the perception of one employee. Hence, there is a need for team implementation as well as management of projects. (Pietras & Szmit, 2003, p. 8) This perspective will be developed later.

Meanwhile, it can be also stated that some of the definitions include the meaning of project in the so-called narrower sense, others in a broader sense. Taking into account the first criterion, the definitions include project as an analytical and research work, the concept and functioning of the system, documentation,[2] and as an action plan or programme. On the other hand, in a broader sense, a project is understood as a model that improves a specific object and system. It can also constitute a base solution, which is a product with an innovative form and structure. This creation enables the implementation of the intended undertaking as an investment, operational, public task, etc. In broader terms, the components of the project are (Stabryła, 2006, p. 31):

- phased studies,
- models,
- technical documentation included in the programme, and
- material effects.

Thus the project, in its systemic (more extensive) approach, assumes that the activities carried out within it should be perceived as a form of transformation of outlays into results. Outlays should be understood as various types of resources, which can include human (Strużyna & Pyka, 2010, p. 409), material, financial, intellectual, organizational resources, etc. On the other hand, the results of the project are products or services constituting its output. The actual implementation of the project is possible by combining all possible resources, which include: knowledge, people, experience, capital, planning tools, and techniques. Only consistent functioning of the aforementioned resources will bring the effect expected by a given programme (Figure 1.3; Drobiak, 2008, p. 14).

At this point, it should be emphasized at this point that the concept of a project should not be equated solely with processes related to maintaining production or providing services. These processes are often continuous, which is why they are called operational activities. However, the project is a unique[3] undertaking, which in a direct sense is closely related to the implementation and maintenance of its individual stages and only indirectly ensures the maintenance of products or services.

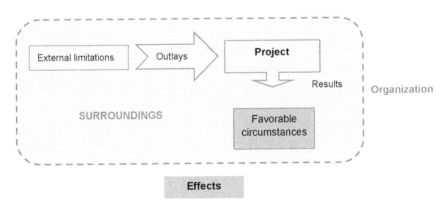

FIGURE 1.3
Project from the system perspective.

Source: Own elaboration based on Drobiak, 2008, p. 14.

Taking all of the previous reflections into consideration, it is possible to conclude that to put it simply, a project may be considered in the categories of a set of tasks that need to be completed to reach a specific goal. Its essence can also be interpreted as a set of inputs and outputs required to achieve a particular outcome. The project should also refer to a specific, well-defined group of final beneficiaries and respond to the identified needs of this group. It is believed that nowadays projects, especially those of an innovative nature, i.e. constituting a response to the challenges of modern times, going beyond the scope of projects previously undertaken by other companies (the authors write more on the types of projects in the next section) may constitute one of the key determinants of the development of enterprises that have to operate in the conditions of a turbulent environment and the development of modern technologies.

Projects currently constitute one of the key factors determining the success of an organization, as they often have an impact on socio-economic development, including, in particular, the level of competitiveness of enterprises. In order to develop dynamically and effectively, every company needs new design ventures. "Increase of the value of the organization and gaining a competitive advantage on the market" (Szymańska, 2012, p. 147) may be the effect of them. For this reason, many researchers see innovative programmes as the driving force of the modern economy, transforming ideas and knowledge into products and services (Krzepicka & Tarapata, 2012, p. 75).

Over the last decades, projects have become increasingly important as a way to organise work. "More than ever before, projects are used to solve big tasks [...]. They operate across organisations and are terminated when the planned task is completed. There has been a significant increase in the amount of [...] projects – not least in sectors such as offshore, infrastructure and information technology. But projects are also organised within individual organisations" (Samset, 2003).

However, this type of approach must be taken with a grain of salt and should be considered in an ambivalent manner. On the one hand, the path of development of modern civilization undoubtedly leads through the achievements of human ingenuity implemented in the form of different projects. Scientific authorities also quite clearly share a positive opinion on the importance of new project solutions. More than a quarter of a century has passed since the significant statement by C. Freeman, who said that not introducing new solutions by companies means for them to die (Block, 2018).

On the other hand, however, it must not be forgotten that in practice many sets of tasks to be completed do not end successfully, and the term "project" itself may not be characterized by the adjective "good" in every case. It is noted in the literature that in terms of the system approach, the project may have a positive, negative, or neutral impact, both on the organization involved in the implementation of the project, as well as on its environment.

Some projects, despite the right intentions of the people who develop them, may be associated with technical or organizational regression, cause losses within the economic or social reality, or may not benefit either the initiator of the project or other people around him. The practical experience of the authors of the book also shows that many undertakings may have a dark side and cause numerous negative side effects. Such projects should be described as not only ineffective but also unnecessary (Jasiński, 2006, p. 12). One of the main sources of this type of negative transformation is the adoption of a management model in which project activities distract the organization from its basic and current activities.

1.2 TYPES OF PROJECTS

When discussing the theoretical underpinnings of projects, one should refer to their classifications due to the non-identical criteria for division. It is because, nowadays projects are classified in various ways and different criteria are used in order to distinguish them. Currently, in the literature, many systematics of project divisions can be found. Their multitude means that the same project can often be included in more than one group, depending on the adopted criterion of division or perspective. When analysing individual types of projects, it is easy to see that the boundaries between them often blur, giving an ambiguous picture. Some changes to selected types of projects combine the features of different projects. Currently, relationships between them can be identified, and this is a consequence of the development of the theory and practice of project management.

First of all, project defined in the categories described in Subsection 1.1 and implemented on the scale of one enterprise may concern individual, specific areas of the company's operations (e.g. marketing, finance, production, or logistics). Depending on the area covered by the project, it can be defined in a non-identical way or even it is possible to identify features that distinguish it from other projects implemented in the enterprise. This is due to the fact that while the essence of the project is the same in every enterprise, one should always remember the specifics of a given venture.

For example, researchers interpret a logistics project as unique tasks, limited in time and financially, the implementation of which serves to improve the efficiency and effectiveness of product flows and accompanying information flows in enterprises, supply chains, or spatial systems (Witkowski & Rodawski, 2007). Taking into account the strategic goal that will be achieved through the implementation of the project, a logistic project is by them defined as a time-cost and organizationally separate project aimed at the implementation of a one-off and unique activity optimizing a specific logistic process (Biernat-Jarka, 2014, p. 3496).

Among the other features that distinguish a logistics project from other projects carried out in the company, they mention, among others, adopting the total cost of logistics as a decision-making criterion, the need to take into account cost factors (trade-offs) that show the relationship between the various spheres of logistics functioning, the necessity to define customer service parameters which on the one hand means improving customer service as a result of the project and, on the other hand, the possibility of the client influencing the project by all the time of its implementation, etc. (Biernat-Jarka, 2014, p. 3496).

It is also possible to make a list of the basic types of projects implemented in enterprises on the basis of the so-called subject division. According to it, the following types of projects can be distinguished (Kasperek, 2006, p. 10):

- projects aimed at product development;
- research, development, and mixed (both research and development – R + D);
- information technology (IT), which is aimed at creating an IT system, i.e. related elements such as software; hardware; human resources; and organizational elements, which together are designed to process data with the usage of computer technology (Snedaker & Hoenig, 2005, pp. 163–165);

- infrastructural in the field of construction and modernization of basic, physical equipment necessary for the functioning of the enterprise (Luger, 2008, p. 25);
- reorganizational ones, aimed at improving the functioning of the enterprise and minimizing the errors that occur;
- investment projects, interpreted as a set of investment tasks that are dependent on each other and jointly strive to achieve the goal of the investment project; and
- organized for the sake of product distribution, and so on.

The duration of the project may also be the criterion for the division. In this case, the following projects are distinguished:

- short-term (lasting conventionally from one month to one year),
- medium-term (over one year), and
- long-lasting. Usually, a project is treated as long term when its duration is ten years or more. In IT, however, a long-term project can last three to five years because short-term ones can last a couple of days or a couple of weeks.

Finally, projects can be differentiated according to the source of financing. Two basic types of them can be distinguished in this case:

1) Standard ones – financed either from the resources of the entity initiating the project or using repayable financing (borrowing funds from various institutions, including financial ones. Examples include a bank loan or leasing). This group also includes capitalized projects without the need to return cash contributions (e.g. financed from venture capital funds), as well as projects using hybrid financing methods that combine both previously indicated groups (e.g. crowdfunding – social financing) (Wanicki, 2017, p. 359).
2) EU constitutes a separate group analysed in the context of broadly understood project management. Such projects are financed or co-financed from EU funds, implemented in accordance with the EU methodology of project cycle management, and their task is to support the economic development of the Member States (Domiter & Marciszewska, 2013, p. 42; Tkaczyński, Świstak & Sztorc, 2011, p. 21). Several facts reaffirm the distinctiveness of the projects financed in this way from traditionally understood

(Trocki & Grucza, 2007, p. 15)

- They involve enormous resources and are implemented in very large numbers.
- Their participants often come from different backgrounds, have different education and professional experience, and represent entities with different organizational cultures.[4] Some of them often come into contact with management in general for the first time (and with project management in particular).
- Such projects are subject to common European rules and regulations, which unfortunately are often very bureaucratic.
- Should be always innovative (solve a matter in a new way compared to the methods used previously), as well as measurable (objectives of the project should have clear, measurable, and quantifiable results. What is more, also any previous analyses concerning the needs to be solved should be also based on tedious collection and analysis of quantifiable and measurable data).

Apart from the aforementioned, many other criteria for the division of projects can also be presented (they are listed in Table 1.1).

Although it has not been mentioned in Table 1.1, one of the divisions of projects classifies them according to their degree of modernity. As it was mentioned previously (in Section 1.2), within this arrangement, one can distinguish between innovative and traditional projects. The latter of them are created in a traditional way, i.e. they follow a previously proven path and/or refer to a specific pattern, e.g. another project arranged at earlier stages of the company's organizational development. They can also refer to good practices implemented in other organizations.

Enterprises implementing such projects limit themselves to quick adaptation and do not have the time, need, or ambition to formulate plans with solutions significantly deviating from the standard ones. They rather derive from the foundations of the concept of benchmarking, otherwise known as creative imitation. In its fundamental meaning, it consists of modelling previously encountered actions and practices that have achieved the intended effect.

On the contrary, a project can also take the form of an overtaking, i.e. be creative, new, entirely in-house developed without looking at the others. It may assume unconventional ways of proceeding, the usage of previously unprecedented practices, and the introduction to the use of new things and ideas previously considered unheard of (both by the people arranging the project and its later implementers).

TABLE 1.1

Types of Projects Due to Specific Criteria

Criterion for Differentiation	Types of Projects	Projects' Characteristics
Scale	Small and big	Projects may vary in scale depending on the amount of involved funds and human resources necessary for their implementation. In this sense, projects can be large, such as the construction of a tunnel under La Manche Channel, or small, such as the computerization of a single office workstation.
Number and type of entities participating in a project	Individual and team projects	In this case, it is possible to distinguish an individual project (whose creator is a single natural person) and team projects – developed and implemented by a group of natural persons or legal persons (institutional entities, e.g. enterprises).
The nature of the impact of the project on the organization – the significance of the effects of the projects for the implementing entity	Strategic, tactic and operational	Strategic projects have a wide scale of impact and relate to long-term undertakings of strategic importance for the organization. They affect not only individual departments but the entire company and its supply chains. They are usually long term in their nature – some of such projects may last for years. In contrast, operational projects are short, run on a day-to-day basis, and relate to current activities. An example of such a project may be, for example, supplementing the IT infrastructure (software) for the needs of office work. On the other hand, the tactical ones are focused on all kinds of temporary changes in such areas as, for example, the technology used, production methods, or organization methods. The aim of such, less significant than strategic, projects is to increase the effectiveness of the functioning of selected functional areas of the organization in order to better meet the needs of customers. They have a slightly wider range than the operational ones because they affect both time and space – their range goes beyond routine activities.

(Continued)

TABLE 1.1 (CONTINUED)

Types of Projects Due to Specific Criteria

Criterion for Differentiation	Types of Projects	Projects' Characteristics
Impact on the economy	Microeconomic and macroeconomic	The microeconomic project concerns the operational technical base of individual enterprises. It is used to acquire, modify, and improve exclusive resources owned by the enterprise necessary for the performance of its activity. The macroeconomic project contributes to the development of equipment necessary for the proper functioning and development of the whole economy, as well as creates a basis for the functioning of many enterprises in this economy, affecting their development.
The importance of the project in shaping the new order	Breakthroughs, modifications, and recombining projects	Some of the transformations resulting from the project are not very visible; for example, they relate to a specific field or sector only. On the other hand, it also happens that the degree of the project's radicalism leads to far-reaching transformations within the social reality. This can be exemplified by the project of placing GPS satellite blocks, which forever changed, among others, common ways of determining the position in the field. Thanks to such (breakthrough) projects, it is usually possible to overcome a specific barrier that until the project seemed impossible to overcome (e.g. navigating in the field without a traditional map). However, such projects are possible thanks to the usage of enormous amounts of human labour and financial resources. Sometimes they require basic research. In opposition to the breakthrough, gradual projects introduce changes to the existing order of things but at the same time do not revolutionize it. The researchers rightly judge that it is obvious that the project of "giving the silhouette of our car a more modern line is not the same as presenting a completely new model with electric drive, made not of steel and glass, but of composite materials" (Tidd & Bessant, 2013, p. 55). Non-breakthrough projects can be further divided into modifications (leading to minor modifications of existing products, technologies, etc., in order to improve them) and the so-called recombining ones based on the use of commonly known organizational, technological, production solutions, etc., in order to develop new products, management systems or technologies. In practice, we often deal with mixed types of projects, groundbreaking to a greater or lesser extent.

Organization of project	Simple and complex	Simple projects do not lend themselves to further differentiation, and they are implemented by one team from start to finish. On the other hand, complex projects are those where, for better coordination and control, a large number of sub-projects implemented by many different project teams are set aside.
The impact of the project on the company's financial situation	Cost, revenue, and investment projects	Cost projects result from the internal needs of the company's operations. Their implementation directly increases operating costs so their implementation is included as an element of the organization's cost plans. Revenue projects are implemented for external clients, generating both sales revenue and project implementation costs. Therefore, the effects of such projects must be included in both revenue and operating cost plans. Investment projects, on the other hand, are internal undertakings carried out to increase a company's assets, i.e. those in which implementation costs are capitalized and shown as capital expenditures, and project products after their completion become assets of the organization. Such projects are included in the organization's investment plans.
Range of impact	• implemented within a department of a single enterprise, • implemented in a scale of a single company, • performed between the links of the supply chain, • with an international scope, • on a global scale.	Many projects are only carried out within one company and even within its single department, e.g. logistics department (an example of such a project may be the reorganization of warehouse space or reduction of inventories). The department can also act as a project coordinator involving the resources of the entire enterprise. A slightly extended scope has projects implemented within the supply chain. Their example may be improving the organization of the purchase and delivery of specific materials from suppliers. Organizing the supply chain in the area of two or more countries may be an example of a project implemented on an international scale, while projects of a global nature are carried out by global corporations or specific state agencies.

Source: Own elaboration based on (Tidd & Bessant, 2013, p. 55; Kasperek, 2006, pp. 10–12; Biernat-Jarka, 2014, pp. 3496–3497; Łady & Kozarkiewicz, 2007; M. Bąk 2010, p. 10).

However, it should be emphasized that innovative projects are always associated with a specific risk. "Constant progress causes a constant expansion of potential possibilities, but also increases the risk that must be overcome: no project can be perfectly planned and none can be carried out strictly according to plan" (Pietras & Szmit, 2003, p. 78). At the same time, however, the innovativeness of the project may lead to gaining a significant competitive advantage: innovation is considered crucial in the management of projects (Barnes, 1991, pp. 207–209).

Besides, there are practical ways to reduce risk that the company can make use of (Kasperek, 2006, pp. 121–122):

- complete abandonment of uncertain activities; risk acceptance is nothing more than taking no action other than observing the status of the risk (Prywata, 2010, p. 6);
- division of the project into smaller parts, i.e. giving up a large venture in favour of many small ones, controlled by independent managers. In this case, a possible problem within a smaller project does not undermine the possibility of achieving the assumed primary objective (a specific loss can be compensated with revenues from other projects);
- project benchmarking, i.e. making usage of proven patterns and solutions that have already proven themselves in the past (or have been successful in other enterprises' project activities); and
- application of the customer's co-responsibility, transferring part (or all of the risk) to the client (e.g. by means of appropriate provisions in the contract for service).

Moreover, it should be noted that in each project, apart from its type, certain limitations can appear, which include scope, cost, and time. These elements set the direction of individual project activities and the level of their achievement affects the final assessment of the of the tasks' performance correctness. The goal of each project is to achieve the aforementioned parameters at an optimal level. The scope determines what should be done in the logistics project and what tasks should be performed in order to achieve the project goal. In the case of project costs, attention is paid to the financial limit which should not be exceeded. Similarly, the project time is the period in which the project should be made and completed. Meeting these three limitations of the project determines its success (Biernat-Jarka, 2014. pp. 3496–3497).

1.3 SOURCES OF PROJECTS

The reason for the creation of a project may be anything that generates specific ideas and may become the beginning of searching for new things and solutions, undertaking projects, and implementing and improving them. Any motive that inspires a person to initiate a process of change should be then considered the source of the project (Pomykalski, 2001, p. 25). Each project has its source, i.e. the place where it was initiated. In the literature on the subject, the impulse/stimulus that inspired the project is identified with its source. Figure 1.3. shows a range of examples of common stimulators that can act as impulses to start a project journey. They are, however, not grouped within specific generic groups.

As shown in Figure 1.4, there are in practice many factors that can stimulate the creation of projects. At the same time, it is possible to try to somehow combine the sources that determine the undertaking of a project work by a person or a team to certain groups. For example, the community and the economy may be the point of reference in classifying impulses for projects. According to this criterion, domestic and foreign project sources can be distinguished. In the first case, it is about the impulses that flow from the home country. For example, the idea of a project venture may arise as a result of the possibility of obtaining a national grant or as a result of getting acquainted with the results of scientific research conducted by both, national individual inventors and institutional units: home universities, enterprises, design offices, experimental centres, entities from research and development back-up which are located outside the economic sphere, etc. (Wasiluk, 2003, p. 337).

In contrast, foreign sources are stimulants coming from other countries (e.g. importing new licenses from other EU countries). It should be emphasized that the appearance of the aforementioned sources depends mainly on the actual country's research capacity and potential, as well as on its development strategy, which is shaped by factors such as the number of funds allocated to research and development, the effectiveness of their usage, the technical level of industry, and its competitive position in the international market (Wasiluk, 2003, p. 337).

Sources of projects undertaken by organizations can be also divided into the so-called demand and supply sources. The two basic components of the impulses in this systematics are not, as in the previously mentioned division, distinguished on the basis of the geographical area where the

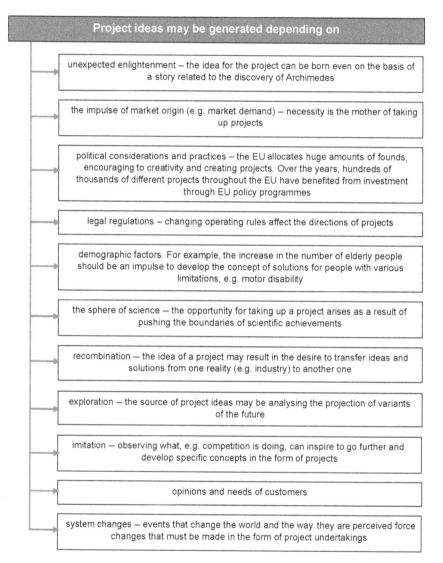

FIGURE 1.4

Common sources of projects.

Source: Own elaboration based on: Tidd & Bessant, 2013, p. 314.

motivation arises. Detailed components of projects' sources are distributed between two sets from the main cause of their occurrence point of view. In the case of demand-driven projects, a circumstance, phenomenon, or an external person is essential for their occurrence – e.g. a client who, in a way, assumes the role of a participant involved in the occurrence of the design of the project's process. Supply-side projects, on the other

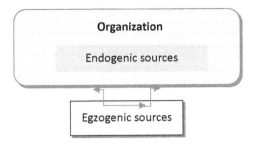

FIGURE 1.5
Placement of projects' sources.

Source: Own elaboration.

hand, have their only source in the activity of the spheres of science and their own ingenuity, and then they are forced into the economy by means of transfer (Figure 1.5.)

The break of war in Europe, high-level inflation, disturbed energy markets, political uncertainty, and climate-induced challenges shape the investment environment and impact the challenges and opportunities for undertaking certain projects.

Nowadays, in the case of all kinds of institutional units, the motives for undertaking project activities should therefore be seen in one of the two basic areas (Drucker, 1992, p. 44):

- the interior of the organization (internal sources – endogenous ones);
- environment (external, exogenous sources) resulting from the market sphere, economic situation, specificity of the sector, etc.

(Knosala & Deptuła, 2018, p. 26)

Generally speaking, the latter ones (external sources) are associated with changes that take place in the environment of the subject. The organization itself has little influence on the possibility of their occurrence. In this context, one can speak of a specific independence of exogenous sources in relation to the subject of their influence. The main sources from the outside of an organization include the following:

- Know-how and licenses purchased or obtained in the frame of cooperation with other companies. Enterprises not only can but also should maximize the effectiveness of partnership cooperation in the context of project development. As R. Luecke emphasizes, licensing or undertaking projects in cooperation allows to make usage of the advantages of the free market in order to generate an influx of new ideas – the basis for projects (Luecke, 2005, p. 68; Veryard, 2000, p. 2). This is of particular importance, for example, in high-tech sectors where, due to the complexity of the processes and manufactured products, the companies operating there are often unable to cope with all aspects of their activities on their own and need a kind of external inspiration. Due to the flexible inter-organizational relations and combining components from various sources, they are still able to continue their operations, and often even obtain a new quality in the form of innovative projects.

- Scientific and popular science literature in which researchers share their findings coming from their laboratories, research, and university centres.[5] An impulse for the project may be, for example, a new model presented in the book, developed by an experimental centre or university.

- Actions of market competitors – for example, the presentation of a prototype of a folded touch screen by a well-known Japanese company coming from the electronic industry has become an inspiration for its competitors to intensify projects on similar solutions.

- New or changed legal and normative regulations to which the company can respond and cannot remain indifferent. For example, when the United States government revoked AT&T company's authorization to provide local telephony services, the company embarked on a project to look for new avenues of development first by focusing on long-haul telephony services and then by engaging in projects related to the anticipated integration of telephone networks with computer systems (Christensen & Raynor, 2008, pp. 17–18).

- Specific needs of target market representatives – organizations can use, for example, market research in order to reveal needs that they can respond to, in the form of a project. An example may be the project of developing a car air-conditioning system as a response to the needs of drivers who wanted to travel in conditions conducive to the feeling of comfort.

- Development of modern information exchange technologies. For example, the development of the Internet has led to a situation where even individuals, not directly related to a specific organization, have the opportunity to submit new ideas to it, which may become the basis for a new project. The transfer of valuable ideas can take place, for example, by using so-called blogs[6] or video blogs. There, in the Internet space, are present both corporate and private blogs run by employees, and often by representatives of the organization's management. These people often encourage the representatives of their audiences to actively respond to the posted messages and share their thoughts, as well as submit their ideas and proposals for changes. It is possible due to one of the characteristics of blogs. It is a platform for creating a social group centred around the author, whose members have the opportunity to tighten contacts and intensify relations thanks to the possibility of exchanging insights, ideas, and views.

Supply-side projects, not based on external but on endogenous factors, should be mentioned here. Their idea is born inside the organization, they are created only on their own, and then they are commercialized (Westland, 2008, p. 8), i.e. introduced into economic practice on market principles (Wiankowski, 2005, p. 213). In this case, there is no "mutual penetration of technologies, solutions and standards between individual participants of the market game" (Lamparska, 2016, p. 42), and the company's interactions with the environment are reduced to the absolutely necessary minimum.

Such projects' ideas come from the interior of an organization – they are the result of the company's individual, creative initiatives and inquisitiveness of people or departments dealing with a specific field. The stimulation to undertake a given project takes place in this case as a result of internal motivation – the work of the members of the organization leading to discoveries or idea generation which are then put into practice. Referring to the previously mentioned example, simple car air-conditioning systems, although sufficient for most users, as a result of the design work of engineers, have transformed over time into complex and extensive multi-zone systems.

Taking up project work as a result of one's own will and ingenuity (internal reasons – supply factors) is characteristic of the classic approach to design work and is reflected in a closed model that has not devalued over time, still well reflecting the approach of many organizations operating in the contemporary environment. In this case, in inseparable cases, the role of an inspirer for new projects is performed by the top management; moreover, employees create research and development facilities, as well as specialists from individual functional departments of the organization, e.g. marketing, production, or distribution ones.

However, all the employees, including these at lower levels in the organizational structure, can be a valuable source of new ideas. Researchers argue that benefitting from the creativity of employees, especially those in rank and file, who are closest to processes, products, and customers, "is of key importance for the continuous organizational improvement" (Dekier & Grycuk, 2014, p. 4).

For this reason, many enterprises have implemented formal organizational solutions in the form of programmes that allow each individual employee to submit new ideas and proposals for improvements, both for his own workplace and other areas and processes taking place within his organization. The submission of new ideas is most often done in writing or in an electronic way. They are then assessed, and the originators often receive awards if their ideas will be considered valuable, implemented, and commercialized (Lamparska, 2016, p. 42).

In the literature, researchers emphasize the importance of the human factor in the development of endogenous projects. They indicate that the creative potential of employees should be considered in terms of the most important factor in the development of each enterprise (Romanowska, 2016). They also draw attention to the fact that the possibility of the emergence of new ideas leading to the project among employees is determined by certain conditions.

Among them should be mentioned, among others, an organizational structure favouring creativity, an organizational culture promoting courage and ambition, an incentive system involving the practice of rewarding new and valuable ideas, the attitude of managing staff that appreciates the commitment and ingenuity of their subordinates, and a leadership style that integrates employees around the company's goals, etc.

The existence of the aforementioned conditions measurably increases the chances of the emergence of valuable ideas and initiatives within the company. Then, however, the evolved concepts have to be implemented in the form of a project. In order for this to happen (transforming endogenous products of human ingenuity into projects), organizations need to rely on specific values and fulfil conditions, which include, among others, proper financial standing, the size of the enterprise, the effectiveness of its information systems, the ability to organize the necessary technical facilities (e.g. machines as well as other devices), complementary resources, human resources, etc. These characteristics affect, therefore, the possibility of financing further works on new solutions in the long term. The options of implementing ready-made project solutions also depend on these conditions.

1.4 STRUCTURE OF PROJECTS

Project management is a field of management dealing with the usage of available knowledge, skills, methods, and tools in order to achieve the assumed goals of the project (i.e. the quality of the intended result, low cost, and deadline). The definitions of project management that can be found in the subject literature indicate the need for planned acting, which to a large extent requires a certain effort to perform all managerial functions, in particular planning, organizing, and controlling. In practice, the involvement of a company in a project, regardless of its type, is always associated with the need to complete a sequence of specific activities (Krakowska, 2016, p. 25). This processes' approach, on which entire project management is based, requires consideration of all processes related to the project: both project progress processes (also referred to as basic or operational processes), consisting in the transformation of project input values into their expected results as well as processes supporting the project course (also referred to as auxiliary processes that do not directly contribute to the creation of the project result, but create the conditions necessary for its achievement) (Trocki, 2010, p. 135).

Mentioned processes are realized through individual phases in which the completion of one automatically initiates the next stage of its implementation. "The project is an undertaking that consists of many phases. Each of the project phases differs in terms of duration, the degree of resource involvement, and the methods used for conducting, planning and controlling. The way of dividing the project into phases and their number in the project depends primarily on the subject and scope of the project" (Pietras & Szmit, 2003, p. 15).

It should be emphasized that the smooth transition from one phase to the other is greatly influenced by schedules. At the beginning of the 20th century, H. Gantt and K. Adamiecki in Poland, drew attention to this challenge, introducing charting techniques that allow for the effective preparation of schedules for implementation programmes (Domiter & Marciszewska, 2013, p. 36). Creating an appropriate schedule allows for the implementation of many activities at the same time, thus shortening the duration of a specific task, contributing to the improvement of communication between individual cells, and reducing the costs of activities.

An example of such a programme is concurrent designing carried out simultaneously by many executive and design units. It means that at the same time particular task or problem is solved by many smaller units which, through mutual exchange of information, limit the time and eliminate errors or defects appearing during the implementation of the project.[7]

It is assumed that the overall structure of a project covers phases ranging from the conceptualization (resulting from the goals and mission) to the audit (effects control). These activities form a series of logically consecutive stages, whose execution, in consequence, measurably increases the chances of success in an undertaken project. In fact, in the case of each type of project, the practical activities shaping its structure will be slightly different from each other because the type of idea forces the order of actions which have to be taken.

In Figure 1.6, however, stages that seem to be common to the structure of the most of projects undertaken currently in the European enterprises have been shown.

A separate part of the work is devoted to the considerations of the executive phase of management activities in projects. This is due to the length of the argument and its importance and worth, emphasizing the role of the stages of planning, organizing, leading, and controlling projects.

All the stages listed in Figure 1.5 make up the so-called project life cycle, i.e. all the processes embracing all stages, from the beginning of the project to its completion. The life cycle defines what kind of work should be done in a given phase of the implementation and who should do it. Analysing and rethinking a company's mission,[8] which is, in turn, a

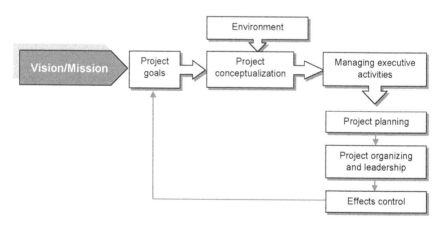

FIGURE 1.6
Common structure of a project.

Source: Own elaboration.

precise expression of the long-term intentions and aspirations of the organization for the future (its vision), should be the starting point for further activity of the company considering involvement in the project. This is due to the fact that the mission (which is the vision articulation) is the primary carrier of the most important and overarching (strategic) goals of the organization (Talbot, 2003, p. 15). The management is obliged to analyse what is really important to the company and determine whether the project will be useful from the point of view of the feasibility of implementing its fundamental plans.

If the answer to this question is positive, the next step is about the move to formulate the strategy[9] and goals[10] of the project. When defining project goals, it should be remembered that they should be understandable, achievable, explicit, and codifiable (possibly to be documented). It is, therefore, necessary to specify their cost, technical, organizational, and personal nature and determine how the result will be measured (they can be expressed in absolute measures – maximum or minimum value of the parameter – a strictly defined value, or in a relative way – a value specified in a range, indicator, percentage, ratio). An example of an absolute way may be shortening the time of shipment delivery to a maximum of 12 hours, while a relative – reduction of the customer service time by 5%–10%.

In practice, in the case of this step, it is all about describing the positive change that the organization wants to achieve as a result of the implementation of the project undertaking (Kopczewski, 2009, p. 25). At this stage, the actual life cycle of the project begins.[11] The SMART (wise, clever) principles may be helpful in precisely defining the guidelines, the achievement of which will be tantamount to the implementation of the project. It is not a goal-seeking technique but rather a set of guidelines defining its characteristics. The acronym indicates that the goal should be: S – specific area – territorially defined, M – measurable, A – ambitious or adaptable, R – realistic (meanly feasible, i.e. possible realization), T – timebound. "If each of these features can be attributed to the goals set for implementation – then they are of the SMART type" (Dadel, 2007, pp. 10–11). Of course, many other, similar goal-defining techniques can be used (STEAM, SMARTER, etc.).

After defining the goals according to these principles, the first phase takes place, which is to create an action plan leading to the implementation of the adopted goals (conceptualization). The general features of a good plan were, among others, formulated by T. Kotarbiński (Polish philosopher, the creator of the science of efficient operation – praxeology), which is the theoretical basis of management. According to the author, a plan is good when it leads to efficient action, and in particular when it is: feasible, purposeful, internally consistent, sufficiently detailed, long-term, timely defined, complete, operative, and rational (Kotarbiński, 1966, p. 114).

Creating a plan usually consists of two basic categories of activities, successive in chronological order: diagnosis (internal and external) and the so-called thinking, which in turn includes two sets of detailed activities, i.e.

- variants' creation and
- selecting the best (most optimal) option.

In the case of diagnosis, it is about acquiring knowledge about the reality in which the project team will be working. It is vital to recognize the potential of the organization and identify internal inhibitory factors, as well as opportunities and limitations imposed by the environment (Webber, 1996, p. 245). This necessity results from the fact that the project cannot be detached from the reality of the organization's functioning and its environment. Internal and external conditions typically have a strong influence on project realization. On the one hand, they condition the possibility of implementing the initial plans resulting from the formulated goals of the project. They may also become an inspiration for completely new ideas and intentions that have not been taken into account so far. Finally, they always define the shape of activities aimed at their implementation.

The described part of the project's conceptualization process covers two categories of detailed activities. The first one is the diagnosis of the organization, which takes the form of verification of the internal factors determining the functioning of the organization (factors that are within it). They are relatively easy to identify and susceptible to the influence of the project's staff. Among them, there are material factors (e.g. technical, complementary, financial, and human resources) and intangible factors, such as culture, values, and managerial style (Harasim, 2004, p. 47).

On the other hand, external verification consists in the diagnosis of factors that may potentially affect the project, located in the further environment (macro-environment) and in the sphere of closer impact (micro-environment) of the organization (Hall, Kraków Hall, 2007, p. 64) (Figure 1.7).

Each organization implementing a given type of project, whether on the domestic or European market, depends on various factors located both in the micro- and macro-environments. Macro-environment means a set of

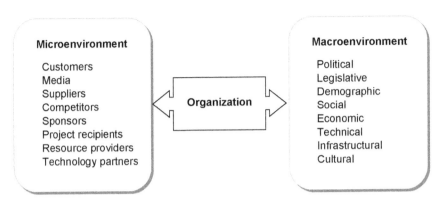

FIGURE 1.7
Areas of external analysis of an entity.

Source: Own elaboration based on Sutherland & Canwell, 2007, pp. 143–147; Gierszewska & Romanowska, 2009, p. 24; Jaśniok, 2007, p. 33; Stoner, Freeman & Gilbert, 2001, pp. 79–81.

operating conditions resulting from the fact that it operates in a specific region (e.g. Europe), in a specific political, legal, economic, systemic, etc., structure. A main feature of the macro-environment is that it strongly determines the possibilities of an enterprise's action and development (Gierszewska & Romanowska, 2009, p. 23). However, the organization is unable to shape or change these conditions to a larger extent. It can only benefit from the opportunities or minimize the threats coming from this type of environment. The macro-environment includes data and phenomena that need to be known and predicted but which are not subject to its own influence (Verbake, 2009, pp. 435–445).

In turn, the environment in the so-called micro-scale consists of external stakeholders of the company who are in constant contact with it. In its primary sense, a stakeholder is any person or group that can influence (or is influenced by) an organization. Stakeholders can be successfully differentiated from the point of view of their significance for the functioning of the small or medium-sized company. "The most important are those without whom it cannot survive" (Molendowski & Polan, 2007, p. 87). There are always present significant cooperative ties between the stakeholders and the organization. The micro-environment affects the enterprise, but in this case, there is also feedback, i.e. the enterprise can also influence the environment, predict its behaviour, and study it (Miłek, 2009, p. 62).

Managers responsible for the project conceptualization phase have potentially many methods useful from the point of view of the analysis of the environment. For this purpose, they can use, among others, scenario methods, SWOT analysis, four-field matrices, Porter's five forces model, strategic mapping, paradox management questionnaires, and many others. Portfolio methods, strategic balance sheets, value chain analysis, benchmarking, and so on are used to study the internal potential of the organization. Integrated techniques are also available, enabling the analysis of the enterprise against the background of its environment (Gierszewska & Romanowska, 2009, p. 8). The choice of the available diagnostic tools should be justified by the possibility of obtaining information which is (Kiełtyka, 2002, pp. 371–372)[12]

- reliable – those that accurately reflect reality,
- complete which run out information needs,
- current (reflecting the present state), and
- responsible, meaning useful in relation to specific needs.

Internal and external diagnosis precedes activities related to devising the main practical issues related to the project. Managers who are already aware of the goals they want to achieve and know the potential of the organization, as well as the opportunities/limitations imposed by the environment, can proceed to develop the general shape of the project. Options for further action can take a variety of forms, from general characteristics to detailed plans defining goals, tasks, division of responsibilities, activities, allocation of resources, and measures of effects, as well as subsequent stages.

Subsequently, the evolved solutions are thoroughly assessed in order to determine whether their implementation makes sense. The variants are verified primarily in terms of the anticipated benefits. It is usually a stage of self-assessment, where decision-makers look more closely at the plans they have developed and accept, in their own group, the one they consider to be the best in the whole pool. At the same time, however, they are often exposed to pressure from various stakeholders of the subordinate unit. Beneficiaries and stakeholders take an active part in determining the scope of the project, which is analysed in terms of feasibility.

After the project's conceptualization stage, there is a time for managerial executive activities (project implementation phase) consisting of performing so-called managerial functions. It is an important issue because the principles of project management boil down *de facto* to four critical functions. These functions are planning (involves defining means to enable results to be achieved), organizing (a process of coordinating task goals and activities to resources), leading (involves motivating the employees to achieve organizational goals – that is why it is sometimes called "staffing"), and controlling (related to monitoring as well as evaluation).

Due to the importance of the subject and the length of the necessary argument, the subject of management activities (functions) of the next stage of the executive structure of projects will be described in subsequent parts of the work.

NOTES

1 In the broadly understood business-related sphere, the concept of project and its management appeared relatively recently. Changes in the functioning of enterprises and organizations related to, among others, globalization of business activity, an increase in the amount of data and information accompanying companies' activities, the need to flexibly respond to changes taking place in the market environment, and the rapid development of modern technologies force the launch of more and more new projects (Pietras & Szmit, 2003, p. 7).

2 The documentation of the project management system should include provisions specifying procedures in the fields of project management, organizational regulations, maps of processes and procedures, documentation of project management methodologies in the fields of planning, scheduling, costing, budgeting, control, acting guides (methods and instructions), model resolutions, and other documentation (expertise, opinions, decisions, letters, etc.). An auxiliary document supporting the implementation of the project is the quality management plan, setting out the principles of quality management. For research projects, the quality management plan also constitutes the project's implementation procedure. This document contains guidelines for the circulation of documentation and the processes of organizing individual activities in accordance with the letter of the law and regulations regarding the implementation of a given project. Procedures often include an organizational chart, a pattern of timesheets, and guidelines on how to assign accounting documents (Stabryła, 2006, p. 110).

3 This is a feature of a project that often causes concern about success in its realization. This is due to the fact that the project is often a new, not typical undertaking that has not been implemented in a given organization before. As a result, the project team may not have adequate implementation experience. Hence, making usage of existing experience, as well as the transfer of newly acquired skills to other teams, is one of the basic principles of proper project management (Biernat-Jarka, 2014, pp. 3495–3496).

4 Culture does not have to characterize only large human communities (national culture). Also, smaller communities, e.g. a team of employees of a specific institution, shape their own organizational culture, which is why "the division into national and corporate cultures, specific to given professions and functions, seems justified" (compare Tidd & Bessant, 2013, p. 687).

5 It is emphasized that the source of progress in the 20th century was the dynamic development of scientific and research centres. Although the creation and improvement of intellectual property is one of the basic roles of every university, as J. Tidd

and J. Bessant point out, laboratories were also created not only in academic centres but also within large companies, becoming specific forges of ideas. Effects of different projects have begun to emerge from them immediately. The tangible effects of them (e.g. mobile phones) began to supply the rapidly growing markets of cars, household goods, etc. (compare Tidd & Bessant, 2013, p. 694).

6   The term was created from the combination of the words web (network) and log (record). It is one of the forms of communication in the Internet space. In practice, it means a website whose administrator has the ability to publish and share content (written word or video material) that he wants to share with the environment. The blog enables two-way communication because the recipients of the content usually have the opportunity of giving feedback, e.g. in the form of leaving a post on the so-called forum. A more developed form of a blog is a videoblog in which the author publishes audiovisual material (McLeod, 2006, p. 9).

7   Information is an integral part of the work of every employee of an organization, especially of a manager (Kiełtyka, 2011, p. 27; Lichtarski, 2007, p. 375; Leibold, Probst & Gibbert, 2005, p. 15).

8   Mission can be defined in different ways. Some authors limit themselves to rather laconic statements considering the term, e.g. that this is a formulation explaining the change that an organization wants to introduce in the world and indicating values that are important to it. T. Sztucki is the author of one of the more elaborate definitions of the concept. According to him, a mission is a set of values that bind employees together and around which their professional activity focuses. Then he concludes that the mission usually defines the meaning of the company's existence and the vision of its further development, as well as the values recognized by all employees, determining the functions and role the company is to play in the market place in relation to buyers and employees (Sztucki, 1998, p. 58, 202; Pakroo, 2011, p. 37).

9   The term "strategy" comes from the Greek language, where it meant managing troops from the position of a commander-in-chief. In the military sphere, strategy is about creating a war plan and defining individual war campaigns. The practice and science of organization and management adopted this term, like many others, after World War II. Initially, it was considered a part of the mainstream of operational research, but at the same time, it had not such a clear meaning as in the military. Nowadays, a strategy can be, for example, defined as a complete plan that defines what decisions will be taken in every possible situation or as a broad program of setting and achieving organizational goals, a general concept of action that is to lead to the achievement of aims, being previously set (see more, Krupski, 1998, pp. 14–15; De Wit & Meyer, 2007, p. 11).

10 The direct mode of formulating goals refers to having the appropriate funds for the preparers to work on a given project. On the other hand, an indirect way relates to Internet communication between the consortia's employees. In some extreme cases, overqualification of the staff related to the project may pose a certain threat to its implementation. These difficulties may result directly from the ambitions of individual managers, which in some cases may disturb the efficient management and implementation of entrusted tasks.

11 This topic has been further developed by Duncan (1996, p. 11).

12 Other properties that determine the quality of information are relevance, content, and usefulness (Kiełtyka, 2002, pp. 371–372.

2

Concept of Project Management

2.1 PLANNING AND ORGANIZING IN THE PROJECT MANAGEMENT PROCESS

The beginnings of understanding the management process (currently including project management) in terms of the implementation of specific managerial functions, the fulfilment of which results in achieving success in obtaining goals, are associated with the achievements of H. Fayol. This French entrepreneur, the manager of a large coal mining centre (Smit, de Cronje, & Vrba, 2007, p. 33), is now considered one of the pioneers of modern management practice. Already at the beginning of the 20th century, he expressed the belief that essential activities such as planning, organizing, commanding, coordinating, and controlling are performed in every enterprise. At the same time, he emphasized that these functions are "neither the exclusive privilege nor the personal obligation of the manager, but are distributed between managers and executive employees" (Martyniak, 2002, p. 99).

Over the following years, until today, the fundamental assumption that management is always (and regardless of the area) based on the implementation of specific functions has not changed. However, since the presentation of H. Fayol's concept, attempts have been made many times to verify the initial set of typical repetitive managerial activities and decisions that have developed around solving problems that still appear before managers. Currently, the management process is usually defined in terms of only four basic functions; subsequently (Schermerhorn, 2008, p. 16),

- setting goals and ways to achieve them,
- organizing tasks and all other resources needed to get the job done,

DOI: 10.1201/9781003309901-2

- inspiring (motivating) people to work appropriately in order to achieve high performance, and
- measuring performance and taking action in order to deliver appropriate results.

J. Zieleniewski concludes that the essence of "management functions as a specific type of functions regulating a task performed collectively by regulating organizational units is in particular, formulating the purpose of action, planning, i.e. organizing structures and controlling the achievement of goals" (Zieleniewski, 1960, p. 477). Therefore, management is framed around the conscious creation of conditions within which the organization can achieve its goals.

Such categorization is often assessed ambivalently due to its brevity, which does not change the fact that it remains widely accepted, and it is usually cited by researchers dealing with the subject under consideration.

It has been noticed that the management process described in terms of the implementation of the four functions indeed represents a series of decisions (Wierzbicki, 1999, p. 16). During planning, as well as organizing, leading, or controlling, managers are always faced with the need to choose one of two or more possible variants. If these decisions are necessary for the implementation of the project, then the decision-making process can be successfully referred to as project management.

The most important functions of project management are planning (combined with anticipation), organizing (administrative and resource-oriented activities), leading (managing people, e.g. by motivating, influencing, giving tasks), and controlling (checking the implementation of the plan):

- focusing on the organization's resources (human, financial, material, and information),
- making specific decisions, and
- performing with the intention of achieving the organization's objectives in an efficient and effective manner.

The essence of the functions in project management relates to regulation of the task performed collectively by the regulating organizational units, in particular, formulating the purpose of action, planning, i.e. organizing structures and controlling the achievement of goals.

(Zieleniewski, 1960, p. 477)

Planning should be the starting point for all further project activities. If we do not want to follow the principle of trial and error, counting on luck, our actions should be properly directed. Planning is aimed at answering the questions of how to achieve the intended goals, by what means, when, in what order, etc. Planning is a mental operation that precedes the actual action and is, therefore, action-oriented towards the future. "Every action should be preceded by thought (…). When the intended goal requires a complex action, there is a need to prepare a plan[1]. And the more complex an individual or collective act is, the more planning becomes necessary. Foresight and planning allow for far - sighted action" (Pszczołowski, 1982, p. 26).

Planning is based on pre-situational approach, assuming the need for thorough and detailed preparation of the action before its commencement. There are many definitions of planning and a review of them gives an idea of its complex nature. Planning can be considered from different perspectives, various aspects (e.g. purpose of planning), time range, minuteness, etc. In practice planning scope includes, among others, the prediction of future changes in the environment that determine the rationality of the preparation of a specific project, the current situation of the company identification (whether it will be able to implement its intended idea), and the precise definition of the goals to be achieved by all units involved in the preparation of the project. Subsequent decisions should concern the determination of the technical, human, and financial resources necessary to obtain a new value, the formulation of necessary actions, the determination of the consequences of taking and not taking certain actions, or the evolution of ways to monitor and control the implementation of plans.

At the project planning stage, it is necessary to analyse in detail the individual relationships and dependencies appearing in them regarding issues related to

- resources necessary to complete the project,
- structure of work,
- time of realization,
- investment outlays, and
- risk, which, if it occurs, may have positive or negative effects on one or more of the project's objectives.

It should be also remembered that each project has its own subject and character, which determine the need to consider some unique issues, specific only to this project. For example, in the case of an initiative involving the desire to open a logistic village, it is necessary to consider, e.g., its location or the architectural design of the building.

In the case of European projects, which are often implemented by teams consisting of employees from different countries and include activities in foreign markets, it is necessary to pay special attention to issues related to cultural differences. For example, the co-author of the book was the implementer of the project, whose source of funding was the European Commission. The Tempus Oflpel Logistics project was the result of signing at the end of 2010 an agreement on improving logistics in Morocco between the Moroccan government and the General Confederation of Moroccan Enterprises. The Tempus Oflpel Logistics project became part of the aforementioned agreement and was intended to implement its priorities, i.e. to reduce the share of logistics costs in Morocco's gross domestic product (GDP) from 20% to 15% and to educate and create jobs for qualified logistics specialists (engineers, technicians, managers) by the end of 2015.

Many people from different cultures were involved in this project, e.g. Spain, Poland, and, of course, Morocco, and its implementation was associated with the need to contact people from even further corners of the world. In many situations, it was a challenge that was as inspiring and broadening horizons as, in practice, not easy.

In this context, it is not surprising that in the literature, the assumption regarding the different cultural identities of individual geographical areas of the world and their impact on the implementation of projects is strongly emphasized (Konieczna-Domańska, 2015, p. 179).

Although challenging, cultural diversity in the project is an opportunity for development, as it not only provides a multiplicity of views but also allows employees to share perspectives, exchange knowledge, develop, and be more creative. Working in a multicultural team teaches empathy, understanding, and respect, and is also a factor that improves the effectiveness of work and the results achieved by the team. At the same time, it remains a fact that downplaying cultural differences (or assuming that they are unimportant) may be a source of complications for organizations conducting all kinds of project activities in an international environment (McCarthy & Perreault, 1993, p. 216).

An example is the story of the Japanese car manufacturer. The company's project was related to the launch of the Pajero model on the global market. In most languages of the world, this word has no deeper, hidden meaning; is neutral; and does not evoke wrong associations. On the contrary: it sounds worldly, original, and easy to remember. It can be associated with the English word power – meaning strength/endurance, which is the right association from the point of view of an off-road car. At the same time, however, in Spanish, "pajero" is not only a colloquial word but also vulgar in meaning.

It is not difficult to guess that as a result of cultural differences (in this case, it comes down to linguistic issues), the company was forced to make additional and costly efforts to change the name of the model in South American and selected European, English-speaking markets (Spain, Portugal). Otherwise, the vehicle, although modern and properly engineered, due to the inaccurate name, would be met with reluctance by representatives of the Spanish-speaking community and would undoubtedly have problems competing with products from other manufacturers.

The term "culture" comes from antiquity (Mazurkiewicz, 2001, p. 26). The etymology of this word should be seen in the Latin phrase *cultura mentis*, meaning the cultivation of the land. At that time, it meant transforming some natural state of affairs into an improved one, more useful, simply more perfect state.

> An anticipation of this use of the term culture was the metaphorical description of Marcus Tullius Cicero in the Tusculo Discourses as *cultura animi*, i.e. the cultivation of the mind or the culture of the spirit. Starting from Cicero, this term began to be associated with any human activity aimed at nurturing, educating, perfecting.
>
> (Sokół, 2011, p. 315)

Researchers agree that nowadays culture defines all forms of social and economic consciousness, "it is the binder of a specific group or society – it is what distinguishes them in the way members interact with each other and on people from the outside, and what determines how they realize their achievements" (Stoner, Freeman & Gilbert, 2001, p. 186).

The concept of culture is one of the most common terms in the humanities and social sciences. In science, there is a multitude of definitions of culture, the core and meaning of which are formulated depending on the discipline and school of science (Rutkowska, 2018, p. 174). Currently, culture can be defined as the entirety of the spiritual and material achievements of humanity collected, consolidated, and enriched by a specific group over the course of its history and passed on from generation to generation. The behaviour of members of a cultural group depends on the history of the people to whom the group belongs.

For a very long time, people adhere to a system of norms, behavioural responses, and actions that are the most beneficial to them. Derived from historical influences, climate, and mentality, culture dictates the type and characteristics of the group. Culture understood in this way includes material products and social institutions, methods of behaving, principles of social coexistence, patterns and criteria of aesthetics, moral evaluations adopted in a given community, and determining acceptable behaviour.

Research shows that two countries, even seemingly very similar to each other in many respects (such as, for instance, Canada and the United States), can in fact be noticeably different in terms of culture (Berkowitz, Kerin, Hartley & Rudelius, 1994, p. 127): all of us are unique. To say, for example, that "Greeks do this" and "Vietnamese believe that" is "both foolish and possibly dangerous" (Galanti, 2020, p. 335). R. J. House, based on research, divided 62 selected countries of the world into groups. Each of them includes countries that are similar to each other (although not necessarily identical anyway) in terms of culture. The affiliation of individual countries to the same group was determined by the significant similarities between them regarding various issues affecting culture, such as, e.g., similar geographic location, similar history or economy but also shared values or approach to work (Browaeys, Price, 2008, p. 39). The research results are presented in Table 2.1.

Differences in the characteristics of representatives of individual nations do not need to be limited to language issues only, as in the example of the automotive company presented earlier. Cultural differences in societies are the basis for distinguishing many cultural groups, cultural orientations, or cultural dimensions – these terms are used interchangeably.

They correspond to a given society or group of societies characterized by similar features distinguished on the basis of a specific criterion. They also provide information on the main characteristics of individual groups, which in many cases are generalizations, but they are successfully a starting point for research and studies. G. Hofstede and R. R. Gesteland are, among others, the authors of well-known models of classification of national cultures. Their taxonomy is presented in Table 2.2.

TABLE 2.1

Individual Cultural Groups and the Affiliation of Selected Countries to Them

Cultural Group	Example of Countries
Latin Europe	Italy, Israel, Spain. French-speaking Switzerland, France, Portugal
Germanic Europe	Austria, Germany, Switzerland, the Netherlands
Anglo	England, United States of America, Canada, Ireland, Wales, New Zeland, Canada
Nordic Europe	Denmark, Sweden, Finland, Norway
Latin America	Columbia, Ecuador, Guatemala, Brazil, Argentina, Mexico, Venezuela
Middle East	Kuwait, Egypt, Turkey, Qatar, Morocco
Sub-Sahara Africa	Namibia, Zambia, Nigeria, Zimbabwe, Kenya,
Confucian Asia	Hong Kong, Taiwan, Japan, South Korea, Singapore, China
Baltic	Lithuania, Latvia, Estonia
Southern Asia	Philippines, Malaysia, India, Iran, Thailand
Eastern Europe	Greece, Hungary, Albania, Slovenia, Czech Republic, Georgia, Poland

Source: Own elaboration based on Browaeys and Price (2008, p. 39).

TABLE 2.2

Cultural Orientations According to R. R. Gesteland and G. Hofstede

Author	Criterion	Cultural Groups
R. R. Gesteland	Behaviour Approach to time Approach to work and business The importance of hierarchy and social status	Expressive/restrained Monochronic/polychronic Pro-transactional/pro-partner Unceremonial/ceremonial
G. Hofstede	Attitude to hierarchy and power Individual or group orientation Attitude towards risk Degree of desire for assertive, competitive attitudes	Power distance (low/high) Individualism/collectivism Uncertainty avoidance – tendency to avoid uncertainty (low/high) Masculinity/femininity

Source: Own elaboration based on Gesteland (2000 pp. 16–17), Bartosik-Purgat (2006, p. 30), and Browaeys and Price (2008, pp. 21–25).

According to R. R. Gesteland and G. Hofstede,[2] what mainly distinguishes the two cultures from each other are the following (Gesteland, 2000, pp. 16–17; Bartosik-Purgat, 2006, p. 30):

- Approach to time. Monochronic cultures worship the clock and love calendars and schedules. The second is flexible in terms of dates and schedules. Treats time like it's made of rubber. Polychromic cultures place more importance on people and relationships than on punctuality. Lateness is treated as something normal there (Pabian, 2008, pp. 79–82).
- Approach to work and business. People from certain cultural backgrounds prefer to work with family, friends, and people they know well, i.e. people they can trust. This can be seen, for example, in the way these people conduct business. The most important task for them is to develop the best possible relations with the negotiating partner (pro-partnership cultures). The opposite is true for people from pro-transaction cultures. They do not feel the need to establish intimate relations with business partners. On the contrary, they do not mind doing business with complete strangers. The most important thing for them is the transaction itself.
- The importance of hierarchy and social status. "The organization of societies with a ceremonial culture is based on clear hierarchies that reflect large differences in social status and power among people". In contrast, non-ceremonial cultures value a more egalitarian organization with fewer differences in social status and power.
- The expressiveness of paraverbal and non-verbal behaviours[3] is, according to Gesteland, the last criterion that distinguishes representatives of particular cultural circles from each other. People from expressive cultures may use conversation overlays during a conversation, i.e. often interrupting the conversation, gesturing in an animated way, not maintaining spatial distance, patting the interlocutor on the shoulder, etc. Such behaviour may seem unacceptable from the point of view of a person from a country at the opposite cultural pole (reserved cultures). Some of these may be perceived as unnecessary acts of excessive familiarity or simply disrespectful or rude.
- Masculinity/femininity. In "masculine" cultures, both women and men are more likely to adopt assertive and self-confident attitudes, generally more aggressive than people from feminine cultures. The latter value modesty and delicacy more, i.e. features generally identified with the fair sex.

These differences in the behaviour of representatives of both groups are a reaction to the goals they are aiming at. In masculine cultures, a priority role is attached to achieving successes of a purely economic nature, related to work. Their implementation often requires adopting more aggressive attitudes. Meanwhile, people from the opposite cultural circle are more oriented towards achieving personal goals (cooperation, building good relations; Browaeys & Price, 2008, pp. 21–25):

- Attitude towards risk. It means to what extent members of a given society are willing to accept uncertainty or instability (Moran, Harris & Moran, 2007, pp. 7–10). This cannot be equated with an aversion to taking risks. People who avoid it fear that something unfavourable may happen, but their anxiety is justified, its source is objective evidence that something may actually go wrong. For example, a student may fear that he will fail an exam because he has not prepared for it long enough. Meanwhile, people described as "uncertainty avoidant" are generally suspicious and distrustful. Referring to the previous example, they are always afraid of exams, even when they are very well prepared for them.

  Nobody knows the future – it is a mystery. However, people from cultures with low uncertainty avoidance accept this fact and are convinced that they can cope with any situation that fate throws at them. Meanwhile, a typical person from a country with high uncertainty avoidance tries to control and minimize uncertainty about the future. He is a supporter of predictability in life. It is guarded by a multitude of formal and informal rules, so characteristic of this culture, regulating various areas of life.

  Their presence creates a semblance of security. Thanks to them, life seems more orderly and can be controlled. In the event of a dangerous situation, their presence gives hope that there will always be a way out. People from cultures with a high degree of distrust of the future are considered to be less creative and innovative than those from cultures where uncertainty avoidance is relatively low. This is because they are afraid of what is new and unknown. They believe that the unknown is potentially dangerous. New ideas and ideas may seem suspicious to them. On the other hand, due to their organization, they are able to assimilate and develop the ideas of others quickly and easily. Hofstede noticed that there are more Nobel prize winners among the British (low uncertainty avoidance) than among the

Japanese (high uncertainty avoidance), but at the same time, it is the latter who have introduced more new products to the world market (Gillespie, Jeannet & Hennessey: 2007, p. 77).

- Individualism/collectivism. Making a distinction between individualistic and collectivist cultures consists in obtaining an answer to the following question: to what extent are individuals in society autonomous and to what extent are they embedded in groups?

  In individualistic cultures, the individual is seen as the basic element of the collective. Great importance is attached to individual decisions because everyone is the blacksmith of his own fate and accepts responsibility for his actions. In addition, all achievements and initiatives are important, and leadership is the ideal. By contrast, in collectivist cultures, there is no place for too much individual independence. Everyone is a member of some larger community (family, clan, nation), and identity is acquired by belonging to it.

  The individual cannot, as in an individualist culture, be guided mainly by his own interest. "In collectivist cultures people subordinate their own goals to the group of which they are members" (Solomon, 2006, p. 545). A collectivist must be able to sacrifice himself for the good of the whole, the group to which he belongs.

  Participation in it is a guarantee of security for its member: after all, he can count on the help of other participants at any time, as all members of the community are jointly responsible for each other. In return, he is required to strictly abide by the rules that govern the community and renounce manifestations of nonconformity. The practice of functioning within a larger community means that for collectivists, unlike individualists, it is extremely important to build deep and possibly friendly relationships with other people.

- Attitude to hierarchy and power. "Indicates the extent to which a society accepts that power in institutions and organizations is distributed unequally" (Moran, Harris & Moran, 2007, p. 17). Unfortunately, this quote does not fully define the essence of the issue, so it seems advisable to recall a few words of additional explanation. Power distance basically determines how important a role is assigned to the hierarchy in society. In some cultures, people are assessed mainly through the prism of their position in a given structure. In others, it doesn't matter that much.

Greater importance is attached to individual predispositions, such as possessed skills or experience. It also indicates how much reserve or restraint is between people at different levels of the hierarchy. "Some cultures are characterized by a rigid, vertical social structure (Japan, for example), while others (as in the United States) prefer equality and informality to a greater extent" (Solomon, 2006, p. 545).

For example, in high-power, distance countries, children are required to obey their parents. Respect for them, and for older people in general, is treated as a virtue. Meanwhile, in countries with opposing cultures, children are explicitly encouraged from an early age to express their individual opinion and to gain personal independence from the family as soon as possible.

The preceding list specifies what, according to the authors, mainly distinguishes the two cultures from each other.

However, not all the researchers agree with them completely – the literature also deals with the subject of the classic anthropological approach developed to compare any areas from the point of view of differences between countries and regions of the world. It lists several basic categories that are usually affected by cultural differences (Table 2.3; compare Moran, Harris & Moran, 2007, pp. 7–10).

Many researchers try to find cultural differences based on an alternative to the previously presented, systemic approach. According to it, culture is the interaction of different elements constituting a system with a specific structure and constituting a logically ordered entity. Just like the roots on a tree, cultural systems develop roots which are impacted by their environment. Eight systems of cultural diversity in the world can be specified and characterized (Moran, Harris & Moran, 2007, pp. 11–13):

- System of education. Cultures differ from each other in the way in which their young or new members assimilate knowledge, skills, or values. Pupils who are raised in different cultural settings may learn and approach education in different ways, In some countries, the education system is more formalized, largely based on public institutions. In others, the role of traditional upbringing in a family or group is more strongly appreciated (for example, in the Polynesian concept of learning, it is acceptable that children are taught by adults from the family or even by older children. Piaget's notions of learning involve the transfer of information from prior knowledge and experiences).
- Political system means political parties, all state bodies, organizations, and social groups (formal and informal) participating in political activities within a given state with general rules and norms regulating mutual relations between them. The key to understanding politics and governance in a given culture is the classification of political

TABLE 2.3

Cultural Differences According to the Classical Anthropological Approach

Category	Characteristics
Communication with each other	Both the usage of the word "communication" and its etymology show that this term means various ways of building a more or less permanent community between people. The community built may concern shared feelings, beliefs, values, meanings, objectives of action, and the actions themselves. In some situations, it may also concern a common arena of struggle, and the ties constituting it are far from friendship. The community in question can be created by moving and connecting people by means of telecommunication devices or by means of linguistic activities and other symbolic behaviours that transfer meanings.
	Linguistic activities are referred to as verbal communication (it takes place through spoken and written words). On the other hand, non-verbal communication does not require words and is otherwise called body language. The implementation of both of these methods of communication differs between individual cultural groups. In Eastern Culture, respect for the interlocutor plays an important role, and for this reason, statements are well thought out, there are numerous breaks between them, which should be used to think over the finished statement and prepare a response.
	A different way of conducting dialogue is presented, for example, by the Southerners. Their statements can be described as overlapping. They are also characterized by a specific, fast, and loud speaking style, also manifested by mutual skewing.
Norms and values	The former can be defined as a standard, recommended way of behaving for members of a given society or social group. Therefore, these are rules, the subject of which are the ways or methods of operation and the means used to achieve the goal. "Social norms result from the adopted system of values and are most often defined as unwritten rules on which social relations in a group are based" (Sikorski, 2005, p. 47) In practice, they are guidelines that tell people what they should and should not do (Browaeys & Price, 2008, p. 10).

(Continued)

TABLE 2.3 (CONTINUED)

Cultural Differences According to the Classical Anthropological Approach

Category	Characteristics
	The individual is always left with autonomy in shaping his or her behaviour, but it concerns issues extending between the indicated extremes. Values, on the other hand, are some kind of priorities that members of society strive for. Different things can be of value to members of different groups. What's more, when striving to achieve them, they may be guided by non-identical standards of conduct.
Relations	In different cultures, the spectrum of relationships between people is shaped in different ways. Some prefer to have a leader at the head of the group, i.e. an individual responsible for others.
	In others, the values of cooperation/cooperation are valued more. In some areas, older people enjoy great respect and esteem, while in others they are downplayed. In low-ceremonial cultures, people recognize equality of status, while in ceremonial cultures, people attach importance to hierarchical order and differences in social status.
Beliefs	A term that is difficult to define, it appears in many different contexts. Generally, these are the views and interpretations created by people about the world around them. They may or may not be verified in practice. They strongly influence behaviour. These are our guiding principles, the inner images we use to understand the world around us. They provide stability and continuity, motivate and shape what people do.
Eating habits	Eating food is undoubtedly an important element in human life. It is not only to satisfy hunger but also to bring people closer together. The things eaten, the ways of eating, and how food is selected, prepared, served, and consumed vary, however, from culture to culture.
	For example, in many cultures, it is natural to eat with cutlery. In others, however, the hands are used for this purpose, which enhances the sensory perception of food by the brain. People from some cultural areas sometimes eat what cannot be considered as a food product in other cultures. As researchers jokingly note, "[O]ne man's pet is someone else's delicacy" (Browaeys & Price, 2008, p. 10).

(Continued)

TABLE 2.3 (CONTINUED)

Cultural Differences According to the Classical Anthropological Approach

Category	Characteristics
Perception of individuality and space	In some cultures, independence, individualism, and creativity are highly valued, while in others cooperation and conformity are highly valued. Individualism is a feature of societies where ties are loose and the individual is focused primarily on himself (his own needs). "Individualism is characteristic primarily of rich countries, and collectivism is the domain of poor countries" (Kosińska 2008, p. 65).
	The latter characterization is characteristic of societies in which people from the moment of birth belong to strong and cohesive groups, providing the individual with care and protection. Their members reciprocate with unquestioned loyalty. This also translates to how much physical distance people from a given culture usually keep in mutual contact. Each person subconsciously sets a specific, imaginary sphere around his body, which he treats as his own space, an area of safety. Its size is not identical among representatives of different cultures.
Time	Often, two cultures differ from each other in the way in which the passing of time is counted. While most people in the world measure time in the hour-minute system, there are still people in many parts of the globe who are not so precise in counting it. However, the differentiating factors within this category are primarily punctuality and the tendency to adhere to schedules. From this point of view, cultures can be divided into monochromatic (e.g. Scandinavian countries, Japan, United States of America) and polychrome (e.g. Latin American countries).
	"In the first case, great attention is paid to punctuality and schedules. On the other hand, time is less important in the second, because good relationships are valued more than punctuality" (Witek & Adamczyk, 2008, p. 135). In monochromatic societies, punctuality is a very important factor. It is considered impolite to be late for meetings (and it is even right to be at a meeting a few minutes earlier). Schedules are treated as fixed once, and the daily agenda as not subject to change.

(Continued)

TABLE 2.3 (CONTINUED)

Cultural Differences According to the Classical Anthropological Approach

Category	Characteristics
	In contrast to these are polychrome cultures, where people place less emphasis on punctuality and are not particularly obsessed with meeting deadlines. People from polychrome cultures appreciate easy schedules as well as appointments where several meetings can take place at the same time (Gesteland, 2000, p. 58). Arriving on time means rather a waste of their own time and disrespect for the time of the person with whom they have made an appointment (they may, for example, want to extend the previous meeting).
Appearance	People are distinguished from each other by their appearance, different anthropological features, e.g. skin colour, body height, dimensions of the braincase and face, their proportions expressed in indicators and descriptive features, including, for example, the shape and profile of the forehead, nose and its numerous details, lips, face profile, jaw shape, and many others. They also have non-identical preferences in terms of clothing, outer wardrobe, and body decoration. Some cultures prefer original and unique elements that distinguish them from others.
Approach to work	Cultures can also be distinguished from each other by comparing the approach to work represented by their representatives. In different cultures, different professions dominate; there is a different division of labour and other practices regarding, for example, ways of motivating effort or rewarding.

Source: Own elaboration based on Waszkiewicz (1997, p. 26); Gajewski (2007, p. 100); Pease (2001, pp. 21– 22); Maksymowicz (2002, p. 29); Moran, Harris, and Moran (2007, pp. 11–13); Olejniczak (2014, p. 117).

systems. The oldest and outdated, yet historically significant typology is the typology of Aristotle already, who distinguished among political systems: tyranny, oligarchy, democracy, monarchy, and aristocracy. In the modern world, in a simplified way, we can distinguish such political systems as, for example, liberal (most European countries), post-communist, liberal, East Asian, Islamic, military regimes. The political system strongly determines the culture of a country or state. In tribal cultures, for example, power is centralized in the hands of one person, i.e. hegemon, who has the exclusive right to make decisions. Others prefer alternative systems, such as a democracy in which formally, ultimately, power belongs to the governed.

- Health system. The ways of treating diseases and caring for the victims of accidents and disasters vary from culture to culture. In some cultures (e.g. in the USA) health care puts a great deal of emphasis on patient autonomy, in others not so much. Individual cultures also differ in the degree to which it is acceptable to use natural healing means (generally alternative medicine) in the medical process. What's more, the health system in individual countries is organized differently. In some of them (e.g. in Poland) a large part of hospitals and other facilities providing health services is under the control of the state. Access to them is not paid, based on the health insurance system. In others, access to health care is associated with the need to spend additional funds, as it is mainly provided by private clinics. Because of these circumstances, health professionals have to always treat each patient with respect, which can make it possible to allow them to avert most cultural problems.
- Economic system. Societies differ from each other in the way in which goods and services are produced and distributed within them. Until recently, the division of the world into countries with capitalist and socialist economies was common. The first group included highly developed countries characterized by a free market economy. Communist countries were centrally planned and less organized economically. The remaining (least developed countries) were referred to as the third world. Today, however, such demarcations seem insufficient. Individual categories are too general and no longer fit contemporary conditions. Currently, many countries are in a specific, unique economic situation. Their economic systems take transitional forms. For example, some post-communist countries (e.g. Baltic countries: Lithuania, Latvia, and Estonia) have recently undergone a significant transformation and are beginning to aspire to be the most developed areas. They are currently in a transitional stage between the so-called first and the second stage of development[4] Also, selected third world countries (e.g. India) break the rules, boasting of extremely strongly developed, selected technological sectors until recently characteristic only for the most developed countries.
- System of kinship. Cultures differ in the way family relationships are maintained and in the way parents raise their children – people from different cultures have different relationships with their children. In certain cultures (e.g. in the United States), a large, multi-generational family is not highly valued. Rather, it takes the form of a small,

independent unit made up of only the closest relatives. In addition, a characteristic feature of the American model of the family is that its members enjoy considerable autonomy. The value of independence is valued there. Therefore, children are left with quite a lot of freedom to make decisions about their own lives. It should be noted that in many other cultures such ideas of family life are socially unacceptable. Families are much bigger there. They consist of several generations of people who form a homogeneous whole. Units have a great influence on the upbringing of their youngest members. In cultures such as Asian, Hispanic, Middle Eastern, and African, individuals heavily rely on an extended network of reciprocal relationships with parents, grandparents, uncles, siblings, cousins, and so on.

- Union system. People from some cultures are strongly collaborative. They often spontaneously form all sorts of associations to accomplish any task (Hampden-Turner & Trompenaars, 2000, p. 11; Jay, 1996, p. 225). Others prefer the pursuit of self-interest. They are characterized by individuality and independence.
- Religious system. Cultures are distinguished by the faith professed by their representatives. Religion can be understood as propitiation or conciliation of powers superior to man which are believed to direct and control the course of nature and of human existence. It has always had (and still has) a huge influence on people. It is the belief in the existence of supernatural phenomena that has been motivating societies to create great works for centuries (an example can be the Egyptian pyramids). In many geographic areas of the world, religion has managed to dominate other areas of peoples' lives. The political or legal systems of those areas are subordinated to it. In many cases, it is therefore impossible to consider the culture of a given country in isolation from the faith professed there.
- Recreation system – the necessity to do something for recreation is an essential element of human biology, but, at the same time, people in different cultures use the time allotted to them for leisure in different ways. What may be considered entertainment in one culture (e.g. do it yourself) may already be considered work in another, and the other way around.

The analysis of the preceding taxonomies leads to the conclusion that cultural differences may concern many issues. Between some areas, these differences are small. They then apply only to selected points in each of the aforementioned enumerations of the basic categories, which usually boil down to cultural differences between countries. Among others, these discrepancies can be significant. At the same time, we can never assume that they don't exist at all. Even between countries that are very similar to each other, there can be significant cultural differences. For example, from the Czech perspective, Polish culture is more open. Czechs are often considered ambitious, but Poles get to work with enthusiasm and are considered more enterprising. The sense of humour is different – refined irony dominates in the Czech Republic, and Polish humour is simpler, more crude. Of course, further examples of cultural differences can be multiplied. They can effectively prevent the implementation of the project.

In order to find oneself in a multicultural environment, one must be firstly aware of the existence of certain differences. Getting to know the culture of another country often requires many years of work. It requires the ability to quickly adapt to new conditions, openness, and tolerance. Therefore, the issues of cultural differences and the potential complications resulting from them should be considered already at the stage of planning and organizing.

Generally speaking, planning and organizing should be considered in terms of managerial functions, the fulfilment of which is to lead to success in the project undertaken by the company. The first of mentioned activities includes, first of all, the determination of the necessary time, expenditures, and determination of the method of their usage in order to achieve the goals in the best, possible way.

"The importance of planning in an organization can never be overemphasized as we know that planning is the continuous managerial process of anticipating and forecasting the future environment of the business organization, the formulation of the long term and short term goals to be achieved and selecting the strategies for their realization" (Ogolo, 2011, p. 25).

The stage of planning the project is followed by the process of organizing, i.e. ensuring all forces and resources necessary to start the execution of the project. During this process, material and financial resources necessary for project implementation are obtained, solutions for the project organization and external communication plans are developed, contractors and project suppliers are acquired, contracts are negotiated with them, etc. (Trocki, 2014, p. 57).

Organizing consists mainly in organizing, established in the previous stage resources (human and other), which is necessary to implement the adopted project assumptions (Boone & Kurtz, 1992, p. 6) but also, e.g., creating an appropriate structure of the team responsible for the implementation of tasks. In this context organizing is to determine how activities and resources in the project are to be grouped (Griffin, 2008, p. 6). In other words, organizing is to develop such a configuration of resources that will allow for the efficient implementation of planned activities aimed at the project's realization. This step should include

- spatial organization;
- developing an organizational structure that is appropriate from the point of view of the assumed goals;
- making an appropriate division of work;
- delegation of responsibility and decision-making powers (including the transfer of some managerial prerogatives and responsibilities to employees appropriate from this point of view);
- creating teams, organizing tasks into processes;
- coordinating activities in time and space; and
- construction of an information technology (IT) system for the transfer of information and a communication system.

Organizing is, therefore, the stage at which tasks are assigned to individual entities and persons, in other words: it is the moment when the previously formulated task structure begins to vibrate with full life and gains regular momentum in its operation. At this stage, working groups and hierarchical dependencies between people involved in the evolution of a new project finally crystallize.

Planning with organizing does not exhaust, of course, the set of challenges that project implementers must face. Already, at the beginning of the last century, the set of managerial functions could not be considered complete without being extended to include ordering, coordinating, and controlling.[5] As the following years passed by, many researchers attempted to verify this set of tasks. One of the most famous concepts was developed in the mid-1950s at the University of California (LA). Academics of this university used the terms "planning, organizing, conducting personnel policy, directing and controlling" as a frame of reference in a textbook which for many years was undoubtedly the better-known and most frequently bought book on this subject (Robbins & DeCenzo, 2002, p. 34).

Currently, the management process, also in projects, is usually defined in terms of four functions. In addition to planning and organizing, they are: leading and controlling (Ivancevich, Lorenzi, Skinner & Crosby, 1994, p. 14). Such a classification (covering four essential functions) is quite commonly accepted in the scientific community and is repeated in most of the literature positions.

The term leadership is generally defined as a set of processes used to cause members of an organization to cooperate in the interests of the organization (Griffin, 1996, p. 43). This part of the managerial activity is considered extremely ambitious. After all, managing people so that they can effectively carry out the tasks entrusted to them requires the initiation of a number of processes and undertaking activities (Griffin, 1996, p. 43). As noted by K. M. Bartol and D. C. Martin, leadership includes, inter alia: communicating with others, defining the current vision of what can (and should) be done in a given, changing situation, motivating project implementers, and, finally, managing their actions.

The final phase of the management process is control. It consists in continuous and systematic monitoring of the entire management process and drawing conclusions that are the basis for corrective decisions (Bartol & Martin, 1992, p. 44). It is used to observe and introduce corrections to the currently conducted activities in order to facilitate the implementation of the previously adopted goals.

A wider consideration of the leadership and control functions is necessary from the point of view of the subject matter specified in the title of the thesis, however, due to the complexity of leadership and control, these functions will be described in the following subsection. At this point, however, the categories of specific activities included in the project planning stage should be listed and discussed (Table 2.4).

TABLE 2.4

Planning Activities in a Logistics Project

Scope	Characteristics
Resource planning	It is a strategic approach ensuring the usage of resources in the most effective way, across a single project (or projects' portfolio). Project team resources consist of the manpower and labour resources needed to complete the task. Their proper planning requires identifying the type of resource being used, determining its availability, and assessing billing rates per unit of quantity (for the sake of further cost planning).
	The next step is to analyse the charge on pre-acquired resources. It consists in identifying their usage in all processes implemented in the company (a specific resource may participate in parallel processes in the company and thus may not be useful (or useful to a small extent) from the point of view of the project).

(Continued)

TABLE 2.4 (CONTINUED)

Planning Activities in a Logistics Project

Scope	Characteristics
Planning of expenditures	Estimating the inputs expressed in machine or man-hours necessary at each stage of the implementation of a given project. This estimation should be done by someone with experience in the field. When executed properly, an organization achieves maximum efficiency and optimization in its usage of resources (without under/overutilizing any one resource).
Scheduling the implementation time	It is performed with the use of specific planning tools. The most common of these is the Gantt (bar) chart. Another noteworthy to mention, time planning tool is the Program Evaluation and Review Technique (PERT) – a method of organizing a project and judging if it is going well (by calculating the length of time needed for each task and the order in which it may be realized). This method enables (in a graphic form of a network) mapping of many activities carried out in a specific time, as well as their logical connections.
Planning of a work structure	It is all about establishing a comprehensive action plan in the form of a realization algorithm for achieving by the project team, the goal initially set for it. The Delphi method or brainstorming can be used in the construction of the work plan. In many cases, however, an external or internal expert is commissioned in order to develop the plan. Shaping the plan, apart from its implementer, always begins with the development of a list of logical and time-ordered elements of the processes that lead to the achievement of the project's goal. It is followed by the stage of a detailed and formalized, graphic mapping of the processes previously broken down into prime factors.
Costs' planning	Regardless of the type of a specific project, it is necessary to plan project costs, i.e. calculate the planned value of resources used in connection with the project implementation. Fortunately, project costs are an internal factor that can be significantly influenced by the company from the early stages of planning. Forming a real shape of the budget, which will allow the covering of all costs related to the project, should not be a huge challenge, especially since there are many methods available to support this process.

Source: Own elaboration based on Grabowska (2015, pp. 25–26) and Kasperek (2006, pp. 70–75).

Planning of the areas listed in the table may have the following character:

- long-lasting – actions specifying what needs to be done to complete the project,
- short term (up to three months) – short tasks to be performed as part of projects and plans with a wider time range, and
- current – daily or weekly (times and dates of project meetings, matters to be dealt with, etc.).

When planning a project, one should also pay attention to the issues related to the risk[6] that is naturally and inherently associated with each type of project: "projects are risky undertakings and modern approaches to managing projects, recognise the central need to manage risk as an integral part of the project management" (Hillson, 2016). A project, like any other implemented in an enterprise interdisciplinary undertaking of a considerable scale of complexity,[7] is at risk of not being successful. Project threats may appear in any element of its environment. At the same time, however, they are easiest to perceive and control if they appear in the immediate vicinity (Figure 2.1). The specific source of failure may be (Tarczyński & Mojsiewicz, 2001, p. 11).

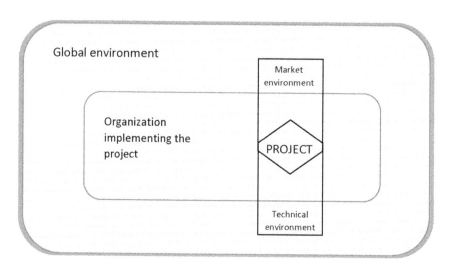

FIGURE 2.1
Project implementation environment as a source of risk.

Source: Own elaboration.

- systematic (external) risk is determined by external forces and is not subject to the control of the enterprise (e.g. demographic factors, legal and environmental conditions, requirements of government institutions, etc.); and
- specific (internal) risk covers the area of operations of a given project's initiator and may be controlled by this entity or person, at least to some extent; thus, internal sources are related to capital and technological resources, competences of human resources, as well as to the skills of planning, organizing, and an efficient communication system.

Among the specific types of project risks in turn, one can distinguish (Kozień, 2007, p. 79)

- proper risk, i.e. risk that can be predicted based on the law of large numbers. It concerns uncertain phenomena (for example, natural disasters, currency fluctuations), but those that have occurred before – with a known and described history and thus subjective to probabilistic description;
- subjective – resulting from incompetence (lack of knowledge and/or experience) of the person (or team) preparing analyses and making decisions in project management; and
- objective – related to the unpredictability of future events, e.g. the emergence of new technologies, political upheaval.

In a project, the objective risk should be controlled, and the subjective risk should be eliminated. In practice, in order to minimize each of the types of dangers, a project risk planning procedure should be applied, which includes three basic and chronological stages: recognition (identification), quantitative assessment, and reduction (Kasperek, 2006, p. 114). The first step is related to the assessment of the complexity of the project[8] related to the prediction of the potential risks arising from it. The most commonly used risk identification techniques include contract, schedule, and final product analysis. Individual conversations with direct task performers, brainstorming sessions, discussions with experts, etc., are also used. Subsequently, the hazards identified in this way should be assessed by performing calculations – estimating the probability of a given risk (PR)[9] and the range of possible effects (potential risk effects – RE). This then makes it possible to quantitatively qualify the so-called rank of risk (RR). It is the product of the risk probability (PR) and its potential consequences (RE):

$$RR = PR^* RE$$

In the next step, an attempt should be made to minimize the negative consequences of the identified problems. The enterprise should reduce the area of unpredictability in the project with a view to minimalize the costs of preventive actions (the price for minimizing the probability of a negative event's appearance should not exceed the costs of its possible consequences).

On the other hand, the first thing to focus on, at the organizational stage of a project is to develop its organizational structure. It should be formed in such a way as to allow for the elimination of problems arising in connection with the implementation of the project. Constructions based on the assumptions of the matrix structure are considered the most appropriate for this purpose. They usually include two basic levels – a periodic structure, i.e. project teams implementing individual sub-projects together with their managers, as well as a superior level created by entities operating in the project for a long time without any changes, including the principal, the steering committee, the coordinator and the audit unit.

After determining the structure of the project itself, its location within the organizational structure should be also considered. It is essential for implementation efficiency. The project can be performed within a single department only or be embedded higher in the organizational structure of the company. The choice of the second option is particularly justified in the case of interdisciplinary projects that require the extension of the range of implementers' competences with various abilities, located in non-identical departments of the organization.

On contrary, however, in projects involving the resources of many departments of the company, personnel problems are often revealed, in particular regarding the reporting of employees. Because often, the contractor assigned to his organizational unit reports directly to the manager of a given project. As a consequence, this may result in a conflict of interest between the line manager and the previously mentioned manager, resulting in an excessive workload for the subordinate. The implementation of the inter-departmental project is also associated with the need to develop a strict plan of burdening the costs of units participating in the project (as well as the settlement and distribution of revenues between them).

It should be emphasized that locating a properly structured project within the organizational structure does not yet complete the set of organizational activities. It is often necessary to develop management documentation of a project or ensure an efficient flow of information both within the project itself and between the project and the organizational structure in which it operates. A careful selection of information flow methods in order to eliminate the excess of information on the one hand and to ensure that the people involved in the project will have all the information they need on time, on the other hand.

The next step is to create a team of specialists competent in the field of project issues, i.e. a project team. Organizing the project team includes determining its composition, formally appointing the project team, organizing its work (internal organizational structure, division of duties, work plan, equipment, communication, financing, development of incentive instruments, etc.), and finally appointing the project managers (leaders). They have to choose the appropriate management style for the project, i.e. a relatively durable, repeatable, and long-lasting manner through which managers' influence their subordinates (Koźmiński & Piotrowski, 2013, p. 761). The superior's behaviour towards employees can be divided due to various criteria (Mroziewicz, 2005, p. 110). The division often cited in the literature is based on the criterion of the degree of participation of subordinates in making decisions. In this case, there are four, basic types of styles (Korzeniowski, 2010, p. 236):

- autocratic style, in which leaders imposes their will on subordinates. They are highly task oriented and low oriented on people. This style is suitable for critical situations, where crises have to be dealt with quickly,
- democratic style – in his case, project managers are highly oriented towards people (subordinates) who can significantly participate in taking decisions,
- liberal (compromise) style where the manager's interference is insignificant and the actual course of events is often out of his control. This style is suitable for project teams consisting of specialists, where the leader's interference is unnecessary, and boils down to administrative coordination,
- partner (friendly) style, where managers care more about relations and integration of the project team, rather than team performance. This style is suitable for start-ups, initial projects, or new team development, where employees do not know each other.

(Wajda, 2003, p. 95)

Traditionally, leadership has been perceived as a single, individual task of leading a number of followers or subordinates (autocratic style with the formally appointed leader). "This relationship has been a vertical one of top-down influence that could also be called 'vertical' leadership" (Pretorius, Steyn & Bond-Barnard, 2018, pp. 161–162). For years, this leadership model has been the principal one in the projects' field. Recently, however, new models of leadership have emerged, leading to the so-called shared leadership approach. Adopting the right style is crucial for the project because "the way of making decisions about the group, the participation of team members in deciding on the group's activities, the freedom to perform assigned tasks and the leader's communication with other team members" (Mruk, 2004, p. 200) depends on it. The authors write more about leadership in the project in line with the adopted style in the next section of the book.

2.2 LEADERSHIP AND MANAGERIAL CONTROL IN PROJECTS

Leadership in projects play a critical role for their in its success. According to definitions, leadership involves modifying the attitudes of subordinates in such a way that they can achieve goals. Referring to the subject of projects, it should be mentioned that project leadership is the skill and art of steering a team towards the successful realization of a project's goals. Leadership ensures that the team together accomplishes more than each individual could do alone because project leadership brings workers together to achieve a common aim.

These leadership functions are performed by the management teams, which consist of all people who have assumed the position of supervisors in the organization implementing the project. By leading functional units, they strive to implement assigned tasks with the help of subordinate staff (Listwan, 2004, p. 188). Their behaviours and their leadership style are determined by the characteristics of the organization, its culture, and the behaviour of its own superiors, and also depends on the attractiveness of the role they play in the organization. Managers make and approve all decisions that are vital to the project. The possibility of achieving success in the intended purpose depends largely on their decisions.

Project leadership requires a core set of competencies. Apart from high professional competences, the project manager should demonstrate an ethical attitude and a clearly defined system of values, pose not only formal authority but also, what is not less important, acceptance of subordinates and even charisma resulting from previous experiences. What's more, he should have empathy for employees, be involved in the functioning of the organization, and constantly raise his qualifications, including those related to motivating and conflict management.

As it was mentioned, a project leader's main role is considered to be dealing with people and addressing interpersonal issues. This is due to the fact that properly selected, involved, and targeted human capital is one of the basic factors guaranteeing the success of any project. However, the figure of the project team manager is often equated quite unambiguously and narrowly with supervision and realization of work progress. However, the spectrum of his duties is much wider. In the case of the implementation of international projects, the key function of a manager is, for example, the ability to navigate within the international framework, i.e. knowledge of foreign languages and cultural differences.[10] "Internationalisation of business leads to creation of employee teams that include foreigners" (Pabian & Pabian, 2021, p. 292).

A number of researchers are convicted that teams which consist of members coming from diverse nations ensure a greater potential for enhanced creativity, innovation, and values in today's globalized world (Daft & Marcic, 2013). Differences between nations should be treated as a team asset. Organizations with diverse people should be treated in the categories of creative and flexible due to different ideas, points of view, and ways of acting. At the same time, however, work in an international environment requires knowledge, effort, and the ability for the manager to go beyond the framework of previous experiences and cultural patterns known to him: "managing multicultural teams requires knowledge of differences and similarities between cultures, necessary in planning and organising work" (Walaszczyk, 2020, p. 56).

Each company strives to succeed in the market through properly led projects, i.e. to stay ahead of the competition by, e.g., offering the best product in the right amount or by responding to the needs of individual customers and the market as a whole. Achieving such goals is usually a long-term process, which however builds a sustainable competitive advantage and creates the image and place of the company in the environment. These challenges are faced by managers who define and plan the future of the company, are responsible for the implementation of projects, and are accountable for the consequences of their decisions.

For example, if they find that there is too small a number of people working on the project, which may delay its completion, hiring new employees should solve the problem. However, in practice, a number of circumstances may arise which will shed different light on this decision. First of all, it is not certain that new employees will have sufficient skills and experience in order to carry out the project. Thus, there may occur delays or inadequate implementation of certain activities. It will also be necessary to use the already working staff to provide certain information and customs, which unfortunately may delay the entire work on the project.

Usually, it is also necessary to modify or change the forms of communication. Information should be transferred to a larger group of people, which may, however, cause disruptions in communication. Its quality will deteriorate, and the time needed to provide important information will be significantly longer (Perlow & Repenning, 2009, p. 195). Everyone will spend less time working on the project and more time determining the data. Consequently, it may happen, for example, that hiring new employees to accelerate project implementation, in fact, will reduce the team's performance (Bracht, Geckler & Motschmann, 2009, p. 19).

One of the most important tasks entrusted to a manager is creating a team of employees, as well as managing this team. The selection of the right employees is crucial during the implementation of projects. A well-selected team is characterized by professionalism and reliability in fulfilling the tasks entrusted to it which translates into work efficiency and reduction of both costs and time of a given project implementation. Appropriate management of a professional team is as important as the qualifications they have. Properly selected management methods help managers efficiently manage the work of individual teams. Planning and logistics management capabilities, as well as the knowledge and precision of employees, allow an organization to reduce the time frame costs of individual tasks.

Another important element in the manager's responsibility is to define the organizational structure of the project. For example, with regard to the international aspect, it is a complex activity that involves the need to include many organizations and is associated with the necessity of the creation of applicable instruments for influencing individual elements of this structure. An additional obstacle in the implementation of the project is the distance between the consortium branches or contractors of entrusted project's works.

The task of the manager or the chief executive in charge of a given project is also its structuring, setting deadlines, and assessing costs. The creation of specific structures will allow the manager to efficiently manage the individual phases of the project, minimizing the impact of dissatisfaction with remuneration in relation to the tasks entrusted. The creation of an appropriate hierarchical grid will allow for the consistent execution of plans, as well as meeting the deadlines for the tasks entrusted to individual executive units. The created structure should be logical, clear, and concise to avoid communication errors between management, supervisory and executive staff in the future. A strict definition of goals and establishing direct authority will allow a company to avoid a situation in which it is dealing with the so-called contradiction of commands, where several superiors give contradictory instructions, and the person carrying them out, due to the resulting information chaos, is unable to precisely execute any of them.

Finally, project manager leadership duties embrace achieving goals in time. To do this, managers have to prepare important decisions and implement them, efficiently delegate tasks and empower participants of the project group, as well as develop tools in order to motivate, engage, and discipline group members. Project managers should also demonstrate the ability to be flexible and adaptable as well as skilfully organize alternative actions when changes occur. They should also be able to ensure the exchange of information between project participants (in a way of, e.g. organizing meetings) and ensure efficient exchange of documents (Pawlak, 2006, pp. 205–220).

The final task of the project manager is controlling (also monitoring), the organization's progress towards previously set project goals. As the organization moves towards the realization of a project, "managers must monitor progress to ensure that it is performing in such a way as to arrive at its destination at the appointed time" (Griffin, 2002, p. 7). Generally speaking, controlling deals with steering, it deals with the coordination of information flows, analysis, and appropriate interpretation of effects. All of this is to ensure the rationalization of decision-making processes in management (Harváth, 2011). It helps to implement and support the company's strategy through specific initiatives and priorities, contributing to the sustainable success of the whole organization (Rump & Schabel, 2010, p. 16).

The need to carry out control should be taken into account at the planning stage, already. In practice, control consists in checking whether the goals set by the management stuff in the planning phase have been achieved. It expresses a close relationship between one of the two initial phases of the project's development structure and the last one being described now. Namely, the evaluation of the project cannot be made without recalling the goals that were to be achieved thanks to it. The degree to which they were realized indicates the effectiveness of the whole project. In other words, the most important measure of the effectiveness of an undertaking aimed at achieving the desired state is the de facto results of the implementation of these previously assumed intentions.

The control process itself is often performed by an external expert, which ensures the objectivity of the process. The most important element is the expert's formulation of positive and negative conclusions that determine what was done correctly and what did not work in the project and why. It should be also emphasized that the implementers of the control phase have a wide range of tools for verifying the degree of achievement of objectives:

> in the field of management science, there are rich sets of analysis techniques that allow to cover all spheres of the company's operation and its environment. The basic principle of effective management of the company is to distinguish by the managerial staff phenomena and factors that can be shaped by them, from those that are beyond their reach.

(Danielak, Mierzwa & Bartczak, 2017, p. 60)

From the point of view of managerial staff, it is much easier to examine internal problems and processes of the company (among others, due to the knowledge and mastery of research techniques). In practice, it seems much more difficult to conduct an analysis of the company's environment and the impact of external factors.

Among the most useful tools that managers may take usage of, researchers mention, among others: the SMART pyramid or the Strategic Balanced Scorecard (Kaplan & Norton, 1992, pp. 71–79).

As already indicated, the effectiveness of the project implementation is indicated by the degree of achievement of specific objectives (of a material or non-material nature), which are characterized by (Trocki, Grucza & Ogonek, 2003, pp. 36–91)

- the scope of the project (what it concerns and what kind of work it covers), including realization quality of its individual phases and the final effect obtained, and
- implementation time, which determines the point of launching/exploiting the project's effects, allowing for reaping economic, organizational, technological, and marketing benefits.

It should be emphasized that the effectiveness of project implementation, depending on its type, can be variously interpreted and measured by what results from the nature of inputs used and results achieved (material/intangible, easily measurable/hard to measure, exchangeable in terms of value/quantity).

On the other hand, the efficiency criterion is closely related to economic issues. Efficiency can be defined as a subject of activities in which the ratio of the value of useful results to the value of the inputs incurred in obtaining them is greater than one (Zieleniewski, 1975, p. 226). Therefore, it should be understood as the relation of the value of the effects of specific activities and processes taking place in the organization to the inputs of production factors used to obtain them (Skowronek-Mielczarek & Leszczyński, 2007, p. 183). It is determined by all elements of the so-called project management triangle (Figure 2.2.).

It is a derivative of the partial effectiveness of the management's activities: the credibility of the managerial staff, clear definition of the project's priorities, achievability of goals, and proper perception of the project by all its stakeholders (Kerzner, 2008, pp. 351–352). The effects of the implementation of individual projects may therefore have different dimensions: tangible and intangible (immeasurable).

The analysis of the economic efficiency of project management is therefore based on the comparison of two different groups: costs and incomes, revenues and expenses, assets, and liabilities. It refers to the phase of developing the initial concept of the project and its definition, as well as to the phase of implementation and commissioning. It plays a very

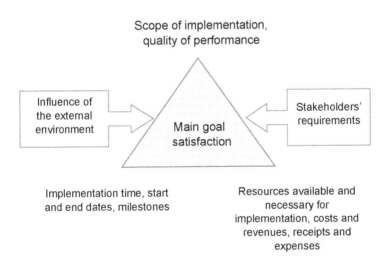

FIGURE 2.2
Project management triangle.

Source: Own elaboration based on Patzak & Ratty, 2009, p. 219.

important role for stakeholders, which can be seen by reviewing the tasks performed at individual positions related to the implementation of the project. The approach to economic efficiency using the division of projects according to the criterion of origin of the order (more about types of projects in subsection 1.2) is presented in Figure 2.3.

Methods for evaluating the effectiveness of projects have evolved and are still evolving. The first and most important event is the development of methods for assessing the effectiveness of projects as components of the programme, including simple and discount methods. The next important step is the usage of IT and communication solutions in enterprises, i.e. the usage of computers, specialized software, the Internet, and telephones or satellite communication (see one of the following subsections). The usage of technological solutions has contributed to an increase in the computing power used for data processing. The effect of this was to enable economic analyses to be carried out almost on a real-time basis and also by people working for the project far from the place of its actual realization.

Another important step was the introduction of spreadsheets, which are used in the economic departments of almost every company. The third breakthrough event is the development of the concept of project controlling, which is a set of measures describing the state of the project

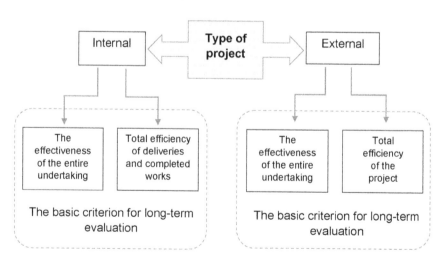

FIGURE 2.3

Project effectiveness criterion.

Source: Own elaboration based on Borowiecki & Rojek, 2011, p. 25.

(Borowiecki & Rojek, 2011, p. 25). It also covers other areas, such as personnel management or logistics management in crisis situations. Unfortunately, despite its importance, project controlling is an issue poorly described in the literature on the subject. At the same time, there are attempts to transfer the concepts of controlling the current activities of the organization to the area of project management, which gives rise to a number of ambiguities and misunderstandings, because the implementation of projects usually does not coincide with the repetitive (process) activity of the company (Bukłaha, 2018, p. 182).

The success of the company is more and more strongly associated with the implementation of projects (Cron et al., 2010, p. 15). However, it should be noted that project implementation failures still remain a big problem and will be also a big challenge in the future. Among the factors responsible for the failure of a project, the following are usually mentioned: improperly defined project's goals from its beginning, bad communication between people working on the undertaking, involvement of people with incomplete or inadequate qualifications, and finally – lack of full resources at the start of the project (Herbolzheimer & Lüthi, 2008a; Spang & Özcan, 2008/2009, http://www.gpmipma; Yeo, 2002, p. 241; Whittaker, 1999b, p. 23). At this point, one should consider whether the aforementioned factors are causes or maybe symptoms of deeper causes. Funding the answer to this question is one of the controlling aims (Patzak, 2009, p. 42; Perlow & Repenning, 2009, p. 195; Abdel-Hamid, 1988, p. 395).

At the end of the section, it should be also emphasized that in order to meet a wide range of leadership and controlling duties, which always depend on the circumstances of a specific place and time, the project manager should have certain key features that will ensure the proper functioning of the project. Among them, should be mentioned first of all (Borowiecki & Jaki, 2011, p. 24):

- ability to behave consistently, inspire confidence, persuasiveness, verbal fluency;
- ambition, activity, the ability to get one's own way;
- effective acting in communication and integration;
- strategic thinking – understood as the ability to plan for the future, generate ideas and implement strategies for obtaining success;
- balance, enthusiasm, imagination, spontaneity;

- listening skills – listening helps understand important information better; moreover, a good manager values and respects his team's insights and ideas by fully hearing what they share;
- the ability to balance technical solutions with time, cost, and human factor constraints;
- good organization and discipline;
- ability to deal with changes – a good manager is adaptable and flexible; when he faces obstacles, he has the ability to react in a quick manner;
- possessing knowledge in many areas (interdisciplinaryness) – being a generalist rather than a specialist; and
- the ability to maintain an appropriate balance in time management.

Experienced managers effectively lead project teams by developing necessary skills. In addition to those listed, project managers must sport the ability to identify problems, devote most of their time to planning, controlling, solving personal problems, and skilfully take difficult decisions. They should be characterized by emotional intelligence which can help them to, e.g. identify a co-worker who is feeling burned out or overwhelmed (in such a case, a compassionate leader may give support or put provisions in place in order to help a struggling subordinate, such as reminding about services and policies that are set to help, offering spare time, work from home day, arranging a flexible schedule). Post-COVID-19 era revealed that assuring the well-being of employees is a key competence of to-date leaders (Dyduch & Bratnicka, 2022).

Training and development is always a valuable route in developing and improving upon managerial skills. Since the mid-1980s education of managers has experienced the proliferation of texts and courses designed to teach managerial skills to people who want to expand their managerial abilities and be more effective leaders. "Today there are at least nine textbooks devoted exclusively to managerial skills, some in their second or third edition. Many MBA programmes have made management skills training a central component of their curriculum" (Caproni & Arias, 1997, p. 293).

In addition to social and personal abilities which can be acquired, project managers need to become specialists possessing appropriate, in-depth, expert knowledge in the field of projects' management, which gives leadership and direction to projects, allows reducing project costs by improving efficiency, mitigating risks, and optimizing resources.

2.3 CONTEMPORARY CHALLENGES IN PROJECT MANAGEMENT

The words "problem" and "challenge" are inseparably inscribed in the subject of project management, so their appearance during the realization process should not surprise anyone. Project management is always a big challenge. Each project has specific features that determine the need to take many actions (Table 2.5). One of the key challenges facing the project manager is minimizing any design deviations. In order to deal with the managerial challenge, it is therefore necessary to adopt the appropriate formula.

One project management formula is broadly understood as "managerial pragmatics", i.e. performing economic and managerial work on the course of the design and implementation process, focusing on the functions of organization of project teams, planning the design and implementation cycle, scheduling, budgeting, analysis of the effectiveness of projects, coordination and control of implementation. The second formula of project management is substantive management over project development and implementation (Stabryła, 2006, p. 34).

The Project Cycle Management (PCM) method recommended by the European Commission – EUROPAID Cooperation Office is of universal

TABLE 2.5

Features of the Project in Relation to Activities

Feature	Action (example)
Dynamic time horizons for changes	Long-lasting projects, long product lifetime
Controlled by multiple feedback structures	Hiring staff, product quality, activities related to management
Delay	Time to build experience, delay in hiring employees
Lack of linearity	Workload effect focused on productivity
Accumulations dependent on the past	Accumulated experience, reputation, standards of safety
Same regulation	Complementary and competing assumptions of project participants
Strongly combined elements	Strong division of tasks and dependencies, high degree of specification
A large number of claim groups	Project managers, clients, politics, competition, society

Source: Own elaboration based on Herbolzheimer and Lüthi (2008a), Spang and Özcan (2008/2009), http://www.gpmipma, Yeo (2002, p. 241), and Whittaker (1999b, p. 23).

importance in the approach to project management. This approach allows the management of many different projects and improves the quality of them over time. It is based on many years of development and focused on organizing and planning projects through foundational principles and defined phases.

Complexity is a specific feature of a system that arises through time shifts, accumulation, non-linearity, and dependencies of feedback. Unfortunately, it is dynamic complexity that should be considered in the case of the main reason why a large part of projects implemented in enterprises finish in failure. Problems related to proper communication and the lack of appropriate staff to manage the project can be caused by dynamic complexity. If we care about proper project management, we can use an integrated feedback model to use dynamic complexity not only in planning but also in controlling and project management (Sterman, 2000). It will be a valuable addition to the controlling instruments and, at the same time, to the controller's skills.

Widespread globalization (has to be considered in terms of all the processes leading to the increasing interdependence and integration of states, societies, economies and cultures,[11] resulting in the formation of "one world", a global society; the disappearance of the nation-state category; shrinking social space; and increasing the pace of interaction through the use of information technologies and the growing importance of supra- and international organizations, in particular transnational corporations) (compare: Campbell, Hamill & Purdie, Stonehouse, 2001, p. 25; Guzek, 2001, p. 18; Lamy, 2004, p. 15; Liberska, 2002, p. 20; Ładyka, 2007, pp. 36–37; Łoś-Nowak, 2000, p. 112; Adamowicz, 2004, pp. 239–237; Adamowicz, 2008, pp. 49–64; Piwowarczyk, 2004, pp. 155–166; Zaorska, 2000, pp. 14–21; Spychalski, 2009, p. 319; Tkaczyk 2005, pp. 12–13; Budnikowski, 2006b, pp. 434–444; Skidelsky, 2009, pp. 2–3; Stoner, Freeman, & Gilbert, 2001, pp. 136–141), in which more and more companies treat the whole world as a sales market (Budnikowski, 2006a, p. 434; Gieryszewska & Wawrzyniak, 2001, p. 19; Siekierski & Popławski, 2006, pp. 123–129; Klimczak, 2002, pp. 39–47; Rynarzewski & Zielińska-Głębocka, 2006, pp. 209–210; Winiarski, 2002, pp. 23–32; Kołodko, 2008, pp. 98–99), currently forces enterprises (or economies) to adapt to the shape of the market on which they operate and which they want to enter.

Globalization is not a new phenomenon in the history of modern civilization. Researchers note that in earlier historical periods, there were also significant transformations in economies, caused, among others, by geographical discoveries of the 15th century or the industrial revolution that began in Western Europe at the end of the 18th century (mainly in the Netherlands, England, France, Germany, Belgium) (Brzeziński, 2016, p. 16).

At the same time, however, the so-called new globalization, whose beginnings should be seen after the end of the Second World War, is characterized by unprecedented dynamics, which results from the rapid development of previously unavailable information and communication technologies (ICT) technologies for data and information exchange. More and more companies, previously operating only on internal and local markets are included in the scope of the global exchange processes that are currently taking place. In connection with this, the prestige of local cultures and conditions of everyday life is of great importance. Therefore, globalization should be viewed not only from the point of view of the offerer but also from the point of view of the consumer.

Implementation of project management in the conditions of widespread globalization and integration, under the influence of exogenous conditions, should be viewed through the prism of the EU market as a single creation – a single whole (Czyżewski, Grzelak, 2011, p. 21).

Mostly, projects are undertakings with a specific goal and realization time. Among their characteristics can be distinguished complexity, unique character, uniqueness in terms of concept and/or realization, equivalence, and formalization of activities.

Complexity (in other words comprehensiveness) is, in the most general terms: a lot of possibilities and activities, a multitude of various connections and influences, and changing and remaining in certain dependencies and relationships. It is possible to distinguish (http://wirtschaftslexikon. gabler.de/Archiv/5074/komplexitaet-v6.htmp; Patzak, 2009, p. 42):

- Detailed complexity – it contains many components in the system that can be combined in various ways. When making decisions, one should consider all opportunities that arise. Among them, there is the one that is the best.
- Dynamic complexity – in this case, there are no simple and direct cause-and-effect relationships. It should be taken into account that in actions it is impossible to plan all moves precisely, forecast, or anticipate certain effects. Undesirable, unwanted events and surprises must be taken into account. It is particularly important when the implementation of the plan requires significant outlays and large investments to contribute to the development of the enterprise or to maintain its current strong position in the market.

These two types of complexity should be of interest primarily to managers, who must at least try to address this division and find appropriate, diametrically opposed means of management. It is easier in the case of detailed complexity, as existing management methods mainly focus on this type of complexity, using, for example, standardization or detailed planning (Figure 2.4).

In turn, the method of integrated qualitative feedback modelling can be used to properly understand dynamic complexity, which, despite a long career among managers, has not yet become a permanent element of leadership behaviour (Smura, https://konteksthr.pl/feedback-jest-klopotliwy-jak-yeti/, reading: 05.12.2022). And it may successfully allow us to better define and describe phenomena that have been difficult to grasp so far.

Managers, undertaking the implementation and realization of a specific project take into account the fact that certain factors can appear that will call into question the final success of their activities (Herbolzheimer &

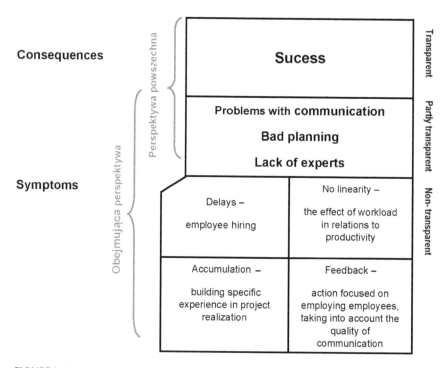

FIGURE 2.4

Features of dynamic complexity as the main cause of project failure.

Source: Own elaboration based on http://wirtschaftslexikon.gabler.de/Archiv/5074/ komplexitaet-v6.htmp; Patzak, 2009, p. 42.

Lüthi, 2008a, p. 14; Spang & Özcan, 2008/2009; Yeo, 2002, p. 241; Whittaker, 1999a, p. 3). Projects usually do not end perfectly as planned and require vigilance and control until the last moment (even when it seems that nothing unexpected should happen). In practice, the list of problems that can be called design challenges will never be closed because the prose of design life keeps adding new items to it. Among the most frequently mentioned factors determining the success or failure of projects these are mentioned:

- communication – incorrect or insufficient;
- not very precise definition of project objectives;
- incorrect valuation of project costs (typically too optimistic);
- underestimation of the project by superiors;
- lack of qualified staff working directly on the project;
- mistakes in change management;
- errors related to the management of the project team; a well-performing, motivated design team can save the worst-looking project, and vice versa; and
- lack of sufficient risk management.

Each project manager in the course of his professional practice completes his own list of challenges containing more or less abstract project risks and at the same time becomes the owner of a growing portfolio of solutions to crisis situations (Pojda & Bukłaha, https://gazeta.sgh.waw.pl/ekonomia-po-prostu/dlaczego-projekty-sie-nie-udaja, reading: 15.05.2022). The majority of these factors are noticed when the project has already ended and has some characteristics of a summary. Unfortunately, such a situation has its downsides – in this case, managers assess certain causes after they have occurred, so they are unable to analyse their development in detail during the project, and they distort certain information. Thus, they do not sufficiently consider dynamic complexity. The managers pay attention primarily to what affects the success or failure of the project at a given moment, collect data, and analyse it but are often unable to see the appropriate symptoms.

In practice, even a seemingly simple action related to project management, such as hiring additional staff to improve project progress, can bring unexpected and undesirable results. Hence, experienced managers are aware of the consequences of their decisions and are able to recognize them and prevent them in time. They are also aware that surprises may appear later, as they can be delayed in time and reveal themselves in unexpected situations. It may also happen that managers, analysing the unfavourable circumstances in the implementation of projects, incorrectly determines the reasons for these circumstances.

To avoid these errors in diagnosis, managers should use controlling instruments and use the skills of controllers in finding the right methods and instruments to take into account, among other things, dynamic complexity in management. Here, the method of integrated feedback modelling is a well-proven method (Sterman, 1980, p. 20; Abdel-Hamid, 1988, p. 395; Williams, 2002). Thanks to it, it is possible to build certain models as modules and use them later, which significantly reduces the costs of their implementation or employee training. In addition, the feedback method advantages are (Patzak, 2009, p. 42):

1) easier and faster understanding of the impacts of project management;
2) knowing the negative effects of certain activities and dependencies; one can react to them in advance by preparing certain models and plans that will take them into account;
3) changes to the project (e.g. scope, implementation time, technology change) can be communicated to people working on the project in a timely manner;
4) possibility to integrate the already used project management methods and focus on the essential elements of this management; and
5) possibility (in the long run), to improve the image of the company among potential customers who will appreciate the right management policy.

Properly defining and determining the reasons for project failures is a major challenge for project managers as well as their supporters, e.g. controllers, as it is their task to identify the features of the management system that are responsible for the causes of failures. It is also not enough to constantly refer to (or use) only, already known methods, the effectiveness of which has been previously checked. It is necessary to focus primarily on the consequences of actions because most often, the majority of problems arise when people responsible for management are unable to predict the effects of their actions.

Only proper knowledge about the causes and relationships between these causes and the ability to reduce them will allow for the proper usage of management methods and limit the possibilities of failure to a minimum.

The currently used methods, although usable, are not fully able to meet these challenges. Therefore, the advantages of qualitative feedback modelling should be used to a greater extent, which gives greater opportunities for broader recognition of threats that may decide the failure of the project (Cooper, 2007, p. 157). Thus, it allows managers to examine the reasons for both the success and failure of undertaken activities. Also thanks to the possibilities offered by feedback modelling, it becomes possible to understand the essence of dynamic complexity and its impact on the causes of failures (Sterman, 2010, p. 316).

The complexity of the project is evidenced by the multitude of institutions responsible for its implementation. Therefore, planning, designing, implementing, realizing, and managing processes are very complex undertakings, requiring participants a lot of creativity, flexibility, responsiveness, regularity, and extensive knowledge not only in the field of management but also in many other areas. The implementation and management of the project is an extremely difficult undertaking that requires diligence, consistency, and enormous determination at every stage of this multi-factor process, both on a national and European scale. Implementation of all planned tasks translates into managerial, infrastructural, and human-related/personal success.

2.4 IT TOOLS IN PROJECT MANAGEMENT

To-date, society is dealing with a growing saturation of life with computer and Internet technologies. Appropriate IT tools have become indispensable in life and work. People using IT or ICT tools can be described as (Sobocińska, 2012, pp. 26–27):

- enthusiasts for whom the computer/Internet is an integral part of life and who attach great importance to the possibility of using it;
- communicators who like to talk and express themselves also in the virtual world and use IT primarily to communicate with others;
- those who like innovation and learning, seek to broaden their knowledge and are characterized by searching for information using IT tools; and
- beginners who have been using computers for a short time and strive to create their own place in the virtual space.

An important and very large group is people using IT tools to perform tasks related to their work (professional users). In this context, IT tools are also necessary to work on projects and to improve their management.

> "Project management as a discipline was born from the combination of several types of engineering studies as early as at the beginning of the 20th century. But it took almost five decades to understand that without the right tools, achieving success in project can be only considered in terms of a wishful thinking".
>
> (Sadowska, https://www.droptica.pl/blog/czym-sa-metodyki-zarzadzania-projektami-i-ktora-wybrac-dla-twojego-projektu/, 2022)

The usage of IT tools is nowadays a prerequisite for the efficient, reliable, and undisturbed implementation of a project's processes, from the simplest ones to the more complex. What's more effective control of decision-making processes in the project is also conditioned by up-to-date and reliable information that is usually obtained and transmitted through technical means of generating and processing information.

Modern IT tools used in projects can be grouped within specific infrastructural components. The term infrastructure itself originates from the words: "infra", which can be easily translated into "beneath", and "structure", which means "to build". Generally speaking, this term encompasses all components that are available beneath the given framework which can be, e.g. an information system. In the physical world, the term generally translates into basic, physical equipment necessary for the functioning of a state or a society (Luger, 2008, p. 25). It often refers to public utilities such as water, electricity, sewage, gas, telephone services, and so on – all the components literally beneath the structure of a city or town (Laan, 2017, p. 37).

There is no doubt that such quite laconic statements in many cases have become an inspiration and a starting point for formulating more detailed definitions of infrastructure, created for the needs of various fields of knowledge, including IT. Thus, in the literature on the subject, many interpretations of the term IT infrastructure have been noted. It is worth noting some examples (Laan, 2017, p. 36):

- IT infrastructure should be considered in terms of reliable and shared services that provide the foundation for the IT portfolio of any organization.

Its architecture includes processors, software, hardware, electronic links, datacentres, as well as standards that ensure components work together, the skills for managing operations, etc.

- Configuration items (hardware and software components) are needed to run IT applications and are necessary to deliver IT services to an organization and its customers.
- A system which underpins the distributed, administrative, and operational computing environment. This kind of infrastructure is hidden from the application-based reality of end users and encompasses the unseen realm of networks, protocols, and middle-ware that facilitate efficient data flow and bind computing organizations together.
- System of hardware, software, facilities, and service components that support the delivery of business systems and IT-enabled processes.

> *(Gartner Glossary: https://www.gartner.com/en/information-technology/glossary/it-infrastructure)*

Without modern IT infrastructure elements, it is nowadays difficult to imagine any aspect of a modern enterprise's activities, including project activities. According to the EU, digital technology is changing people's lives. The EU's digital strategy aims to make the IT transformation for people and businesses while helping to achieve the target of a climate-neutral Europe. The EU Commission is determined to implement the "digital decade" for Europe. According to European officials, this continent must now strengthen its digital sovereignty and set standards, rather than follow others' solutions (with a clear focus on data, technology, and infrastructure).[12]

IT infrastructure has been identified in recent years in some businesses as having a critical impact on the firm's ability to act competitively (Duncan, 1995, p. 37). A flexible, reliable, and secure IT infrastructure can help a company to achieve business goals, as well as a competitive advantage. Conversely, if the IT infrastructure is not implemented properly, the company may face connectivity, performance, and security issues, such as system disruptions and security breaches.

Figure 2.5. shows the components of the IT infrastructure enabling the processing of information streams necessary to steer a project's processes, for which, apart from traditional computerized office equipment, modern multimedia computer systems and accompanying ICT systems supporting process management are used.

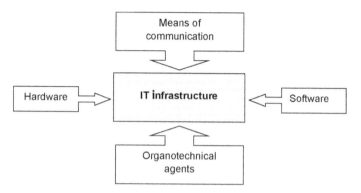

FIGURE 2.5
Components of the IT infrastructure.

Source: Own elaboration based on Wojciechowski, Wojciechowski & Kosmatka, 2009, p. 15.

The IT infrastructure finding usage in projects consists mainly of independent elements that can be divided into hardware and software components (Neuhold & Paul, 1992, p. 9):

- IT equipment (hardware) means a set of technical devices, including computers with the necessary cabling, network devices (e.g. modems), and accompanying sets of peripheral devices, intended in accordance with the definition of IT for information processing.
- Software is a set of applications and computer programs (operating systems, utility, and utility software), defined as a sequence of commands entered in a fixed manner and executed by a calculating machine in order to achieve a specific goal, perform a task, etc. It enables the use of computer hardware in order to perform a specific task work.

The hardware does not work without software, such as an operating system. Apart from them, the elements of IT infrastructure include means of communication, as well as an organotechnical means. Table 2.6 lists specific elements that make up each of the IT infrastructure's components.

The aforementioned division shows that IT tools supporting projects can beclassified into two groups: tools having a physical form (computer and communication devices), as well as tools not having a physical form[13] (all information in the form of a set of instructions, implemented interfaces, protocols and integrated data intended for operate computers and execute specific tasks).

TABLE 2.6

Detailing of IT Infrastructure Components

Hardware	Software	Means of Communication	Organotechnical Means
Hardware (abbreviation HW) refers to all physical components of a computer including devices connected to it (e.g. modems). It is neither possible to create a computer nor to use software without HW. Hardware components include, but are not limited to: • personal computers (laptops and desktops); • microcomputers; • portable terminals; • servers, i.e. computers that allow multiple users to access and share resources; • centres of data processing; • concentrators; and • routers.	Software can be defined as a set of instructions which makes machine with information processing capabilities capable of performing specific tasks (those instructions are placed on a medium from which the machine can retrieve data). In practice, it is easy to identify obvious software components, such as operating systems, spreadsheets, office packages, or graphics processing packages. Generally, however, it can be noticed that • system software and • device software are the two main types of software which are necessary in projects. System software acts as a basis for software applications. It governs a computer's internal operation, mainly by operating system (manages the resources and equipment of IT systems) and controls peripherals such as displays, printers, and storage devices. It allows the machine to operate effectively. It is also responsible for managing components of hardware and providing basic functions that are non-task-specific. In contrast, application software guides the machine to perform user-given commands and can assume to include any programme that processes a user's data. Office Suite is an example of application software. Software for applications may be a single programme or a series of tiny programmes. The third category of software is network software, (which coordinates communication between network-connected computers) and programming software (tools for writing programmes to support developers).	Means of communication means tools or mediums intended for sending and receiving information. They take the form of technical solutions, including devices of ICT as well as software tools cooperating with them, enabling individual communication at a distance using data transmission between ICT systems. This group includes, among others: • telephones, • smartphones, • faxes, and • telexes.	These are auxiliary, technical measures used in the process of mechanization and automation of data processing, e.g. • wires, • nests, • connectors, • concentrators, • switches, • extension cords.

Source: Own elaboration based on Abt (2001, p. 131), Behan (2018, p. 47), and https://www.javatpoint.com/software-definition (reading: 15.07.2022 r.).

Due to the possibilities of computerization and digitalization available in Europe (the phenomenon of the digital economy has begun on a large scale in Europe at the end of the twentieth century), the number of Internet users is increasing, a catalogue of available public online services is increasing, the ICT infrastructure develops, and new business models are being identified. As a consequence, the digital economy constitutes an important component of the contemporary economic landscape in Europe[14]) and worldwide, organizations increasingly focus on the automation of their activities and project management procedures. Computers have become ubiquitous and are undoubtedly one of the most effective tools for all business activities, including project management processes. Used for data processing formerly, they are nowadays used to collect, store and share large amounts of data,[15] which can be used in the implementation as well as management of the project. The development of a network of computer systems means that nowadays computer systems effectively act as a source of information, necessary in project work.

Nowadays, both project implementers as well as managers have many helpful tools at their disposal. Unlike other inventions, the purpose of the computer has changed over the years. At the beginning (mid-20th century), the computer was only used as a high-speed counting machine, performing different types of calculations. Various kinds of calculating devices were already known in ancient times and they played a similar role as today's calculators. For example, as early as in the 10th century BC in Central Asia and Greece, a board or a clay tablet was used, in which stones were placed in carved grooves (the so-called: *abacus*), to facilitate calculations

The first device that can be called a computer is the Electronic Numerical Integrator and Computer – ENIAC. It was created over 70 years ago and constructed by J. P. Eckert and J. W. Mauchly at the University of Pennsylvania in the United States (Moore School of Electrical Engineering). It was presented to the public in February 1946 at Princeton University, and its usage was discontinued not earlier than nine years later.

ENIAC consisted of 42 steel sheet cabinets, which were over 2.4 metres high and 24 metres long. It occupied 167 m^2, and its total weight exceeded 27 tons. Despite these facts, it worked with a clock speed of only 0.1 MHz. Contemporary low-end smartphones are on average 50,000 times faster and over 43,000 times lighter than ENIAC (McCartney, 1999). Later, the technology developed, but still only a few were able to make use of computer and network solutions.

Today, the computer and the associated Internet are basic work tools, and modern computer systems are very extensive and complex structures, which enables their usage in projects. However, please note that complex systems inherently have more potential failure points and are more difficult to correct implementation. What is more, a complex system is harder to manage, much more knowledge is required to maintain it, and errors appear more often.

When it comes to computer hardware, its significant development has taken place in recent years, which has definitely facilitated work on projects and their management. The progress in hardware that has been made since the aforementioned ENIAC has significantly expanded the usability of computers. The first devices available for commercial usage appeared on the market, no earlier than 40 years after EINAC (the 1980s of the 20th century). However, unlike the first computers, they already successfully fit on a desk thanks to small tin or plastic housings (a good example is the so-called Cray-2 computer, which was at the time considered an unmatched formula of computing power). During this period (the year 1982), the Microsoft Windows operating system also made its debut on computers (initially it was an overlay for MS-DOS).

It was crucial innovation that contributed greatly to the further development of desktops, which due to their ease of use became more and more desired by a large number of private as well as commercial buyers. Nowadays every single person knows what the word "computer" means. We can find computers everywhere around us. In fact, the modern world would be incomplete without computers and their applications. It's almost impossible to even imagine modern facilities without the use of computers (Horst, 2012, pp. 69–70).

The answer to this mentioned interest was, among others, the Commodore 64 computer. It took the form of a small, beige unit attached to a TV set. This computer already offered, among others, basic office software, and its processor's clock frequency was 1 MHz. However, it was the 386-type processors that brought a real revolution in the industry. Equipped with such a unit was, among others, Compaq Deskpro (1986) – one of the oldest computers that found wide usage in homes. It cost a lot but was worth its price: it had, for example, a 32-bit processor with a clock frequency of 16 MHz.

Stationary computers were still dominant during the 1990s, and engineers competed in designing more and more efficient constructions. The appearance of the first portable computers, i.e. laptops, is connected with the late 1970s. The first commercially available laptop appeared on the market then. Alan Key, an employee of Xerox PARC, is today considered the originator of the concept of the laptop, originally referred to as "Dynabook".[16] It was a step towards mobile computers that can be used in not only one strictly defined place. As their power was increasing, their size and weight were dropping away, making laptops gradually become the basic equipment of ordinary users, as well as companies. Entrepreneurs began to use them widely and for many years it was believed that a good laptop was the end of personal computer development.

However, at present, the pinnacle of computer technology are rather 2-in-1 devices (Microsoft was the precursor of 2-in-1 devices with its line of Surface devices, which debuted on the market in 2012), which can function as tablets (equipped with touch screens) but also as laptops thanks to the keyboard attached to their screens. Their main advantages are mobility and multifunctionality. Thanks to their low weight and size, they can be taken almost everywhere. More and more often they are used by private users and organizations implementing projects, especially those carried out in conditions requiring speed and efficiency of operations.

It seems that the next steps in hardware development will be the introduction of laptops with double screens (which can be used in two modes – a tablet with two independent screens or a compact laptop, including a screen displaying the keyboard) or the development of the idea of a "Password-Free World" developed by, among others, Microsoft. Consists in abandoning passwords as a sequence of characters typed from a computer keyboard – this idea means extensive use of biometric data, which is to allow for more effective protection of computer interfaces (Maziarz, Benchmark.pl: https://www.benchmark.pl/aktualnosci/historia-rozwoju-komputerow-i-laptopow.html, reading: 29.08.2022 r.).

The market for personal computers does not stand still. Designers of the next generations of devices are trying to equip them with new technologies. Due to them, computers are becoming more and more attractive and useful products. So far, the goal is one and clear: to maximize the comfort of usage. At the same time, thanks to the use of new solutions, computers are becoming more and more user-friendly and safe.

The degree of maturity of modern computer hardware makes it indispensable in projects. It enables users to perform routine activities related to the implementation of the project (communicating with other team members, storing information in databases, performing calculations using spreadsheets, etc.). However, from the project contractors' point of view, this is only the first stage in the development of using computers in their daily work (Woźniak, 2005). It is possible to list further computer functions that facilitate the work related to the project:

1) Computer as a tool for solving decision-making tasks. It is required in this case to take into account the specificity related either to the nature of the reality to which the task relates or to certain distinguished typical functions. The entirety of the problems at this stage can be called problem-solving engineering. It uses methods and algorithms for optimization, identification, recognition, control, decision-making, etc.

2) A computer as a means of collecting and processing information. It performs functions the subject of which are information and information sets. The subject matter of this stage can be called information engineering, using methods and algorithms for processing and collecting information, and algorithms for managing information sets.

3) Computer as an expert, supporting the process of solving problems with the usage of registered knowledge representation and reasoning algorithms. Knowledge engineering deals with these issues using the methods of description, collection, and supplementation of knowledge, as well as methods and algorithms for the use of knowledge according to the appropriate rules of reasoning.

It should be emphasized at this point that even the latest and the best hardware solutions cannot be effective for project contractors alone, without the use of appropriate software. Working with a project often requires individuality in the selection of appropriate software solutions; therefore, when choosing a programme/programmes, one should precisely define the goals of working with a computer and evaluate the formal features of the programme in terms of the following:

- Communicativeness and ease of use – the quality of information generated by the computer should be assessed in terms of its ability to be understood by the user.
- Availability, expressed, inter alia, in the amount of financial resources that are necessary to be spent for the use of software.
- Time and pace – the programme should be designed in such a way that the time needed to complete the tasks is as short as possible so as not to cause a feeling of weariness and discouragement in the user.

- Programme manual – the programme should contain an overview of its functionality along with the methodological cover.
- Sound and/or visual attractiveness.
- Polysensory and multitasking – the programme should enable the simultaneous impact on all senses and perform many operations simultaneously.
- Easy possibilities of integration with other software solutions.
- Openness of the programme – the ability to adapt it to the needs and abilities of end users.

An appropriately selected programme can become a recipe for challenges arising in connection with the project and become a motivating factor for work. Of course, the type of software used depends on the specific project, but at the same time, project implementers have a wide range of solutions that they can implement in order to facilitate their work and management in the project. This collection includes both simple, everyday tools (e.g. word processors) and comprehensive computer software for project management, i.e. scheduling, budget control and management, resource allocation, quality and documentation management, risk management, and management of variance in projects.

"Project management software is a term covering vast types of software" (Kundu, 2015, p. 91). It allows us to collaborate, plan, and share the effects of work. It helps to organize the flow of information, ensures timely execution of tasks, and proper distribution of resources. The market is full of such tools, such as IC, etc. From the functional point of view, among the available modules of software solutions for project management, there are certain types of them (Modliński, 2015, pp. 67–70):

- Project Portfolio Management (PPM). Software enabling centralized management of a group of projects. It allows, among others for more efficient use of resources. From the shared pool one can use currently needed resources for several projects, so there is no need to allocate them separately and independently to each of them.
- Database Management System (DBMS) is a software or IT system designed to manage a database. Projects contributing to the implementation of an organization's goals, use the company's information resources and creates a database for their needs. "A database can be defined as a set of interrelated collections, together with the software enabling their collection, storage, analysis, access which

are stored in the memory of computers and used by application programs of instructions or organizations" (Szymonik & Nowak, 2018, p. 187). Databases always have a data source, users, and connections with the represented reality (tools for processing, adding, updating, searching, and correcting data, as well as tools for presenting the obtained information in the form of, e.g., a report). Databases are of key importance in many projects, but their exploitation is neither an easy nor a stable process. During the implementation of a project, the closer and further the environment changes, the more the input and output parameters of the system also change. It is therefore necessary to adapt the system to the changing reality.

- Groupware. Support for team/group work (GW) is software aimed at facilitating the work of a group of people involved in a project – both gathered in one place or geographically dispersed. It enables, among others, work on shared data and allows for mutual synchronization (e.g. calendars, task lists) as well as communication thanks to the most common solutions, such as e-mail (both traditional e-mails and internal messages between employees using the tool), through various types of text and voice communicators, videoconferences, etc.

- Time Scheduling (TS). The purpose of such software is to allocate owned resources (including time) to individual tasks in order to maximize the efficiency of their usage. In practice, they are most often associated with additional methods of analysing such schedules as the Critical Path Method (CPM) or PERT, allowing users to find activities critical for the success of the project, both in terms of time and usage of other resources.

- Document Management System (DMS) covers software tools that allow for recording, classification, archiving, etc., of all documents related to the project. The software of this type may also contain elements of the Optical Character Recognition (OCR) type, allowing for the recognition of the written text on the basis of, e.g., a scan (and then processing it with the usage of tools operating on the text).

- Time Management (TM). Software that allows the determination of what specific resources were used at a given time. In particular, it is used for project teams' reckoning – it allows users to determine how much work has been put into the implementation of a specific task (that is part of the project), not in an estimate, but in real terms.

- Analysis and Reporting (AR) – these are the tools that allow for the presentation of a project's elements in a synthetic and condensed way, e.g. by presenting a cross-section of certain data. An example may be the total amount of work done so far (man-hours) and the degree of advancement of the project defined as the number of completed tasks. This type of analysis allows users to control the course of work and detect possible deviations from the assumed schedule on an ongoing basis.

Specific programmes from the mentioned categories of tools can be acquired (licensed) in various ways. There are two basic types of software in terms of licensing: freeware and commercial. The term freeware is formally a specific type of license, but colloquially, this term is used to describe any software distributed under non-commercial licenses. It is characterized primarily by the possibility of free use, often also introducing individual modifications.

Regarding the installation method, project management software can be implemented as a programme that runs on the desktop of each user. It typically gives the most responsive style of interface. Project management software can be also implemented as a web application, accessed through the Internet. In this situation, a project's information is not available when the user, or server, is offline, but such an option still has some advantages. Among them, it supports multi-user access, only one software version and installation is to be maintained, data can be accessed from any type of computer without installing software on the user's computer because the original software is installed on the application server, and so on.

NOTES

1 The concept of a plan is an ambiguous one. The dictionary of foreign words lists several meanings of this term but from the point of view of project management, two of them are important: "a schematically mapped image of an object" and "a program of tasks, works in a certain field to be performed within a certain period of time; schedule of activities foreseen to be made". Compare: *Słownik wyrazów obcych*, PWN, Warszawa 1980, p. 576.

2 The fact that individual countries differ in terms of culture was shown by him on the basis of research conducted among employees of the IBM corporation. Based on the analysis of questionnaires completed by 116,000 people employed in 72 subsidiaries of the company, located in more than 69 different corners of the world, similarly to the other author, he came to the conclusion that these differences concern four fundamental issues (compare Gillespie, Jeannet, & Hennessey, 2007, p. 72).

3 There are three basic ways of communication between people: verbal (using words), paraverbal (e.g. how loud we speak, what colour our voice is, what is the importance

of silence during a conversation, speaking at the same time), and, finally, non-verbal (body language) (compare Pabian, 2008, p. 83).

4   Researchers note that currently almost a billion consumers live in most developed countries. First of all, due to the current and historical economic success, the following markets should be considered the most developed: Great Britain, the United States, Sweden, France, Japan, the Netherlands, and Germany. Over time, they were joined by Canada, Israel, and some of the previously unmentioned European countries (e.g. the Benelux area), as well as the countries of the Asia-Pacific region (Australia, New Zealand, Hong Kong, Singapore). This does not change the fact that almost half of the world's population (three billion people) still populates the least developed markets, i.e. those where fundamental living needs are not met on an ongoing basis, and those of a higher level are often not even defined (see more: Hampden-Turner & Trompenaars, 2000, p. 11).

5   According to the concept of H. Fayol (compare Donnelly, Gibson & Ivancevich, 1992, p. 102).

6   Generally interpreting the risk, it should be understood as any uncertainty, also one that may favourably change the course and effects of any undertaking. A project risk should be understood as an uncertain event that may (but does not have to) occur during a project or (according to PMI): as an uncertainty to the occurrence of an event or condition that, if it occurs, will have a significant (positive or negative) impact on the course of the project (compare D. M. Kirschbaum, "Calculated Risk. Good Surprise, Bad Surprise: The Law of Unintended Consequences". Community Risk Management and Insurance. Washington 2000; www.pmi.org (reading: 25.07.2022 r.)).

7   Each work (activity) performed by any organization is a composition of processes and projects. The processes are performed in a routine (repeatable) manner, while the projects are performed on a time basis, and each of them is different. Each organization usually undertakes both types of activity, although many organizations (e.g. offices or manufacturing companies) mainly work in a process mode – they perform routine operations on a daily basis. These operations are improved in an evolutionary way and relatively rarely require fundamental changes, which is why they are usually not burdened with high risk. Conversely, projects are made not only to improve the existing processes, but they often launch completely new, previously non-existent processes and products which require greater attention of the teams involved in them.

8   The complexity in the project should be equated with its size, understood in terms of a certain number of interrelationships between the individual elements that make up the basic dimensions of the project (compare Haffer, 2009, p. 30).

9   Knowing the probabilistic model to which a given risk is a subject, it is possible to carry out a classical probability analysis using the theory of random variables. Simulation methods such as Monte Carlo may be useful in this case.

10 Culture was defined by Linton as a configuration of learned behaviours and results of behaviour whose component elements are transmitted and shared by the members of a particular society. Individual countries and areas of the world (to a greater or lesser extent, but always), differ culturally. Not knowing the differences between people from different cultures may result in specific problems during the realization of projects. Because of that, national culture awareness is considered one of the main conditions of effective cooperation between the members of project teams coming from different parts of the world (compare Linton, 1945, p. 32; Pabian, 2008, pp. 77–78).

11 Culture is defined as "a specific set of elements that are related in a specific way, and both the elements themselves and their connections have a specific meaning for

the people who use them". A slightly extended definition of this term, closer to the sociological way of understanding it, says that culture should be interpreted as a set of artefacts and symbols created by a given society and passed down from generation to generation as determinants and regulators of its members' behaviour. They take a tangible form (e.g. works of art or other material products of human thought) or abstract (e.g. values, beliefs). Each society creates its own symbols that are fully understood only by its members. For people coming from a foreign cultural circle, they may be understandable only partially or, in extreme cases, have no meaning at all. The more antagonistic two cultures are to each other, the more difficult it is for a representative of one of them to find himself in the reality of the other (compare Santon, Etzel & Walker, 1991, p. 118; Filipiak, 1996, p. 42).

12 On 2 May 2017, the European Commission published the Staff Working Document Digital4Development: mainstreaming digital technologies and services into EU Development Policy (D4D) setting up its vision, priority areas, and future actions in using digital technologies and services as a cross-cutting tool in the EU development interventions. Based on existing policies and partnerships involving the public and private sectors, the Commission is mainstreaming digital technologies across four main priority areas: promote access to affordable and secure broadband connectivity and to digital infrastructure, including the necessary regulatory reforms; promote digital literacy and skills; foster digital entrepreneurship and job creation; and promote the use of digital technologies as an enabler for sustainable development (https://ec.europa.eu/futurium/en/eu-au-digital-economy-task-force/eu-digital-development-policy-0.html).

13 The entire set of applications, protocols, and processes involved with a computer system's operation uses the software (Osterweil, 2018, pp. 59–70).

14 Improving access, usage, and quality of Information and Communication Technologies has become one of the 11 thematic objectives for the EU Cohesion Policy between 2014 and 2020. Over €20 billion from the European Regional Development Fund (ERDF) was available for ICT investments during the 2014–2020 funding period. These investments have been vital for the success of the Commission's objective of making Europe fit for the digital age (compare Moroz, 2017, p. 175; EU portal: https://ec.europa.eu/regional_policy/en/policy/themes/ict/;   https://ec.europa.eu/info/strategy/priorities-2019-2024/europe-fit-digital-age_en (reading: 15.08.2022)).

15 One of the manifestations of these changes is, for example, the fact that the term "control of electronic data processing" has been over time replaced in the literature with such terms as "control of information technology" and "control of information systems" (compare INTOSAI Working Group, 2016, p. 8).

16 However, the solution he proposed did not enter general circulation. Only the '90s brought a real boom for laptops and a leap in development of this category of equipment.

3

Small and Medium-Sized Enterprises in Poland: Organizational Design Supporting Innovative Projects, Crisis Management and Prospects for Development

3.1 SMEs IN POLAND – GENERAL CHARACTERISTICS

SME stands for "small and medium-sized enterprises". The SME sector includes every entity that, regardless of its legal form, conducts regular economic activity. Therefore, the SME sector is made up of entrepreneurs operating on the market, most often as family enterprises, partnerships, or consortia (Krezymon, 2018, p. 23). These businesses' personnel numbers fall below certain limits.

The category of micro SMEs includes enterprises that employ fewer than 250 employees (employment level is treated as an absolute measure for classification because its value is not subject to rapid obsolescence and does not depend on the economic situation of the country); what is more, the data themselves are easily accessible (Drab-Kurowska & Sokół, 2010, p. 14) and annual turnover does not exceed EUR 50 million or the total annual balance sheet does not exceed EUR 43 million. The main advantage of such a distinction is the measurability and objectivity of these indicators and the ease of their use in statistical comparisons.

Among firms from the SME group, there are a lot of so-called family businesses. One of the first definitions of family businesses was created by R. Donelley. The author understands it as one in which "at least two generations of the family can be identified and when this connection (between generations) influenced the policy of the company and the interests and

DOI: 10.1201/9781003309901-3

goals of the family" (Donelley, 1964, p. 93). In the world literature, a family business is nowadays defined similarly as an enterprise that may take any legal form. Its ownership is fully or partially held by a family (at least one family member holds a managerial position), and there is the intention to keep the organization in the hands of the family (Frishkoff, frishkoffbus. orst.edu, reading: 12.11.2022). "Defining the concept of a family business is usually based on two criteria: management and ownership understood as an impact on decision-making. The way these criteria are delineated, however, tend to vary from country to country" (Głód & Głód, 2017, p. 40).

Family enterprises are the oldest and at the same time one of the most numerous business entities (Leszczewska, 2016, p. 7). At the same time, however, the issue of family businesses has been undertaken relatively recently. The influence of the family on the company for many decades was overlooked in scientific and political discussions and was not treated as a significant factor influencing the conduct of business. The situation began to change at the turn of the 1970s and 1980s – since then, the topic of family businesses has been gradually included in scientific and political discussions, both in Europe and around the world. A similar tendency can also be observed in Poland in recent years (Krynicki, 2009, p. 6). It is so, e.g. because nowadays, family businesses in the EU account for more than 60 percent of all operating enterprises: "depending on the adopted definition, it is estimated that family businesses in the former EU-15 and in the United States constitute from one third to over 70% of all economic entities operating on the market, generate between 20% and 70% of GDP and employ from 27% to 70% of all employees" (Astrachan, Shaker, 2003).

Family businesses are a specific type of enterprise. At the same time, one can list characteristics that determine the specificity and competitive advantage of family businesses (Kałuża, 2009, pp. 52–55):

- their main purpose of functioning is usually to provide financial security for family members and to maintain control over the company;
- founders most often build their company from scratch, investing all their own capital, time, and energy in it;
- they perceive their company from the beginning as "their child", another family member whose proper formation will ensure its good functioning in the future;
- in family businesses, more than in other types of companies, full commitment and dedication to what they do is visible because the family is more emotionally connected with the company;

- family entrepreneurs are not immediately focused on maximization of profit in a very short period of time. This fact makes the actions aimed at return on investment rather long term and carefully thought out;
- a very official nature of business running is usually not needed. Family businesses are usually not large organizations that have been formally established and for the operation of which bureaucracy is needed. Less formalized family organizations are therefore more flexible, they adapt more easily to changes, which makes it easier for family members to make decisions and easier to set goals, as well as their possible correction if necessary;
- in family businesses, there is a stronger identification with the values of the enterprise itself or internal conviction as to the mission of a given company. This is due to the sense of community, belonging to the firm, and the generational identity that its members have;
- many large global corporations grew out of family businesses, and some of them still remain under the control of the descendants of the founders.

Today, SMEs, including these of a family nature, are associated with a number of positive attributes. They have a significant role in modern economic processes both in European countries and in other regions. Actually, the SME sector plays an extremely important role in a modern economy. This role is fulfilled through a significant share in the domestic product, creating new jobs, productivity, investment outlays, and entrepreneurial activities conducive to economic development.

Micro SMEs are considered to be the driving force of the European economy. They stimulate job creation and economic growth and ensure social stability. In 2013, over 21 million SMEs provided 88.8 million job places across the EU. Nine out of ten enterprises were small and medium. SMEs create two out of every three jobs (Komisja Europejska, 2019, p. 4). SMEs also stimulate entrepreneurship. They are believed to be the most attractive and tremendously innovative system.

SMEs come in many different forms and sizes (family ones have been already mentioned);[1] however, in today's complex business environment, they may have close financial, operational, or administrative ties to other companies. These relationships often make it difficult to draw a precise line between small, medium, and larger enterprises. Hence, managing an SME requires not infrequently many skills from the entrepreneur and manager due to the specificity of their business, limited resources, and the constant need to respond to changes in the environment. On the other hand, however, such units' advantage is the speed and efficiency with which they can take advantage of unexpected changes in the environment (Danielak, Mierzwa & Bartczak, 2017, p. 7).

The SME sector is undoubtedly an important part of the Polish economy, and the COVID-19 pandemic did not change it much. This sector is still representing a large majority of companies in Poland. While the enterprise sector generates over 72% of the Polish GDP, the SMEs themselves contribute to creating nearly 50% of the GDP (PARP, 2021).

Among 2.2 million enterprises operating in Poland, 99.8% of them are micro-, small, and medium-sized ones. Every second company operates in services, every fourth in trade, and every eight in construction.

In the second quarter of 2022, over 93,660 enterprises were registered in Poland, which is 1.3% more year to year. Only 80 enterprises declared bankruptcy, which is 4.8% less year to year. In the second quarter of 2022, more enterprises were registered in the information and communication branch (by 37.5%), transportation and storage (by 13.9%), while some decrease was observed in accommodation and catering (by 15.6%), trade, repair of motor vehicles (by 6.1%), services (by 3.8%), industry (by 3.1%), and construction (by 2.5%) (Statistics Poland, https://stat.gov.pl/en/topics/economic-activities-finances/activity-of-enterprises-activity-of-companies/registrations-and-bankruptcies-of-enterprises-in-the-second-quarter-of-2022,21,14.html; accessed 16 November 2022).

The SME sector, covering companies with 10 to 249 employees, has an unleashed potential to develop and grow in the Polish economy and sports the power of entrepreneurship that is yet to come. The sector, since being smaller than in other EU countries, is still not saturated, and many entrepreneurs can start and grow their businesses, as there is room for them on the market in many branches.

Even though the Polish economy is developing dynamically and the GDP growth was not very much harmed by the COVID-19 crisis and the war in Ukraine, there is a relatively low unemployment rate, the export stays strong – some barriers to developing new SMEs are indicated (https://www.politykainsight.pl/multimedia/_resource/res/20105186, accessed 16 November 2022). First, the SME sector is smaller in Poland than in other EU countries, which represents both an opportunity and a threat. The opportunity derives from the fact that there is still a lot of room for the development of the sector. However, the faster development of the SME sector in the EU signals that the ease of doing business in Poland, entre-preneurial policy, and conditions to start up still require improvement (https://archive.doingbusiness.org/en/rankings, accessed 16 November 2022). The majority of the SMEs in Poland are just small businesses, with only 23% innovative enterprises, while in the EU the proportion is reversed.

Second, even though services took the floor in recent years, the SME sector in Poland is still predominated by industrial and trading firms. This of course creates great opportunities to export goods like furniture, elec-tronics, white goods, fast moving consumer goods (FMCG), etc., but makes companies in other countries competitive in advanced services. Third, SMEs are more heavily indebted than large companies, and they are more sensitive to economic fluctuations than large firms. What is more, SMEs' development depends largely on increasing productivity, even though these enterprises invest relatively more in people than tangi-ble assets compared to large corporations. Fifth, the SMEs have difficulties accessing financing and finding skilled workers, which inhibits innova-tion to a certain extent. Finally, as SMEs cooperate with large corporations (as subcontractors or in a symbiotic model of controlling the pie) not all the SMEs are able to look for key partners, develop relations with large firms, enter networks, and build social capital with other stakeholders.

Other barriers include a lack of resources, as well as a lack of know-how and management competences, which results in designing inappropriate structures and implementing ineffective strategies. At the same time, entrepreneurs in Poland are regarded as creative and hardworking, able to look actively for opportunities, which often translates into the overall con-dition of many small and medium-sized firms.

The latest Global Entrepreneurship Monitor report (GEM, 2022) indicates that the COVID-19 pandemic influenced largely both entrepreneurial intents and the number of start-ups launched. Even though the percentage of mature SMEs tends to be high, and the conditions to start up are generally improving, the motives for starting up have changed – opportunity-based motives were replaced by the concern about financial stability and safety; at the same time, the number of people fearing a start-up does not decrease.

It can be noticed that the environment has been perceived as difficult and more complex – the number of owners knowing someone who was forced to close the company recently has increased. However, despite the dynamism of the environment, there is still a high self-assessment of the personal com-petencies to start and run their own companies among Polish people. Poland faced the pandemic during the dynamic economy growth and a very good situation in the labour market. For the past two years, despite lockdowns and other restrictions, thanks to public support, the unemployment rate was low, and the demand for employees started growing in 2021, which strengthened the conditions for employing people by SMEs (PARP, 2022).

The positive assessment of conditions to start up did not translate into entrepreneurial intents of Polish people: in 2021 only 3% declared that they plan to start their business activity (5% in 2020, 6% in 2019, the EU average is 13%, PARP, 2022). Nearly every second adult person admitted that the risk of failure discourages them from starting their own company. This means that Poland is dominated by mature SMEs whose number is five times higher than the young ones. The leading motives to start up are financial ones (getting richer and assuring employment).

Neither the desire to change the world or continue a family tradition is a popular motive to start a company. Start-ups are assessed well as far as co-working and mentoring are concerned; however, there is a need to improve the competences to build relationships between large and medium-sized firms with start-ups, financing possibilities, and public programmes oriented towards helping young businesses (PARP, 2022). The summary of the advantages and disadvantages of the SME sector in Poland is presented in Figure 3.1.

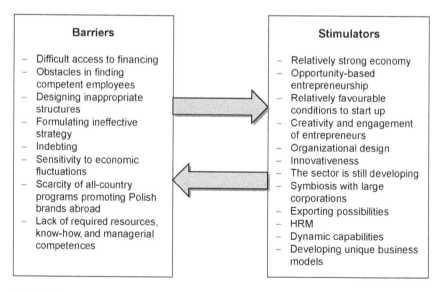

FIGURE 3.1
Barriers and stimulators of SME development in Poland.

Source: Own elaboration.

Having identified the advantages and disadvantages of the sector, it is worth answering the question about the pillars of SME success in proper project management and innovativeness. Entrepreneurs who have the intent to start their own companies are advised to plan their business well, analyse the environment, identify the competitors, carry out market research, define the target group, offer a unique value proposition, and continue planning, especially in crisis times, as well as developing with the help of dynamic capabilities that facilitate adapting to a dynamic environment and shifting the resource base to exploit opportunities that appear.

Many success factors can be identified for SMEs: consistent vision implementing, creating value for customers, caring for competent employees, innovativeness, environment scanning, and assuring financial liquidity. For SMEs, a key success factor is also to shape an idiosyncratic business model – with hard-to-imitate sources of value creation and to formulate a unique strategy – understood as an efficient commitment towards a future that no one has thought about before.

3.2 ORGANIZATIONAL DESIGN FOR PROJECT MANAGEMENT AND INNOVATIVENESS

SMEs require proper organizational design to effectively manage projects and to prepare and commercialize innovations (Dyduch, 2019). Firstly, however, it is crucial to understand what innovation is and what it represents.

This concept has not been strictly defined in economics and in the discipline of management sciences. This is mainly due to the interdisciplinary nature of research on innovation (Sławińska, 2015, p. 158). On the one hand, interdisciplinarity is still declared as one of the essential features of the modern way of doing science. On the other hand, however, such an approach is a source of specific problems, including, for example, those related to the unambiguous definition of concepts introduced by the argument that assumes the demarcation of science. Researchers, however, agree that the etymology of term "innovation" can be seen in the Latin word "*innovatis*", which for the former inhabitants of the Apennine Peninsula meant "renewal", alternatively "creation of something new". It is also not uncommon that "the concept of innovation is treated as derived from another Latin word, namely *novus*, meaning novelty" (Sikora & Uziębło, 2013, p. 354).

The extremely dynamic development of the concept of innovation takes place today, i.e. the beginning of the 21st century (Białoń, 2010, p. 95). Researchers agree that the realities in which enterprises have to manage today cause the need to increase "the adaptability of business entities and are a premise for the search for new and sustainable sources of economic growth based on innovations" (Szaflarski & Markiewicz-Halemba, 2014, p. 237). In other words, in an economic situation characterized by strong competition and permanent and dynamic changes in the market situation, company development strategies must be based on the introduction of innovations.

Obtaining and then maintaining a competitive advantage and the development of business entities in turbulent realities are conditioned by the creation of new solutions in the form of products and processes, as well as the development and implementation of unprecedented business models (Porter, 2001, p. 27).

Nowadays, innovations are therefore one of the key determinants of the development of enterprises that have to operate in conditions of a turbulent environment and the development of modern technologies. "The effect of innovative activities is to increase the value of the organization and to gain a competitive advantage on the market" (Szymańska, 2012, p. 147). Innovation is seen as the driving force of the modern economy, turning ideas and knowledge into products and services (often through project work) (Krzepicka & Tarapata, 2012, p. 75).

This approach is in line with the words of H. Ford, who stated that companies that grow through development, improvement, and innovation will not die. But when a company stops being creative and starts thinking that it has achieved perfection and only has to produce, then it is doomed to failure (Joseph & Rodenberg, 2007, p. 234).

There are many definitions of innovation in the literature that characterize it in a non-identical way. In the dictionary of foreign words, innovation is defined as a change involving the introduction of something new, or novelty understood as a newly introduced thing (Kopaliński, 1983).

In its fundamental meaning, the term, therefore, means something new and different from the solutions used so far. As researchers write, "[I]nnovation is an idea, procedure or thing that is new and qualitatively better" (Czakon & Komańda, 2011, p. 19). In a broad sense, it means change of a creative nature, which can occur in any given social, economic, technical, or natural system. Such transformations take place as a result of the activity of people who adopt a

sequential set of procedures, consisting of creative preparation and formation of a new state of substance (thought) that meets the specific needs of
consumers, and then transforming it in a certain segment into one of the
subsystems of global system.

(Janasz, 2011, p. 269)

In this sense, the term "innovation" should be identified with any transformation of the current state of an arbitrary and purposeful arrangement of elements, which has a specific structure and constitutes a logically
ordered whole. As a consequence, this leads to the creation of a good,
idea, practice, or process that is perceived as new by the person or other
receiving entity. This way of defining innovation indicates its further key
features:

- Innovation can be a new solution both on a global and regional scale
  and even on a single market or institution.
- The concept of "innovation" should be understood as changes of
  various nature.
- Innovation must have a practical application.

At the same time, it should be emphasized that in the economic literature
the concept of "innovation" has a slightly narrower and more precisely
defined meaning. Although there is no full agreement among researchers
as to the definition of this term, most of them agree that innovations can
be considered in terms of a deliberate, systematic, and organized search
for new solutions by entrepreneurs who, due to their activity, acquire the
name of innovators (Drucker, 2004, pp. 32–40). The changes made by
them may be of a non-identical nature:

- Technological. New technologies are defined in terms of technological knowledge in the form of intangible or legal assets, in particular, the results of research and development works acquired from
  scientific units. This knowledge enables the production of new or
  improved products or services, or the improvement of processes, and
  should not be used in the world for more than five years (Ustawa z
  dnia 30 maja, 2008 r., Dz. U. 2008).
- Non-technological, e.g. in the field of marketing or organizational
  activities.

In turn, the aforementioned novelty does not necessarily mean that, in objective terms, the solution will be something very modern, previously unavailable in any other form. One has to agree with the researchers who claim that the concept of novelty is very subjective, so the use of this term depends only on the perception of the author of a new idea or the person to whom it directly or indirectly relates, for example, advanced IT systems at such giants as Shell or IBM are standard, but for a small trader or food manufacturer, using even an ordinary PC to navigate the Internet can be a real challenge (Rogers, 1995, p. 15).

The presented way of understanding innovation does not differ significantly from the thoughts of J.A. Schumpeter (born in 1883, an Austrian scientist and politician, minister of finance of Austria in 1919–1920, considered one of the greatest economists of the 20th century[2]), who first used the term, associating innovation with a new combination of factors of production. In a work dating from the beginning of the 20th century entitled *Business Cycles – a Theoretical, Historical and Statistical Analysis of the Capitalist Process*, this researcher emphasized that the search for new solutions, already indicated in the aforementioned definitions, may be carried out in specific areas of the company's activity. Thus, he narrowed down the meaning of innovations, describing them in terms of (Glapiński, 2012, pp. 3–5)

- introduction of new or improvement of existing manufacturing and/or sales processes;
- launching a completely new or possibly only improved product on the market;
- entering a new market, i.e. one where a given type of industry has not been introduced before;
- obtaining a new source of raw materials or semi-finished products for production; and
- introduction of a new organizational form of production.

Researchers note, "[F]or many years Joseph A. Schumpeter's theory of innovation was not applied in economic practice. This was due to, among other things, the relatively slow economic development in the first half of the last century" (Postawka, 2018, p. 5). However, this does not change the fact that the categories of innovation listed by J. A. Schumpeter are accepted by the scientific community to this day.

They are considered in terms of a set of traditional innovations. They also belong to the group of creative changes, which in the literature on the subject are called "closed" due to the limited participation of various entities involved in their creation. The classic approach to innovation, evolved by J. A. Schumpeter, assumed the development of a new idea exclusively in-house, and then its commercialization, i.e. introducing it to business practice based on market principles (Westland, 2008, p. 8).

Because the term innovation has been already clarified, in this section, some conceptual findings are given concerning the organizational design that supports project management and innovation development (Tushman et al. 2010). The management literature tackles the problem of organizational design either as designing proper structures (e.g. Oe, 2021; DeSanctis, Glass & Ensing, 2002) that will cope with project management complexity or designing a coordinated system of integrated actions allowing for effective information processing in the times of uncertainty (Puranam, Raveendran & Knudsen, 2012, p. 419). These two perspectives will be considered here to offer a framework for developing the organizational design that facilitates project management and stimulates innovativeness.

Some recommendations are given concerning the organizational design for better project management (DeSanctis, Glass & Ensing, 2002, p. 64):

- designing strategic mechanisms that support creativity and idea commercialization (e.g. high priority for research and development (R&D) expenses),
- top management team engagement in project management and new product development,
- developing an entrepreneurial culture,
- knowledge sharing throughout the whole organization,
- searching for opportunities outside the organization, and
- readiness for changing structures, designing hybrid structures for quick responding to signals coming from the environment.

The strategic design of a creative organization needs to sport the following features: (Bilton & Cummings, 2010, p. 207):

- formal structures that create a skeleton for the whole organization, with informal structures promoting idea generation and bottom-up experimentation;

- strong but adaptive organizational culture that on one hand integrates and unifies the whole organization but on the other hand allows it to adopt to environmental changes and introduce innovative ideas;
- meritocratic organizational climate, where promising creative ideas are assessed objectively and promoted depending on their value, regardless of where they come from and by whom they are introduced;
- knowledge management environment that leaves room for idea exchange between experts and naive enthusiasts;
- intrapreneurship processes and autonomy, with new idea generation both inside and outside of the organization;
- environment promoting multitasking, holistic thinking, and using various perspectives;
- optimal approach towards introducing change; avoiding change just for the sake of changing; and
- ambidexterity, understood as managing paradoxes present in all the dimensions of organizational design.

It is worth looking closer at the offered dimensions of the organizational design promoting creativity and innovativeness. The first of them, organizational structures, are an important element of organizational design. Centralized, formal, bureaucratic structures are perceived as appropriate for large organizations with big R&D departments making it possible for introducing new products (DeSanctis, Glass & Ensing, 2002), while informal and loose structures are associated with SMEs, where they can be the source of radical and discontinuous innovations (Chell, 2001). To manage projects effectively, the structure of the SME should evolve, depending on the lifecycle of the enterprise, or the phase of projects being developed: idea generation, idea selection, and commercializing.

During the initial phase of SME existence, the dominating structures should rather be organic, informal, project, or virtual, allowing flexibility and dynamics in teamwork, opportunity identification, and idea generation. This phase focuses on informal relations in the teams, moderate pressure on deadlines and effectiveness, informal planning, and flexible work division. However, during the next phase of selecting ideas that will be turned into innovations, the organizational structure should be more formal – functional or divisional, requiring diligent planning effort from other functional units. Finally, the phase of commercialization of innovations requires divisional, matrix, or hybrid structures for bringing marketable ideas to life. Moreover, this phase requires building relations with stakeholders, as well as creating network structures outside of the organization for acquiring complementary resources beyond the organization's control.

The second important component of the design promoting innovativeness is the organizational culture. On one hand, it should be strong and built around commonly shared values and norms that create a spine integrating members, providing the perception of a community. On the other hand, the organizational culture should be flexible enough to allow openness to change and adaptative enough to promote bottom-up experimentation, new idea acceptance, and dynamic capabilities development. Underestimating the organizational culture may lead to market failures (Aboramadan et al., 2020).

The third important element of proper organizational design promoting innovativeness is the organizational climate, where valuable ideas are being recognized and selected on a meritocratic, not political, basis. A climate of trust and teamwork requires strategic mechanisms of valuable ideas recognition already in the moment of their appearance, as well as proper filtering and selection of marketable ideas. The fourth component of the design is stimulating knowledge management by sabotaging and questioning expert and specialized knowledge for new idea appearance, improving the learning processes, and seeking new perspectives in problem-solving. This approach based on questioning the existing *status quo* results in better problem-solving, as well as identifying common areas between various points of reference.

When promoting new idea generation and innovativeness, it is vital to mention intrapreneurship (Pinchot, 1995). It is not only about giving autonomy and financial support to certain organization members responsible for creating new products and services. The idea of intrapreneurship lies in recognizing complex sources of new ideas. Hence, the organization uses products and ideas created by its members, but also resorts to products and services generated outside (extrapreneurship), often imitating, improving them, and applying firm-specific marketing strategy.

In order to stimulate the work dynamics and keep the interest of the team members, proper organizing should involve multitasking and changing perspectives, i.e. frequent shifting roles, assigning tasks that are not directly connected to one's expertise, occasionally shifting specialists into the project teams, and using various perspectives in idea generation and innovation preparation. This component of organizational design requires avoiding problem-solving within one unit of the organization, by the same team.

On the other hand, seeking heterogeneity and promoting multitasking should not lead to organization member dispersion. Still, multitasking based on empowerment and designing project teams with members from different organization parts may result in better cooperation and a higher level of creativity. A vital component of the design facilitating project management and stimulating innovativeness is designing places to work that would allow for concentrated and creative work. The former can be designed around closed areas that help to work effectively on the assigned projects and tasks. The latter is more open, therefore facilitating communication and idea exchange, allowing people to meet, talk, and inspire each other before concentrating on work.

An important aspect of the organizational design is proper intensity in introducing change that does not overwhelm organization members' capacity to accept them. It requires developing the ability to cope with the changes introduced. At the same time, this characteristic of the organizational design requires strategic mechanisms that reject changes that are trivial, unnecessary, or are introduced just for the sake of change.

Finally, ambidexterity is the organization's characteristic in which all the other aspects of the design are merged. Ambidexterity means reconciling paradoxes – managing contradicting situations that appear at the same time, and none of them can be removed (De Wit & Meyer, 2010) – in order to revive and integrate the entire organization (Weick, 1987).

The dimensions of the organizational design facilitating project management and promoting innovativeness described earlier can lead to offering a conceptual framework (Figure 3.2).

It assumes that in the first-place proper structures for units managing projects and preparing innovations should be chosen, depending on the innovation phase: it would be different for the stages of idea generation, preparing innovations, and commercialization. For the organizational creativity phase, the choice would boil down to simple, organic, adhocratic, flexible, and virtual structures. For the innovation preparation phase, the structures would be more complex, usually functional, divisional, or project teams. The phase of commercializing innovations would already require complex divisional, matrix, network, or hybrid structures for effective R&D, complementary resources organization, and seeking support from external stakeholders.

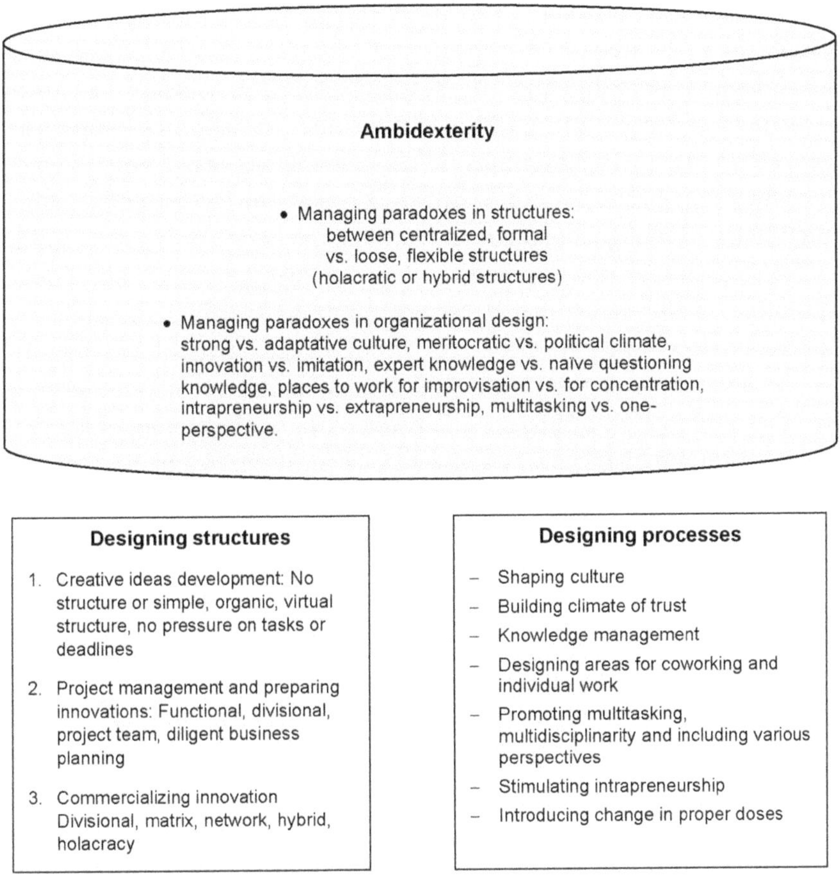

Ambidexterity

- Managing paradoxes in structures:
  between centralized, formal
  vs. loose, flexible structures
  (holacratic or hybrid structures)

- Managing paradoxes in organizational design:
  strong vs. adaptative culture, meritocratic vs. political climate,
  innovation vs. imitation, expert knowledge vs. naïve questioning
  knowledge, places to work for improvisation vs. for concentration,
  intrapreneurship vs. extrapreneurship, multitasking vs. one-
  perspective.

Designing structures

1. Creative ideas development: No
   structure or simple, organic, virtual
   structure, no pressure on tasks or
   deadlines

2. Project management and preparing
   innovations: Functional, divisional,
   project team, diligent business
   planning

3. Commercializing innovation
   Divisional, matrix, network, hybrid,
   holacracy

Designing processes

- Shaping culture
- Building climate of trust
- Knowledge management
- Designing areas for coworking and
  individual work
- Promoting multitasking,
  multidisciplinarity and including various
  perspectives
- Stimulating intrapreneurship
- Introducing change in proper doses

FIGURE 3.2
Conceptual framework of organizational design supporting innovativeness.

Source: Own elaboration on the basis of Bilton & Cummings, 2010.

Apart from the structures, the conceptual framework considers other elements described earlier: organizational culture, climate of trust and meritocracy, knowledge management, places of work stimulating creativity and concentration, multitasking environment, intrapreneurship and extrapreneurship, and change management. At the same time, it is important to concentrate on developing the characteristics of an ambidextrous organization that is capable of managing the tensions resulting from the paradoxes present in the element of organizational design promoting project management and innovativeness. As a result, explorative and exploitative learning with the autonomy of members, cooperation, and involvement in processes management, strategic control could well translate into value creation.

A relatively recent survey (Dyduch, 2019) suggests that the majority of the researched SMEs are able to shape project management-oriented organizational design promoting innovativeness quite well. Young enterprises (up to 14 years of existence) can have more difficulties in designing proper elements than mature organizations (14–22 years). It can result from the fact, that when organizations become grown corporations the design is mature and developed enough, not requiring continuous change, acting as a routine for R&D, project management, as well as new idea generation and implementation. It also seems that larger organizations sport a better ability to design both loose and tight structures, strong and adaptive culture, organizing for flexible and concentrated work, change management, multitasking, etc., that promote innovativeness. When looking at the sectors of activity, construction and financial services seem to be most able to organize a proper design, while production and industry enterprises are less able to do so.

The survey also reveals that the vital components of the organizational design facilitating project management and promoting innovativeness were

- the ability to create both organic, loose structures allowing for bottom-up experimentation and centralized structures, assuring diligent preparation of projects;
- the ability to create strong organizational culture, making an organizational spine and being adaptive at the same time for new idea creation; and
- the meritocratic climate of trust, with some presence of organizational politicking.

These three elements scored highest on average. It is also evident that for effective project management diligent planning and precise preparation of business projects are more important than uncoordinated processes of opportunity identification.

3.3 INNOVATIVENESS, VALUE CREATION, AND VALUE CAPTURE

Shaping proper organizational design in SMEs can be a foundation to develop innovativeness. The research results clearly indicate that innovativeness, traditionally understood as supporting the processes of new product or service development, coupled with protected know-how, can be the source of survival and competitive advantage (Anning-Dorson & Nyamekye, 2020).

In this context, one should agree with the opinion of researchers that "the globalization of economic activity, the development of new technologies, the increase in the importance of competitiveness and cooperation cause the need to put more emphasis on innovation and the ability to cooperate" (Wyroba & Tkaczyk, 2015, p. 5).

Therefore, this relatively new conceptual category has been included in recent years not only in the subject of scientific research but also in practical initiatives and programmes of the EU. Already in the Europe 2020 strategy of the EU, which is a continuation of the Lisbon Strategy, one of the priorities was to meet the need for the so-called smart development (Markowska, 2014, p. 23).

The concept of smart development is a new approach to economic development. The first research on intelligent development took place no earlier than the 1980s. The very concept of "smart development" should be identified with taking actions aimed at increasing the role of knowledge and innovation as the driving force of future development (Serwis Rzeczpospolitej Polskiej, Ministerstwo Rozwoju & Strategia Europa, 2020, https://www.gov.pl/web/rozwoj/strategia-europa-2020, reading: 15.05.2022).

The source of innovation, in this case, is apart from research centres, also commercial enterprises. The aforementioned document emphasizes both "the need to increase spending on research and development by the private sector and to improve the conditions for private research and development activities in the European Union" (Firlej, 2020, pp. 75–76). According to the document, the creation of new, unprecedented solutions should take place, e.g., thanks to (Ministerstwo Funduszy i Polityki Regionalnej, 2020, pp. 2–7)

- strengthening mutual relations between the spheres of business and science;
- creating general conditions conducive to the development of a competitive, cohesive, and more environmentally friendly economy;
- support for the environment of enterprises (maintaining the transfer of technology and know-how, pro-innovative services for enterprises, support for investments in infrastructure consisting, among others,

in organizing institutional infrastructure that creates innovation such as technology parks), as well as creating a system of financing and risk guarantees of new ventures in the field of advanced technologies; and

- support for the potential of enterprises to conduct R&D and innovation works.

R&D activity is defined in terms of creative work, which is carried out in a methodical manner and conducted in order to increase knowledge resources and create new applications for existing knowledge. Activity in the field of R&D is characterized by such attributes as (Główny Urząd Statystyczny, 2018, p. 15)

- inventive – focused on creating new, unique solutions;
- unpredictability – lack of knowledge about the final result, cost, and effort;
- creativity – relying on original, non-obvious hypotheses and concepts;
- proper methodology (conducting research based on a plan evolved on the basis of objectives and with an indication of funding sources); and
- reproducibility and dissemination (striving for results that can be reproduced and disseminated).

The authors of the strategy are of the opinion that the effects of enterprises' involvement in creative activity may also bring benefits to the general public, primarily by accelerating the development of civilization.

Innovations, however, are important primarily from the point of view of the possibility of achieving success by the economic entity itself. This view is represented, e.g., by T. Kalinowski. He states that innovations can successfully form the foundation "to ensure the company's development and increase the attractiveness of the offer for customers" (Kalinowski, 2010, p. 44). Other researchers agree with this opinion, stating that

> innovations are necessary in all phases of the existence of an enterprise, starting from the creation of an idea, through the phase of establishing and starting a company, entering and surviving on the market, success, development, maturity, until the phase of decline and death, when they can become the beginning of a new life cycle of the company.
>
> *(Wasiluk, 2002, p. 335)*

In the modern, globalizing world, there are changes in the functioning of all structures and transformations in the ways of thinking. All existing elements must therefore adapt to the turbulent environment, including economic entities. Those among them who cannot adapt must accept defeat or the necessity to drift into undevelopmental stagnation. "Those who want to succeed or exist must show initiative and innovation" (Janowicz, 2016, p. 175).

At the same time, it is worth emphasizing that the ability to create or develop specific ideas is still one of the greatest challenges for contemporary economic entities.

Despite many pro-innovation initiatives, projects, and policies undertaken by various institutions and administration bodies, both national and reaching beyond the territorial borders of individual countries (in the modern economy, innovative processes are primarily subject to market regulation. However, it is also accompanied by a certain scale of political intervention. Such interventionism takes the general form of the so-called innovation policy, often also referred to as "science and technology policy", although there are slight differences between them (Jasiński, 2006, p. 190)), many economic entities remain passive in the development of innovations.

It should also be noted that sometimes the terms innovation and invention are treated in terms close to synonymous and translated in a similar way. In fact, however, innovation is a broader concept. Researchers explain this by emphasizing that an invention is a new solution to a specific issue, but only one that is of a technical nature. Meanwhile, innovation is defined as a novelty that is deliberately introduced not only in technology but also in organizations, economic activity, or in any sphere of human life. "Innovation may also concern the transformation of an invention into a product or process suitable for launching on the market" (Adamczak & Gędłek, 2009, p. 5).

This attitude may seem understandable in some circumstances. Generating new ideas is a difficult task, requiring the involvement of time, personnel, and conceptual expenditures. At the same time, many enterprises have achieved a satisfactory market status quo. The traditional type of activity continued by these entities brings them the expected results, and current operational needs involve most of their creative reserves. From this point of view, additional involvement in innovation activities may seem unnecessary or unprofitable to such companies.

Naturally, on the contrary, there are also entities on the market that have based their entire activity, and even the meaning of existence, on the belief that it is necessary to create and implement specific new solutions. They can be called "start-ups". At the same time, both theoreticians and practitioners of doing business do not express unambiguous opinions on which specific entities can be called a start-up. However, they agree that this English-derived term covers all temporary organizations that are looking for a scalable, repeatable, and profitable business model (Blank & Dorf, 2012).

A start-up is a creation that is based on a specific vision and a set of ideas. According to the assumptions of the customer development model, these ideas are then consulted with potential recipients. In this context, they verify the ideological foundations of the start-up and, in a way, participate in its development, the ultimate goal of which is to transform it into a traditional enterprise (Blank & Dorf, 2012).

In practice, the category of start-ups includes all young companies that are trying to enter the market and whose activities are characterized by creativity. At the centre of their interest is not so much the development of their own business as doing it based on a new idea – an innovative solution that has not been used on the market so far or had it in a different form (Skala, 2019, pp. 15–25).

Start-ups are based on technologically innovative solutions and on combining known methods and techniques with new media and technologies. They are a relatively new phenomenon in the economic world (Skoneczna, 2020, p. 283). Such entities usually have a short history and are in the initial phase of their life cycle (they are in the development phase). For this reason, they are not a dominant force in the market from the point of view of criteria such as size or market share.

What is more, the prospects for their development are not clearly defined. After all, there is no certainty that the new, previously untested ideas pushed by him will be successful in the long term and in the prevailing environmental conditions. Hence, the individual contribution of individual entities to the implementation of the goals of innovative activity of the broadly understood market (primarily those considered on a macro scale) does not have to be large in practice.

Despite this, many researchers still believe that nowadays innovation is everywhere – both in start-ups and in other companies. What's more, the path of development of modern civilization undoubtedly leads through the innovative achievements of human ingenuity. Scientific authorities also quite clearly share a positive opinion on the importance of new solutions.

On the other hand, however, one must not forget that in practice many new ideas do not end in success, and the term "innovation" itself cannot be treated synonymously with the word "progress" in every case. Some inventions and discoveries, despite the right intentions of the people who develop them, may be associated with technical or organizational backwardness, cause losses within the economic or social reality, or be of no use to either the initiator of the changes or other people from his environment (Godin, 2008, p. 5).

The history of farming practice knows as many examples of successful innovations as unnecessary ones, i.e. those that did not catch on in the long run. According to the researchers, "the creators of new ideas who wanted to turn them into products, services, solutions did not always meet with the kindness of the environment" (Glinka & Gudkova, 2011, p. 88).

A proper illustration of this fact can be, for example, the history of a photographic company from the USA, which in the early 1980s developed and commercialized the idea of a camera with an unusual and virtually unprecedented type of film in the form of a specially developed rotating disk.

The American company had high hopes for the described product innovation. First of all, this was due to the fact that the use of a new type of camera was associated with specific benefits for users. The device itself was characterized by an acceptable price, an attractive design, and a small, compact size. The use of disk technology contributed to the fact that it was not difficult to use (Poli, 1982, pp. 72, 182).

On the contrary – its operation was not a challenge even for people with little knowledge of photography, and taking a large number of readable photos in a short period of time did not require special knowledge. Despite certain advantages, the new solution did not catch on in the long term. The reasons for this state of affairs can be sought in many factors, such as the unsatisfactory quality of prints for many users or the not fully thought-out composition of activities in the field of integrated marketing communication.

The disc camera was undoubtedly a testament to Kodak's innovation potential. Its failure, however, contributed to the growing financial problems, which had unpleasant consequences in 2011 when the company was declared bankrupt (Levitin, 2016, p. 120).

Supporting innovations that can prove new and useful requires diligent planning with flexibility allowing bottom-up initiatives, explicit and implicit knowledge management, free information flow, and expertise sharing, as well as resources to prepare and rationalize innovations. Innovativeness in SMEs can be perceived as processes of both discovering existing ideas (observing and discovering phenomena that have existed but were not made explicit) and generating new ones (through ideas, opinions, and knowledge exchange), questioning the existing status quo and sabotaging the available knowledge (Dyduch, 2019).

It is possible to distinguish a universal set of recommendations and guidelines that can help develop the innovation capacity of any organization. The mere awareness that innovations are an impetus for the success of business ventures is insufficient from the point of view of companies considering the possibility of introducing new solutions. Suggestions on the practice of generating innovations arising from the literature should therefore be considered. Guided by them should lead to the success of the process of creating innovations in every enterprise.

First of all, the researchers emphasize the need to show an open attitude towards non-identical sources of inspiration. In practice, a large part of the new solutions is still internal, which means that they are created only within a single economic entity as a result of the individual ingenuity of its employees and using its own technological and competence base. At the same time, however, nowadays definitely more numerous groups are progressive changes, resulting from interactions between enterprises and the environment in which these entities operate (Kozioł-Nadolna, 2012, p. 298).

Changes taking place in the organization's environment force the need to constantly adapt to them. This is always the case in a dynamic environment. On the other hand, a "more static environment promotes routine and anticipation by extrapolation from previous experience" (Davis, 2007, p. 83). This principle also applies, and perhaps above all, to innovations, which by definition are to lead to changes in the environment and constitute a response to specific transformations of the reality around the company.

It is also important, as noted by M. Sawhney, R.C. Wolcott, and I. Arroniz that in order to create innovations, enterprises must also go beyond the traditional areas of activity (i.e. product and technology), and focus more on business and social processes to look for new development opportunities there (Sawhney, Wolcott & Arroniz, 2006, pp.74–81).

This is due to the fact that innovations, which at first may seem unrelated directly to the mainstream of activity, and thus little needed, in the long run can bring measurable benefits to the organization and stimulate innovation in traditional areas (for example, financial innovation in the form of replacing a deposit from a domestic bank with a loan from a foreign bank may result in the release of additional financial resources, which can then be allocated to the improvement of manufactured products).

It is also important to remember that studies on the gradual change process indicate that the benefits of changes made in a gentle and incremental way often outweigh those that can be achieved by a one-time breakthrough.[3] Therefore, regardless of the chosen area of development, the sought-after innovation does not have to be radical and far-reaching. Innovation may not go beyond introducing a change to already existing products or services.

For example, one can consider introducing the so-called corrective innovations, i.e. such that are focused on repairing an already existing, but defective element that is not conducive (in a technological or organizational sense) to increasing resource efficiency (Fudaliński, 2002, p. 200). "Such innovations are usually quick and easy to implement; examples relate to new colors, flavours, features, benefits, or aspects of customers' experience" (Kaplan, 2017, p. 20).

Researchers even encourage us to use the method of small steps and move in scope: we do what we are good at, but better. They propose to focus on the pursuit of small changes made overnight (so-called rolling innovation). A simple improvement in a product, process, or, for example, a social issue, in consequence, can still be associated with achieving specific benefits.

Another tip concerns the technical side of the process of generating new ideas. Special attention should be paid to it. It should take an organized form, the course of which is determined by specific stages, which together form a sequence of proper conduct. It is true that history knows cases in which unprecedented solutions arose spontaneously and even unintentionally. Nevertheless, one should be aware of the fact that most of the new solutions introduced by modern companies are not the result of a sudden, unexpected epiphany, but they are rather the result of an intentional and organized creative process involving task forces implementing formalized plans and projects.

Innovations, regardless of their type, should appear as a result of a sequence of strictly defined activities (innovation process) (Harvard Business School, 2005, p. XVI) – Figure 3.3. These activities form a series of logically successive stages, the execution of which, as a consequence, measurably increases the chances of achieving success understood in

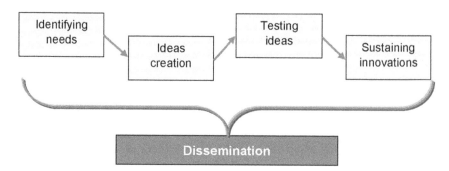

FIGURE 3.3
Phases of the innovations' generation process.

Source: Personal studies based on: Murray, Caulier-Grice & Mulgan, 2010, p. 55.

terms of the dissemination of new ideas. As noted by J. Baruk, "[I]n general terms, the innovation process can be understood as a sequence of activities necessary to implement a specific innovative concept and transform it into a new state of affairs (product, technology, organization)" (Baruk, 2001, p. 76).

The first of the phases listed in the figure is the identification of needs. It consists in determining all the factors that show the need to introduce a new solution. Motives for undertaking innovative activities can be very different. For example, an inspiration for social innovation may be the deteriorating living situation of the community in which the company operates. The idea of creating an innovative strategy is dictated by something completely different (e.g. the ineffectiveness of the plans made so far). Financial innovation may result from the depletion of funds needed to settle current liabilities.

It is very important to prepare a comprehensive description of the problem that leads to innovative actions, i.e. to carry out a thorough diagnosis of the sources and causes of particular problems. In other words, one cannot limit oneself only to specifying the symptoms of a given phenomenon but also turn towards outlining its causes. R. Murray, J. Caulier-Grice, and G. Mulgan emphasize that a comprehensive understanding of the company's situation, as well as the circumstances in which it has come to operate, is halfway to success in terms of innovation (Murray, Caulier-Grice & Mulgan, 2010, p. 12).

After the recognition stage, one can move on to the next phase, i.e. generating and developing ideas that respond to the observed issues. Ideas for dealing with identified problems can come from a variety of sources. The company can look for solutions both outside the organization (using, for example, the so-called banks of ideas) and reach for the intellectual potential of its own employees. For instance, if a new solution is to be an answer to a social issue, it is worth seeking the opinion of the people most interested in it: citizens, members of the local community, or employees of social organizations.

When generating new ideas (regardless of which area they concerns and whether they are a breakthrough idea or an extension of existing practices), one should always assess whether its implementation will be beneficial for the company.

Some of the innovative projects may not look promising at first, e.g. due to the fact that they remain detached from the core area of the company's activity (this is often the case, for example, in the area of social innovations, generally understood as new solutions that may contribute to the development of the quality of social life in the environment in which companies operate).

In practice, however, they may turn out to be very interesting and useful ideas, spreading the vision of achieving specific benefits aimed at the company and/or the environment. Similarly, other innovative projects may at first glance seem very promising and perfectly matched from the point of view of the company's business profile and end in failure.

To avoid such problems, the next step should be a phase that consists in testing the innovation in practice. The new solution should be tested to assess whether the innovative idea can be considered functional. In practice, this means its pilot implementation, evaluation, and introduction of possible improvements. This is a necessary stage to obtain information on the usefulness and desirability of a particular solution. So testing is preventive. It serves to prevent a situation in which, even though we carry out all the planned activities, the innovation will not work in practice, and the company will not achieve the intended benefits.

Carrying out such an initial, common-sense opinion is usually not an easy task, because such an assessment concerns new, sometimes even revolutionary ideas, often ahead of the current technical and technological level and in no way previously verified in practice. Enterprises, however, have specific instruments at their disposal that can be successfully used to improve the evaluation stage. One or several of the methods grouped within the four basic sets of methods for assessing innovative projects can be used to evaluate innovative projects. These are (Table 3.1) (Krawiec, 2000, p. 152):

TABLE 3.1

Methods of Evaluating New Ideas

Category of Methods	Types of Methods	Characteristics
For assessment of profitability	Static ones (usually refer to one calculation period, e.g. year): • regarding measurement of economic efficiency and • relating to the measurement of the time of return on invested capital. Dynamic (taking into account the change in the value of money over time): • based on a comparison of input streams over the life of the project.	They do not differ fundamentally from the methods used to assess typical investment projects known from the economic literature. The commercialization of most innovations (including primarily product innovations) is usually associated with the need to launch an investment process in which the financial resources required for project implementation must be determined. The usage of these methods also allows one to obtain important information from the investor's point of view on the expected rate of return or risk.

Multi-criterial of decision support	• Additive:
	  • SAW (Simple Additive Weighting Method)
	  • SMART (Simple Multi-attribute Ranking Technique)
	  • SMARTER (Simple Multi-attribute Ranking Technique Exploiting Ranks)
	• Of analytical hierarchy and related:
	  • AHP (Analytical Hierarchy Process)
	  • REMBRANDT (Ratio Estimation in Magnitudes or Deci-Bells to Rate Alternatives which are Non-Domina Ted)
		Multi-criteria methods allow for a comprehensive assessment of innovative projects, as they are based on a certain set of criteria determining the usefulness of a particular innovation for the enterprise. However, due to the large variety of available methods (each of which has both specific advantages and disadvantages and limitations), it is necessary to carry out a detailed qualitative analysis in order to select the most appropriate technique for a particular decision problem.
		Multi-criteria analysis should be used when the choice is made between many possible variants of innovative projects and ways of their implementation. Important in these methods is the proper selection of evaluation criteria and the precise assignment of weights. Depending on the issue, the criteria should reflect non-identical aspects, such as implementation possibilities, costs, time, environmental requirements (both measurable and immeasurable parameters can be used).
		The purpose of the analysis is to select the optimal variant from the point of view of the adopted criteria. When performing the analysis, a set of specific variants of solutions is assumed $W = \{W_i: i = 1,2,3...,m\}$ and a set of criteria: $K = \{K_j: j = 1,2,3...,n\}$, according to which the individual variants will be assessed.

(Continued)

TABLE 3.1 (CONTINUED)

Methods of Evaluating New Ideas

Category of Methods	Types of Methods	Characteristics
	• F-AHP (Fuzzy Analytic Hierarchy Process) • ANP (Analytic Network Process) • MACBETH (Measuring Attractiveness by a Categorical Based Evaluation TecHnique). • Verbal • Of reference points' usage • PROMETHEE (Preference Ranking Organisation METHod for Enrichment Evaluations) • ELECTRE (from French language: *ELimination Et Choix Traduisant la REalia*)	The next step is to assign a value for each criterion that is a measure of the Wi variant according to the Kj criterion. The assigned values can be placed in the data matrix $Xij = \{xij: i = 1,2,3...,m; j = 1,2,3...,n\}$, in which the i-th row presents variant values according to successive criteria, and the j-th column – values of all variants according to a given criterion. In addition, each criterion should be assigned a weight.
Mathematical	• Linear programming • Dynamic programming • Making usage of artificial intelligence[4]	They are used for quantitative evaluation and selection of innovative projects. With their help, you can also optimize the benefits from the adopted portfolio of innovative projects. In practice, they are not very widespread due to the specific conditions of innovation processes, which cannot be easily represented by the mathematical equations on which the methods are based.
Subiective of assessment	For example: • Q-sort • Delphic • Methods inspired by the previously mentioned	These methods use the knowledge and experience of opinion givers who, in accordance with the adopted work schedule and specific procedure methodology, make a qualitative assessment of the projects presented to them for review. In less complex cases, ideas for innovations are evaluated by members of numerous evaluation teams (including people holding lower positions within the organizational structure); in more complex cases, only experts and authorities in a given field takes part in assessment.

Source: Own elaboration based on Szatkowski (2016, p. 94–114), Kukułka and Wirkus (2017, p. 613), and Trzaskalik (2014, pp. 240–250).

- cost-effectiveness assessment methods,
- multi-criteria methods,
- mathematical methods, and
- methods of subjective assessment.

The next stage, referred to as maintenance, is the implementation and popularization of an innovation that has successfully passed the testing phase. For such an innovation, a business model must be developed that will ensure its financial success and stability. Dissemination means, in turn, attempts to increase the impact and range of innovation through its expansion, attempts at replication, and diffusion among entities, groups, communities, and communities interested in change (e.g. through franchise or licensing).

It should be emphasized that the implementation of the stages of the innovation creation process presented in such categories measurably increases the chance but never guarantees the final success of the new solution. Earlier, in a different context, the case of Kodak company had already been written about. At this point, it is worth turning to the automotive industry, which is the source of as many successful and unsuccessful innovations.

One can mention, for example, the Sinclair C5 car. It was a small, three-wheeled, one-person microcar of British production, equipped with an electric drive and not requiring registration. The unfulfilled intention of its creator was to revolutionize urban transport. Although extremely innovative for the 1980s, Sinclair failed to live up to expectations. This was determined by the vehicle's limited practicality, controversial design, limited range, and lack of dedicated infrastructure (Clough, 2016, p. 225).

In terms of the process innovation, which evokes mixed feelings among users, as well as the process innovation assessed ambivalently by researchers, one can consider the payment system at self-service checkouts, introduced in many retail chains, also in Poland. In principle, this procedure was to result in significant savings in the conducted activity, primarily by enabling the reduction of staff involved in the process of charging and collecting payments for purchases.

In practice, he did not meet with a clearly positive response from customers, especially traditionalists accustomed to the classic way of service. Some of them went so far as to reduce the volume of purchased goods, and even to change their preferences regarding the place of making purchases in favour of competing shops. The stimulus in this case was the reluctance to use the new solution along with the accompanying lengthening of queues at traditional checkouts (as a result of reducing their number at the expense of self-service counters).

Research indicates that the innovator mindset can be a relatively good predictor of innovativeness (Stauffer, 2015a), as it assesses how entrepreneurs follow the innovation cycle (Stauffer, 2015b) and react to the useful novelty that appears in the environment. The innovation cycle covers four phases (Stauffer, 2015b):

- generating or discovering ideas,
- implementing feasible ideas,
- commercializing, and
- assessing.

The popular belief suggests that SMEs are more flexible as far as implementing ideas is concerned, as they avoid organizational inertia when managing projects and preparing innovations. However, large organizations benefit from the better possibilities of finding complementary resources, funding R&D, and launching production. It also seems that in spite of higher flexibility and adaptability, the effectiveness of implementing innovations is higher in large firms (Terziovski, 2010). Still, SMEs are capable of benefiting from creativity to generate unique innovations (Hitt, Ireland, Sirmon & Trahms, 2011, p. 61). Preparing a totally new good or service based on radical innovation requires large investments, financial capital, and investing in new technologies (Sood & Tellis, 2005). SMEs typically do not have the demanding resources to launch breakthrough innovations; they often reach for external sources, develop networks, and enter cooperation with universities or companies that can assure necessary resources (Gretsch, Salzmann & Kock, 2019).

Preparing and commercializing innovations is strictly connected with the problem of value creation and value capture (Green & Sergeeva, 2019). It is interesting that some companies can create and capture more value from the innovations commercialized than the others (Kim, Tang & Bosselman, 2019). This can happen since preparing innovations requires time and financial resources, but they can quickly find imitators. Although the relationship between innovativeness and company growth has been identified, imitation can have a higher impact on performance (Hashai & Markovich, 2017).

The literature review identified a number of value creation and value capture (VCVC) processes and mechanisms present in organizations, as well as variables that describe these processes. A recent survey indicates that VCVC processes mostly depend on (Dyduch, 2022)[5]

- SME's strategic potential,
- resource-based value creation,

- value capture through interactions with stakeholders,
- value capture through interactions with the task environment,
- legal mechanisms of value capture,
- patents and intellectual property rights,
- value creation for customers, and
- appropriation rents.

The survey carried out among Polish SMEs suggests that few organizations prepare and commercialize breakthrough technologies or develop unique products or services. The managers at the researched companies identified that value is created by possessing adequate competencies, employees, and a proper organizational design. Possessing or developing high technologies and breaking-through innovations that require complementary resources is a feature of a few SMEs, which is not surprising given the amount of funds and resources required. The overall conclusion that can be drawn from the survey among SMEs is that the main source of value creation at the researched organizations is creating value for customers and offering attractive products that customers are willing to pay for.

The majority of managers indicated that their organizations prefer to invest in incremental innovations, imitate other firms, and exploit existing ideas rather than generate new ideas as a strategic choice. Relational, marketing, or financial capabilities were indicated to be of most importance. The SMEs are aware that quality products and marketing are the sources of value creation, so they invest in high-quality materials and spend money on developing marketing strategies.

As far as the competitive environment is concerned, the researched organizations indicated that the existence of many competitors who can observe and imitate some unique solutions is seen by them as the biggest threat. At the same time, the managers who participated in the study indicated that they do not think that their value is captured by competitors. They also took the expectations of the task environment actors into consideration and sought to divide the value created among actors involved in value co-creation accordingly.

To subjectively assess what is the potential of SMEs to prepare and commercialize innovations, and how innovativeness translates into value creation and capture, the *Innovalue* tool can be used (Table 3.2).

The previous section looked closely at shaping the elements of organizational design that facilitate project management and promote

TABLE 3.2

Innovalue Control List

Statement	No	Difficult to say	Yes
We prepare innovative goods and/or services based on new and useful ideas, and we commercialize most of them.			
We prepare innovative goods and/or services based on new and useful ideas, and we commercialize them together with other stakeholders, strategic alliances, or partnerships.			
We prepare innovative goods and/or services based on new and useful ideas, and we sell the projects.			
We prepare innovative goods and/or services based on new and useful ideas, and we make them available as open innovations.			
We are a proactive player with complementary resources competent to prepare and commercialize innovations as well as to use first-move advantage.			
We quickly lose the first-move advantage, as imitators copying our ideas appear.			
We are able to patent our solutions quickly.			
We can access Valuable, Rare, Imperfectly, Imitable, and Non-substitutable (VRIN) resources and enter cooperation with key stakeholders.			
Our company imitates other firms' solutions. We observe and implement best practices already existing in the market.			
We possess high organizational competences; therefore, we can co-create innovation and offer tailored solutions.			

Source: Own idea based on Fisher (2011).

innovativeness. The attention was given to generating, selecting, and commercializing innovations, as well as to the problem of value creation through innovating, and value capture. In the next part, some insights will be presented as to how Polish SMEs survived the coronavirus crisis and what managerial decisions, actions, and measures have been introduced in order to overcome the sudden and unexpected crisis.

3.4 SMEs IN CRISIS, AND WHAT COMES NEXT?

Various factors might act as barriers to companies' development. Barriers to the development of small and medium-sized firms can be divided into internal and external ones. The first of them is identified as the company's weaknesses and usually refers to its size, strategy, structure (organizational and costs), technology and production capabilities, management competences, or employee qualifications (Figure 3.4). Internal barriers result from the weaknesses of the entities.

They are related to management, poor competences, knowledge and qualifications of the staff (managers and regular employees), production problems, and problems resulting from insufficient premises and related to the size of the business (Matejun, 2007, p. 122). Also, the lack (or insufficient amount) of financial resources can be a serious barrier to the dynamic development of a small and medium-sized company.

External barriers, on the other hand, are related to the environment and the risk of volatility of its factors. Refer to those influences which are a result of issues generated in areas outside the domestic firm. They can be considered on a national scale and on a local (micro) level. Macroeconomic conditions affecting the development of SMEs include the level of economic development, level of income, legal and infrastructural barriers, etc. (Figure 3.4).

The recent unforeseen phenomenon in the environment that has strongly affected the SME sector was the coronavirus pandemic. Earlier there were mass-scale virus threats in the form of SARS (2002–2003), avian flu (2003–2006), swine flu (2009–2010), Ebola (2013–2016), and measles. At the same

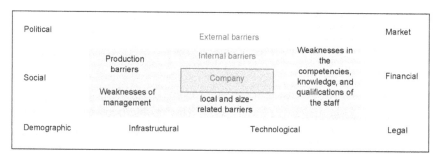

FIGURE 3.4
Internal and external barriers to the development of SMEs.

Source: Own elaboration based on: Danielak, Mierzwa & Bartczak, 2017, p. 7.

time, however, their range and impact were much weaker. Only a new virus from a city in central China quickly began to spread around the world.

Coronavirus disease (COVID-19) is an infectious disease caused by a newly discovered coronavirus SARS-CoV-2 (Pabian, 2020, p. 212). For years, coronaviruses were treated as mild pathogens, causing mild respiratory symptoms that subsided within a few days. Only the emergence of new, highly infectious species has caused growing problems with these pathogens. Coronaviruses are one of the largest RNA viruses in terms of virion size and genome length. The name "coronavirus" comes from the Latin word: *corona* and refers to the structure of the shell of these particles, which under the electron microscope is seen as surrounded by a ring of small structures (Wawrzyniak, Kuczborska, Lipińska-Opałka, Będzichowska & Kalicki. 2019, p. 1).

The new strain of SARS-CoV-2 appeared at the end of 2019 and began to spread around the world at a very fast pace. The first confirmed cases were reported in December in Wuhan, China (Sokół-Szawłowska, 2021, p. 57): "the appearance of an unusual form of severe pneumonia in December 2019 first surprised the health services of the city of Wuhan, in the Chinese province of Hubei, with a population of nearly 9 million, and soon after, the entire province with a population of 58.4 million" (Duszyński, Afelt, Ochab-Marcinek, Owczuk, Pyrć, Rosińska, Rychard & Smiatacz, 2020, p. 7). Due to the course of the disease and complications, the coronavirus was quickly recognized as a great threat to the physical and mental health of people around the world.

Typical symptoms were fever or chills, cough, shortness of breath and difficulty in breathing, rapid breathing, weakness, muscle or body aches, headache, loss of smell and taste, sore throat, runny nose, nausea or vomiting, diarrhoea. The most important disease in the course of infection is pneumonia. In turn, the way of infection was touching surfaces or objects on which there were viruses and then touching the nose, mouth, or eyes. One could also get infected by droplets when coughing, sneezing, or talking. Droplets containing viruses can reach the mouth, nose, or by inhalation into the lungs, between people who are in close contact (less than 2 metres for a long time, conventionally more than 15 minutes).

It has been confirmed so far that the SARS-CoV-2 coronavirus causes severe acute respiratory syndrome and causes damage to many organs (lungs, kidneys, heart muscle). Infection may cause gastrointestinal symptoms (gastritis, enteritis) or changes in the nervous system. Previous research indicates that the virus can infect specific cells in the nose, lungs, or intestines. According to World Health Organization (WHO) reports, mortality of people diagnosed with COVID-19 is more common in the group of the elderly, with comorbidities such as chronic obstructive pulmonary disease, cancer, hypertension, diabetes, coronary artery disease, hepatitis B, obesity, chronic kidney disease. SARS-CoV-2 virus infections are extremely dangerous for immunocompromised people.

Some data indicate that smokers are worse affected by the infection than non-smokers, although recently such reports have been questioned. What is more, men are likely to get sick and die more often from COVID-19 than women. Research published in the European Heart Journal has shown that men have in blood higher levels of angiotensin-converting enzyme (ACE2 – which is the receptor for the virus) than women, so they may be at higher risk of SARS-CoV-2 infection (Nowakowska & Sulimiera-Michalak, 2020, p. 227).

In Poland, the pandemic appeared in the first quarter of 2020. On 4 March 2020, the first case of SARS-CoV-2 was recorded. The following week (11 March), the director general of the WHO announced the beginning of the COVID-19 pandemic. Countries around the world introduced restrictions that were also implemented in Poland (Marcinkiewicz, Nowak, Popielec & Wilk, 2020, p. 9).

At the beginning of the pandemic, it was recommended to use personal protective equipment and isolate oneself from society to the minimum necessary. On 11 March, most sectors of the economy were closed in Poland (except for the most necessary for the safety of inhabitants). Schools have been closed and strict restrictions on movement within and outside the country have been introduced. The restrictions introduced by the state also resulted in problems for many enterprises. Restrictions translated into the closure of some of them, a reduction in the level of salaries, or even layoffs. A nationwide collective quarantine was introduced in Poland, and it lasted from 12 March to 3 May 2020. After its completion, the functioning of hotels and shopping malls resumed, and the possibility of free movement around the country was restored. Schools, universities, services, and medical care (teleconsultations) continued to operate, to some extent, remotely.

In the unpredictable conditions of the COVID-19 pandemic, many companies on the market had to start acting "in the dark", resigning from strict adherence to the assumptions of strategic plans and adapting to dynamic changes in the environment on an ongoing basis. Unfortunately, this approach did not save many of them from complications. In 2020, there was a significant increase in the number of business entities (mainly from the SME sector) in Poland that suspended their operations (a defensive reaction to the special economic situation, as well as to restrictions imposed by the government). In addition, there were noted already 282,000 indebted companies in the National Debt Register, for a total amount of PLN 11.6 billion. Among them, the most significant share was held by one-man companies, which constitute as much as 65% of the total number.

In the conditions of crisis, the most serious problem for 48.7% of enterprises was maintaining financial liquidity. "As the main reasons for problems with this imbalance, the following were indicated: difficulties in obtaining new contracts (45.2%), difficulties in retaining existing regular contractors (40.5%), delays in payment of invoices issued for products delivered and services rendered, difficulties in obtaining funds for running a business (32.4%), maintaining regular semiconductor suppliers (24.4%)" (Zioło, 2022, p. 20).

In April 2021, one month after the first COVID-19-related lockdown in Poland, a survey among 151 SMEs operating in Poland was carried out (Chudziński et al., 2020). The goal of the survey was to seek answers to the question of which activities, managerial decisions, or measures were undertaken to counteract the sudden and unexpected crisis. The results indicate that SMEs mainly decided to shift to online work, reduce CAPEX, send employees on leaves and furloughs, and extend the payment deadlines for key stakeholders. Some of the SMEs reduced the working time or limited the production capacity. The least common decisions were closing part of the company, reducing employment (only every fifth company decided to reduce employment) looking for new markets, looking for alternative distribution channels, or offering totally new goods or services.

The introduced changes coupled with care for human resources, mainly for specialists, indicate strategic protection of employees. Indeed, those companies that panicked and made many employees redundant in the first months of the lockdown had difficulties finding competent workers after the crisis was gone. Reducing CAPEX indicated that the SMEs attempted to sustain the cash flow to survive. At the same time, the researched managers indicated that the most important goals during the crisis were maintaining liquidity, sustaining current revenues, and the employment level.

To identify which managerial decisions influenced the strategic goals of the SMEs, further analyses have been carried out (Chudziński et al., 2022). They clearly indicate that these enterprises that shifted to remote work had higher chances to keep the operations at the current level. However, SMEs dealing with export activity had lower chances of survival compared to those that did not due to border closure or supply chain breakage. The SMEs that reduced employment during the crisis had lower chances to acquire skilled and competent workers after the crisis. The enterprises that prolonged payment deadlines were seen as more stable, trustworthy, and able to survive the crisis.

The research also indicated the influence decisions had on firm performance. The SMEs that were able to acquire external financing and organize virtual teams to shift to remote work had higher chances of sustaining cash flow and revenues. Low turnover and autonomy in decision-making translated also into firm performance, as they limited organizational inertia and promoted adaptability, agile attitude, responsiveness, and fast decisions without waiting for acceptance from the higher level. What is interesting, these SMEs that exploited opportunities during the crisis and introduced innovations despite difficult times, had higher chances of keeping competent employees and maintaining cash flow. It seems that good work organization and strategic planning, coupled with developing efficient IT systems, translates into sustaining financial liquidity (Brzozowska et al., 2015).

The research also revealed (Dyduch et al., 2021), that dynamic capabilities, which influence the organization-environment fit, facilitated firms' survival during times of crisis. The ability to exploit opportunities emerging during a crisis, as well as imitating, innovating, and diversifying products and services, has an impact on financial liquidity while developing modern technologies and orchestrating resources reduce the chances of maintaining revenues at the current level. This may be due to the fact that orchestrating resources and investing in modern technologies are capital-intensive, and they do not immediately result in increasing revenues as this would happen in the longer period.

Management and strategic management are based on visualizing and proactively adapting to the future that nobody thought of. The reality is hard to predict, and probably only a few expected the influence of the corona crisis or the war in Ukraine on the everyday functioning of SMEs. First, an almost instantaneous, necessity-based shift into home offices, telecommuting, and digital work resulted in a quick increase in the usage of digital communication tools. The possibility of working from home will make this form of working stay with SMEs. For SMEs, this means shifting expenses from keeping office facilities into software for monitoring telework, service testing, and application testing. For employees, this means lower costs of transportation and more time not devoted to daily commuting. It only remains to hope that most advances and comforts of digitalization will remain. Recently, the idea of Work From Anywhere (WFA) was offered (Smite, Moe, Klotins & Gonzalez-Huerta, 2021).

Second, it is safe to say that SMEs will focus more on online shopping. So far, around 80% of revenues of firms selling goods were created by physical shops, with only 20% through online shopping. This proportion may be reversed in the future. Third, some weaknesses of certain industries were revealed, while other branches were strengthened. While car, fashion, or tourist industries recorded a sudden drop in revenues, FCMG, packaging, and sanitary products – on the contrary. This might be a recommendation for SMEs to diversify their portfolios and create new businesses to avoid prospering from one type of product or service.

Fourth, the uncertainty of the future, and fear of unpredicted situations will push enterprises to design temporary, flexible, and agile structures, with dispersed, reversed, or substitute leadership holacracy where quick reactions can be applied to events appearing in the environment. It could have been observed already after the crisis breakout. Some companies suspended their activities, while others recreated their structures, developed mobile apps for online orders, shifted resources, and reorganized their activity to exploit new opportunities that paradoxically appeared. Dynamic capabilities, the ability to orchestrate resources or to shift them where the opportunity appears, and quick adaptation to changes in the environment will be important elements of survival and development strategies. Dynamic capabilities, understood as reconfiguring a company's resource base to better sense and seize opportunities, are seen as one of the key drivers of a firm's performance in changing environments. They focus managerial attention on conscious and skilful modification of the firm's strategic potential (Schilke et al., 2018). Surely, the basis of strategic management will not change – competitive organizations thinking proactively will be successful.

Fifth, supply chains will be transformed. They will be shorter, and maybe tight; firms will seek resources and workforce closer to their markets. Production can move to home markets, despite seemingly higher costs. However, the costs of the next crisis and interdependencies on external suppliers might be incomparably higher. Polish SMEs can benefit from this by promoting high-quality products and know-how, and fighting the stereotype of cheap-labour-based competitive advantage. The SME sector will be further developed and advance innovations that will strengthen the economy. Sixth, increasing costs of energy will foster a move into energy saving, looking for alternative sources of energy and eco-friendly solutions.

Finally, digitalization and automatization of production will result in lower demand for certain professions (e.g. call centre workers), while new competences will be of value (robot training, administrating transactional bots, online consulting, 3D-printing services, freelancing). It will not always be possible to shift workers from traditional professions into emerging ones with high demand. Therefore, SMEs that will invent new professions for which the demand will be high will capture more value in the future. In organizations, more focus will be put on the collective wisdom of organization members; the power of intuition, experience, and emotions; and strategic support of creative ideas appearing within organizations, building a climate of trust. The role of social capital and relations, network-based leadership, as well as stakeholder synergy will grow.

Strategic management has undergone certain changes after the corona crisis. Traditional ways of strategic analysis, strategy formulation, and implementation were quite often replaced by experimenting and scenario planning, as well as improvising and emergent approaches (Bhattacharyya & Thakre, 2021). Additionally, organizational elements with so far well-defined status quo were highly affected by COVID-19 and hybridization (Schieman, Badawy, Milkie & Bierman, 2021). Work models changed due to digitization, designing workspaces and ICT solutions changed as virtual teams and online working dominated the organizational reality, business models were shaped as various new ways of creating value appeared, and supply chains got shortened. Leadership turned from task-orientation, inspiring and transforming into assuring the well-being of employees.

Today's SMEs touched by crises, in order to develop and fully benefit from their potential, need to be aware of numerous tensions that appear both on the organizational and strategic levels, as well as be able to manage these tensions. At the same time, reconciling contradictions, especially as far as requirements, approaches, tasks, and goals are concerned, can be demotivating for employees (Nadiv, 2021). To overcome the despondence, it is crucial to promote a certain mindset that allows employees to shift between different logics (Miron-Spektor et al.). This requires proper leadership that supports well-being, stimulates creativity, and maintains team engagement and open communication (Pradies et al., 2021).

NOTES

1 Currently, there is no single universal classification of SMEs in the world. This category is subjective and depends on the internal structure of the economy. However, entities from the SME sector are generally a heterogeneous group of enterprises, including mainly service, agricultural, manufacturing, and trade organizations (see more: Łuczak, 1995, p. 7).

2 He contributed to the development of the neoclassical paradigm, e.g. proving that the main determinants of economic development are not external forces but factors inside the organization, including a tendency to undertake innovative activities (compare Swedberg, 1993).

3 This fact is confirmed, for example, by S. Hollender's research carried out at DuPont's manufacturing plants (see more on this topic: Hollander, 1965, pp. XII–270).

4 Nowadays, it is still difficult to consider innovations in terms other than the product of human ingenuity. However, researchers remind us of the rapid and unrestrained development of artificial intelligence systems. It is possible that in the near future, artificial intelligence will become, if not a performer, at least a source of progressive innovations. More on the development of artificial intelligence can be found, e.g., in Jones (2015).

5 We kindly acknowledge the financial support from the National Science Centre in Poland (grant no 2015/17/B/HS4/00935) that made possible to carry out research and present its results in this book.

4

Experience in Applying European Project Management Models in Enterprises from the Small and Medium Sectors

4.1 METHODOLOGICAL FOUNDATIONS OF EMPIRICAL RESEARCH – OUR RESEARCH METHODOLOGY

Acquiring and then implementing a project financed from European sources is not a simple challenge, among others, due to the high degree of bureaucracy of all procedures and large initial requirements. This is particularly evident in the example of SMEs, which often encounter problems in the implementation of projects because they do not have enough resources. Also, the practice of their management processes is often not adapted to the high requirements imposed by the EU. The issue of EU project management is, then, a significant, although not sufficiently widely discussed, research problem.

The use of knowledge and skills in the field of management and economics, as well as the knowledge of the SME sector and the financing structure recommended by the European Commission, necessitates an interdisciplinary approach to this subject. The spectrum of the research problem is also determined by the wide range of EU projects, i.e. by their nature – development, investment, social, organizational, research, or IT.

The multifaceted analysis of the research problem has begun with the indication of the essence of modern management. The two-level nature of the management process in the 21st century is seen in the identification of contemporary trends and directions of management development and in its definition in the implementation of EU projects.

DOI: 10.1201/9781003309901-4

As the own research has proven, the paradigms of companies' management are the basis for the first of the aforementioned planes, which was found by means of a critical analysis of the literature and verification of the existing analyses and research works created as a part of the research on these issues.

The characteristics of the EU project management process, i.e. the second of the qualified planes, were made on the basis of a critical analysis of the role and importance of projects for the functioning of enterprises, and thus the entire economy. It is emphasized that the prelude to this part of the considerations, necessary to develop part of the book, was the analysis of source documents of the European Commission, as well as national documents related to the financial perspective for 2014–2021.

The selected research procedure, dealing with the aforementioned problems, was considered to be coherent and logical, which was confirmed by the implementation of several dozen operational programmes (at the EU, national, and regional levels). The result of these activities is the establishment of institutions in Poland responsible for the process of distributing funds and handling projects.

Since Poland's accession to the structures of the EU, a total of over 200,000 infrastructural, social, and development projects have been implemented, which have contributed to the unquestionable development of the Polish economy, ergo, increasing the level of competitiveness of both enterprises and domestic trade on international markets. It is emphasized that since 1 May 2004, the number of enterprises (including SMEs), local government and state administration units, clusters, and consortia using EU funds and thus implementing projects in various areas (including areas of goods, services, processes, new technologies, and social projects) have dynamically increased.

An important issue of the discussed problematic is the process of managing EU projects. When talking about the efficient implementation of projects and their success, it should be noted that the knowledge of general management issues is currently treated as a necessary requirement but not the only sufficient one. The earlier statement results from the specificity of projects and is the effect of different requirements in different operational programmes. The excessive number of entities distributing funds in Poland should be pointed out as the main reason for the complexity of the EU project management process. Unfortunately, each of these entities has different rules for preparing and settling projects. What is more, the European Commission only defines the general framework of individual operational programmes, but the details are developed by the financing institutions of the Member States.

A query of the literature on the subject (the bibliographic query was conducted in accordance with the adopted methodology of a systematic literature review,[1] i.e. one that focuses on a clearly formulated research question and uses the described scientific methods of identification, evaluation, and synthesis of all sources adequate to the question guiding cognitive effort; Tranfield, Denyer & Smart, 2003, pp. 207–220) led to the conclusion that due to the implementation of appropriate operating principles and the implementation of the correct methodology of project implementation, the procedures related to them are factors significantly influencing the way of managing the enterprise.

Therefore, rational management of EU funds which are granted to economic entities including small and medium ones, depends on the management processes of the enterprise itself. Taking up the issue of proper administration of EU projects, it should be remembered that the basis is the creation of appropriate mechanisms for project realization management, correlating with the material and financial schedule and parallel fulfilment by the company of other activities and operational goals. Ergo, entrepreneurs who undertake the implementation of an EU project often also have to face a change in the management model.

The priorities of the EU's policy regarding SMEs are an important part of the development potential of the regions, which in turn determines specific, dedicated, supported, and promoted aid programmes. It is emphasized that enterprises in this sector constitute over 96% of all business entities in Poland – the same statistics are presented throughout the rest of the EU. SMEs stimulate de facto socio-economic development of countries, affecting every part of the economy and the entities participating in it.

Significant changes taking place in the aforementioned economic circle mainly concern the role and function of project management in small and medium enterprises. The clou of the aforementioned topic is the specificity of European projects precisely defined by EU's guidelines for their implementation.

Management of SME enterprises is an essence of EU project management, which determines the use of the latest design methods in the aforementioned entities.

The literature query proved that there are cognitive gaps regarding comprehensive solutions intended for enterprises from the SME sector that implement EU projects. The aforementioned deficiencies and shortcomings were defined primarily in three aspects. The gaps are visible in the following areas, primarily,

a. systematizing the scientific achievements concerning the management of EU projects by small and medium enterprises in the example of Poland;
b. identification of determinants and organizational aspects of management of EU projects in SMEs; and
c. lack of an EU project management model in SME enterprises in the example of Poland, taking into account the project cycle management model, SME strategic management, and the process of innovation implementation in SME enterprises.

The presented research gaps are the reason for undertaking research on the issues of EU project management on the example of small and medium enterprises in Poland. When trying to fill up inaccuracies in the literature on the subject, it was necessary to define and indicate the most important activities aimed at improving the process of managing EU projects in the aforementioned enterprises.

The main objective of the research is to examine the management of EU projects and to introduce changes to the existing management model of SME enterprises while determining the impact of new solutions on the increase in the competitiveness of small and medium-sized Polish enterprises in the international arena.

4.2 PROJECT MANAGEMENT IN SMALL AND MEDIUM ENTERPRISES TAKING INTO CONSIDERATION ORGANIZATIONAL ASPECTS

Globalization is an important determinant of the dynamic development of scientific disciplines dealing with management – including project management. It should be emphasized that this has an impact on SMEs that create GDP, which in turn is the essence of the efficient functioning of the state economy (Przychocka, 2012, pp. 13, 22–23).

The increase in the effectiveness of the functioning and development of modern enterprises depends on many factors, including chronic improvement of project management processes. As the literature on a subject treats, project management processes are considered in several aspects – namely,

- teleological,
- functional,
- subjective,
- structural, and
- instrumental.

Reorganization and improvement of project management processes depend primarily on the methods used in them. They are systematized ways of proceeding, developed on the basis of the literature on the subject and aimed at eliminating problematic issues arising during the design process. They include, above all (Cabała, 2016, pp. 34–35),

- defining the scope of the project,
- analysis of preferences and decision-making,
- time management and resource planning,
- management of project teams,
- quality management,
- risk management, and
- management of cost (including processes of project control).

As discussed in the literature on the subject, the last years of research and updating of data on the aforementioned issues are the most dynamic period in the development of project management. The disadvantage is the lack of official statistical data, presented in numerical form and lack of presentation of the dynamics indicating growth; however, observations and popular science articles indicate that the mentioned development is noticeable in Poland. It is emphasized that nowadays, an increasing number of enterprises' activities are carried out in accordance with the principles of project management, which are one-off undertakings coordinated by project teams. This applies to manufacturing enterprises, as well as public administration, non-profit organizations, and many others.

The project approach is both a response to the most important challenges of the present day and a way to quickly introduce changes within the organization. The first of them is implemented as the adaptation of the product offer to the specific requirements of customers and flexibility in operation, which is determined by the volatility of the economic environment. The implementation of new IT systems and new training programmes (Section 2.4) is, therefore, a reflection of changes taking place in enterprises.

The development of new technologies, i.e. IT, telecommunications, media, as well as sectors based on knowledge and relationships (consulting, marketing agencies), determines the growing interest in the management of individual projects, as well as project portfolios and entire project organizations. Meeting the expectations, needs, and goals of the parties to the project (both the principal and other parties involved in the project) is carried out on the basis of an agreement concluded between these parties. The terms of the contract specify the subject, cost, time, and scope of the project, the needs and expectations of the project's principal, and requirements – both defined and undefined. The following three parameters are considered the basis for defining project management: customer requirements, cost, and time. The correlation of them determines the shape of the project.

As can be seen from the aforementioned, project management in an organization has a multifaceted character. Currently, it is believed that the introduction of appropriate techniques and procedures only is not a sufficient solution, in order to talk about effective acting, it is necessary to transform and adapt to the current needs of the organizational structure (Spałek & Bodych, 2012, pp. 42–43). This leads to the conclusion that the most important issues are as follows (Jędrych, Pietras & Szczepański, 2012, pp. 116–117):

- Acquiring appropriate competencies in the field of managerial functions, i.e. planning, organizing, directing, and controlling. This translates into the elaboration of project issues and increasing knowledge about the project.
- Creating a project team that cooperates effectively.
- Appointing a person responsible for running the project.
- Giving a support – both from leaders and employees – manifested by the involvement of the parties.
- Maintaining permanent contacts with suppliers and determining the adherence to appropriate deadlines in the project.
- Communicating in the enterprise, with horizontally and vertically disseminated information,
- Selecting documentation management methods, which translates into possibilities of careful storage, readability, and archiving.
- Preparing for possible conflicts in the organization – both of financial, interpersonal, and resource character. Leaders readiness to make decisions on how to solve them.

The basic goal of enterprises' operations in Poland (including SMEs) is the effective management of organizational aspects that determine the success of the other directions of the entity's policy. Enterprises should skilfully find partners and build lasting relationships with customers and suppliers. The determinants of the aforementioned are the competences of both leaders and employees. As S. Spałek claims, an equally important factor in effective project management is an efficient flow of information (Pietras & Szmit, 2003, pp. 18–36).

SMEs are the basis for the development of the economy in many European countries, including Poland, which translates into the social climate in the country, incomes, creation of workplaces, and social advancement of citizens. According to the latest report of the Polish Agency for Enterprise Development on the sector of SME, in 2019, there were 1.77 million non-financial enterprises in Poland defined as active enterprises. SMEs account for as much as 99.8%.

It should be emphasized that in the scale of the EU, Poland ranks sixth in terms of the number of enterprises (despite the difference in data, because according to Eurostat, there are 1.5 million enterprises in Poland), after Italy (about two and a half times more than in Poland), France, Spain, Germany, and Great Britain (where a similar number of enterprises operate as in Poland, i.e. approx. 1.7 million). According to the statistical data, the SME sector is responsible for generating 48.5% of Poland's gross domestic product, and among all groups of enterprises, micro-enterprises have the largest share in generating GDP – approximately 30%.

Developing an action strategy for project realization should adequately secure all resources enabling action. The clou is the development of organizational goals, focused on specific activities. It is of crucial importance because it stabilizes the course of processes, especially when the company's environment is characterized by volatility. Clearly defined goals determine the adjustment of operational activities to the conditions and areas of change, ergo, carrying out the project based on an earlier needs analysis. Objectives make it easier to understand the meaning of one's own activities and monitor their progress when they are formulated as the results that the project is supposed to bring to, both participants as well as recipients.

Project management is defined as a set of activities aimed at effective control of actions performed in order to create products, services, or implement specific processes. The successful implementation of projects requires that the very objectives of the project and all activities carried out within them will be measured in a timely manner. A project, on the other hand, is defined as a form of planned activity that requires rational decision-making (section 1.1.). As proponents of design methods treat, every process – even minimized to stages – is in practice a project. As an example, they give not only complicated activities but also the implementation of basic everyday activities – ad exemplum, preparing a meal, organizing holidays, and shopping. Each of them requires an intuitive plan, implemented at a given time, includes the sequence of activities, and uses such resources as its own time, money, or transport. Such activities also require an analysis of the effectiveness of operations, possible adjustments to the original plan, budget management, failure risk analysis, and appropriate preparation for corrective actions. All of these activities are, de facto, characteristic of project management (Pietras & Szmit, 2003, pp. 8).

Project management is related to the team form of work organization, taking place in transitional conditions and with the occurrence of changes in the human resources system. Ergo, it determines the risks of various social problems appearing at the individual level (project team member), group, and organizational levels (Batt & Doellgast, 2005, p. 139).

Therefore, SMEs play a key role in building economic growth and innovation in all industries, as they stimulate socio-economic development, affecting almost every part of the economy, entities participating operating there, as well as high values of individual macroeconomic indicators and changes in local markets. New jobs appear in the SME sector, which determine structural changes in society, innovations' stimulation, and integration of the country with the global economy (Skowronek-Mielczarek, 2005, pp. 33–34). It should be emphasized, however, that it was large enterprises that first saw the need to change methods of operation. However, due to their size and complex organizational structure, they encountered difficulties in achieving the necessary speed of acting (Piasecki, Rogut & Smallbone, 2000, pp. 41–42).

When talking about project management, attention should be paid to unofficial entities, i.e. smaller groups combining employees of various organizational units, able to propose useful solutions and quick implementation of project activities. Currently, there are organizations in the market that largely or even entirely base their work on projects. This determines the speed and efficiency of their work and the allocation of employees' surplus time and energy for other activities.

As they grow and enter a phase of growth, small and medium-sized organizations can use project work to manage formal processes judiciously, *ad exemplum*, by establishing project teams responsible for specific tasks or assigning new formal structures and positions as far as orders increase. In the case of reduced orders, project activities can direct the energy and time of human resources to internal activities, i.e. conducted within the given entity. For comparison, in large organizations, it is difficult to conduct internal work, because employees and specialists are focused on a narrow spectrum of their own duties.

As can be seen from previous considerations, effective management and implementation of MSP projects are based on five basic aspects, as presented in Figure 4.1.

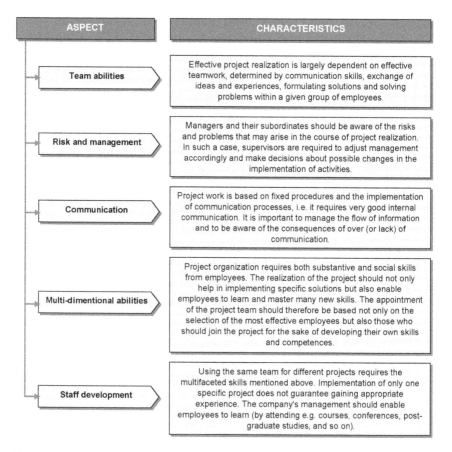

FIGURE 4.1
Basic aspects determining effective and efficient management and project leading in SMEs enterprises.

Source: Own elaboration based on Skorupka, 2008, pp. 120–129; Winkler & Chmielecki, 2015, pp. 87–99; Stabryła, 2015, pp. 169–178.

As can be seen so far, SMEs are inclined to the method of management which is project work. It should be emphasized, however, that in the case of SMEs, this method of work is risky. Although it enables effective operations, as indicated in the literature, it also limits to some extent employees' attachment to the organization. In order to avoid a too high level of lack of the aforementioned connection, a necessary condition for the implementation of projects is a constant and lasting investment in employees (Stabryła, 2015, pp. 176–178).

Project management takes various forms, affecting almost all organizational units of the entity, which determines the emergence of new or modernized material and/or intangible value. The interdisciplinary nature of activities undertaken by project teams and their correlation with only selected tactical and strategic goals of the organization make it almost impossible to identify a model management model that always ensures efficient project implementation. Organizational factors of SMEs, especially those focused on profit, allow us, however, to define a general model of project management (Pietras & Szmit, 2003).

The specific nature of the functioning of SMEs, based on their definite specialization and strictly defined economic relations gives a functional organizational advantage over larger market players. This is determined by a broader spectrum of economic outlays' investment opportunities for the sake of the purchase and acquisition of technologies or resources necessary for the effective implementation of a specific project.

As it was mentioned in one of the previous chapters, the clou and the basis for choosing the method of managing and working on a given project is an idea or a vision. At this stage, among the tasks of the enterprise, the following stand out:

- defining the area and reasons for taking up a project;
- analysis of the available and needed resources, determining the real possibilities of using the possessed potential of the entity (material and intellectual); and
- an indication of the degree of change and/or innovation that would accompany the finalization of the project.

Reliable performance of the tasks of the first stage allows us to start working on the most extensive and at the same time complicated element of the project, i.e. planning. Small and medium entities should focus this stage on the analysis of the closer environment of the organization while taking into account the individual needs of external stakeholders. Projects aimed at restructuring internal processes including employee improvement and motivation should, however, be directly correlated with the organization's development goals. At this stage of activities, T. Błaszczyk and T. Trzaskalik distinguished, among others (Błaszczyk & Trzaskalik, 2007, pp. 64–67),

- determination of the budget that is available for the implementation of the project;
- strategic analysis, estimating the risk;
- development of the project's realization of three variants, i.e. full success, partial success, or no success;
- creating procedures regulating the course of the project;
- determining the time for the implementation of individual tasks and time for the project finalization, as well as observing specific changes and profits; and
- indication of interested parties, i.e. employees responsible for coordinating the project, contractors, addressees, stakeholders, etc.

The third stage of project management is its implementation, which, it should be emphasized, is characterized by incredible organizational dynamics. Organizational dynamism is especially noticeable when SMEs use simple planning and control tools for project implementation as well as less formalized evaluation and reporting methods. Such a nature of activities' organization definitely facilitates the implementation of specific processes, which is unfortunately associated with the risk of deficiencies and deviations from previously defined plans and goals. Among the tasks at this stage, the following stand out:

- changing the organization of work of the entire organization (from process changes to product changes), and
- changes in the way the technology is used, i.e. adapting it to new needs, new information, and IT infrastructure determined by the implementation of the project.

The last stage of project implementation is its audit. As was already emphasized in the previous subsections, this activity is inter alia characterized by the fact that consists of two sub-processes, i.e. the control stage and the closure and conclusion stage. As part of the audit, K. Dziadek determines the following activities (Dziadek, 2010, pp. 254–255):

- Control stage: analysing obtained results and comparing them with the goals planned at the beginning
- Closing and concluding stage: final closing of the work related to project management and formulation of conclusions by the leader

As can be seen from the preceding considerations, project management, as well as its organization, is a process that requires the involvement of almost all company units. Despite this, many SMEs base their activities on the implementation of projects because the estimated profits are greater than the possible risks. The benefits of this type of activity include a comprehensive way of communicating the organization with the environment, obtaining information, or an innovative approach to management.

As research shows, small, medium entities are able to quickly and effectively identify the goals and needs necessary to start work on the project. At the same time it is emphasized that entrepreneurs often strive to achieve many goals within one project, the implementation of which is mutually exclusive. In such cases it results in project failure or fulfilling only partial profits. This requires further research on how to optimize internal processes and adapt the company's strategy to forecasts that determine the direction and development of a given entity in the future (Bizon-Górecka, 2009, pp. 21–25).

Planning and managing a project requires distinguishing three basic factors, i.e. cost, quality as well as time (Pietras & Szmit, 2003, p. 12). These parameters fulfil specific functions, which are presented in Figure 4.2.

As was already mentioned, a project is usually a complex undertaking, which determines the use of an appropriate management method, correlating technology, technical tools, knowledge, and human resources. Project management refers to the execution of a process aimed at producing the desired product. Literature defines the process itself as a set of related activities and actions aimed at delivering a specific set of products, results, or services, which is reflected in project management.

Each management process is a described set of information, taking into account the necessary input data, tools, techniques, and obtained results. Project management processes are linked by inputs and outputs – the result of one process becomes the input of another, but, it should be emphasized, not necessarily belonging to the same group. It is possible to

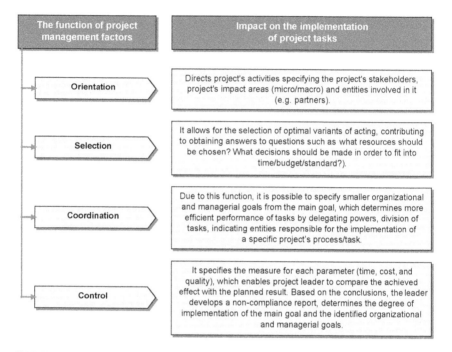

FIGURE 4.2

Functions of project management factors and their impact on the implementation of project tasks.

Source: Own elaboration based on Pietras & Szmit, 2003, p. 12.

categorize processes according to the nature of their interactions with each other and according to the nature of the purposes they serve.

With this in mind, the following five sub-processes of project management can be specified (Pietras & Szmit, 2003, p. 12):

- Initiation sub-processes – they are based on the analysis of business needs and real possibilities of project implementation, which translates into the indication of the main expectations, the initial scope of work, and the involvement of initial resources. Due to the high probability of impact on the finalization of the project, an analysis of both internal and external stakeholders should be performed at this stage. The project leader/manager should be also selected during the initiation process.
- Planning sub-processes – consist in creating a comprehensive project management plan, which will be implemented at a later time. The plan includes the scope, deadline, available resources (human and

financial), and the definition of risk factors, methods of communication, control, quality, purchase, and integrity of the project, as well as archiving of knowledge gained during its duration.

- Implementation sub-processes – specify the activities necessary to perform the tasks specified in the project management plan, i.e. coordinating personnel and other resources, shaping stakeholder expectations, and performing activities in accordance with the project management plan.
- Monitoring and control sub-processes – within this category, the following sub-processes can be additionally distinguished: monitoring, checking, and adjusting the progress of work and the actual implementation of the project; identifying areas for change; and initiating these changes. These activities determine the measurement and analysis of project performance, which aims to identify aberrations in the project management plan. Constant monitoring allows realizators to understand the actual state of the project and identify areas that need improvement and/or control.
- Final sub-processes – their purpose is to formally summarize, accept, and close the project, carried out by completing, e.g., contracts with subcontractors and preparing final documentation. The final product of sub-process should be the final audit, summarizing the actions undertaken and showing the achieved project effect.

As can be seen from the aforementioned, the project management process is a set of input data aimed at determining specific actions for specific output products, correlating either with the project or used as input data for subsequent processes.

So far considerations lead to the conclusion that SMEs play a significant role in the development of the economy by, inter alia, securing employment, exploiting innovations, and contributing to gross domestic product growth. Statistical data show that in the EU, SMEs constitute 99.8% of all companies, generate 60% of GDP, and employ 70% of employees in the private sector. For comparison, in Poland, 25% of their turnover falls on new and improved products – the achievement of such results is determined by the fact that SMEs spend 3% of their turnover on innovations. SMEs undertake the implementation of operational, as well as innovative and development, projects.

As the literature on the subject indicates, projects account for an average of one-third of small and medium enterprises' turnover in Poland, which translates into one-fifth of economic activity. It is interesting and worth noting that this is more than is spent on large infrastructural projects in Western markets. Small and medium businesses also undertake the realization of more formal processes which is to manage a bigger number of professionals and coordinate the interface between them.

The literature on the subject indicates the following key differences between SMEs and larger organizations:

- Small and medium enterprises' processes require simple planning and control systems, as well as informal reporting.
- Their procedures are characterized by a low degree of standardization with idealistic decision-making.
- SMEs use projects in their companies to a large extent – both to manage internal innovation and development undertakings and to work externally for clients.
- Micro and small enterprises need less bureaucratic and more people-oriented forms of project management, which facilitate their work and development. Medium and large organizations, as emphasized by T. Oleksym, need more formal approaches to project management in order to coordinate the work of teams of specialists, while medium-sized enterprises still need simpler forms of project management than large entities (Oleksym, 2009, pp. 18–19).

Statistical data indicate that the Polish economy, like most of the current European markets, is dominated by micro-firms, which have the largest share in the creation of GDP among all groups of enterprises – 30.6% (data from 2019) and assuming the value of GDP generated by the enterprise sector as 100% – 41.8%. We have a similarly high share of micro-organizations when considering the provision of the workplace – 44.9% of jobs in the entire sector of the Polish economy (the number of people employed in such companies is over four million). According to the data of the Central Statistical Office from 2016 to 2019, most micro-enterprises at that time were sole proprietorships, and the average number of employees in this group of entities was approximately 1.4 million people (GUS, 2019).

The SME sector (of micro, SMEs), constitutes therefore the vast majority of enterprises in Poland. The most numerous group (almost 87%) are micro-enterprises. The share of small enterprises in the structure of the Polish economy is 2.4%, medium-sized enterprises – 0.7% (15.2 thousand), and large enterprises – only 0.2% (Raport o stanie, 2020, p. 8).

The determinants of the above data and the development of scientific disciplines based on management (including project management) can be seen in the processes of globalization and technology development.

Summing up previous considerations, we can point out that it is not sufficient to introduce only appropriate management techniques and procedures in the organizational structures of SMEs. Changes and amendments are also required in the field of projects, consolidation of knowledge and data is necessary on increasing the value of projects in the broad sense, largo. In order to maximize the effectiveness of enterprises' activities, a team cooperating with each other is necessary, using its knowledge resources to solve problems effectively and innovatively, and appointing a person responsible for the project's team. This determines the involvement of all participants in the process, which translates to keeping with the proper deadline for project implementation.

In order to increase the efficiency of project management, the authors suggest developing appropriate methods of documentation management, taking into account papers' storage, readability, and archiving. An important element of management (including project management) is also preparation for conflict situations in the team and taking into account the risk at every stage of implementation. This is justified by the fact that the essence determining the effective management and realization of projects in SMEs are team, leadership, communication, multidimensional skills, as well as staff development and risk management. These features can be coupled with proper organizational design including project-oriented structures (e.g. holacracy), dynamic capabilities, crisis resilience, the ability to create and capture value, as well as work organization flexibility.

4.3 BENCHMARKING OF SELECTED SME MANAGEMENT MODELS IN THE SURVEYED ENTITIES

A literature search led to the conclusion that benchmarking was not always an integral part of defining strategy and strategic planning, moreover. So far, it has not correlated or interfered with any of the areas of project management. Recent years of development of management methods (including project management) show that without the possibility of comparing and justifying the strategy, plans, and goals of the company against external reference points, the management staff will not achieve specific effects and will not be competitive in a given market.

Some well-prospering companies experienced activities that prove the lack of analysis and implementation of appropriate actions by observing competition (Borowiecki, Siuta-Tokarska, 2016, pp. 4–7). Similarly it has been noted, that, if managers had collected appropriate benchmarking information, a significant part of their activities, aimed at shaping the level of competitiveness, would not have ended in discredit (Bogan, 2006, p. 221).

Benchmarking – as it was already defined as a process of continuous comparison with a model to follow (benchmark) – consists in tracking, analysing and copying effective practices used by other companies, often competing (Watson. 2007, p. 5). As the researchers emphasize, this determines goal setting pursued by the organization in product and process quality, time, costs and consumption of production factors (Czekaj, 1995, pp. 5–7).

The purpose of using the benchmarking method is also to analyse the solutions used by managers of other organizations, which can contribute to the introduction of innovations or improvement of processes taking place in one's own enterprise (creative imitation, taking the pattern of the best practices of outstanding enterprises) (Kozak, 2004, pp. 5–7).

The goal of this chapter of the book, was to analyse the existing project management models, which was intended to collect information about the possibility of implementing in the frame of benchmarking their individual elements to the original project management model. The strategic management model was analysed first – its general concept is presented in Figure 4.3.

When analysing the diagram in Figure 4.3, particular attention should be paid to the informational and functional feedback, which proves the dynamic nature of strategic management in the enterprise. This type of management model should take into account changes in the company's environment and their impact on the implemented strategy. In extreme cases, the company's mission, i.e. its main strategic goal, may also be modified.

On the basis of the general scheme of the strategic management model, a model was indicated, classified as currently functioning in the SME in Poland, which is presented in Figure 4.4.

Analysis of Figure 4.4 indicates that such a model most often functions in Polish small and medium enterprises, with some elements implemented

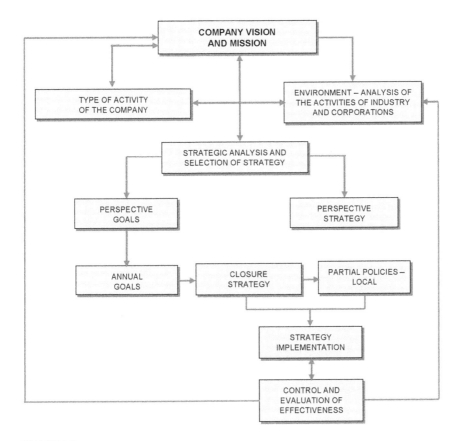

FIGURE 4.3
Scheme of strategic management model.

Source: Stabryła, 1995, p. 34.

in relation to the original model. In point 1, taking into account SME as a type of activity, its type turns out to be important, with the idea and innovation correlating with the type of activity being the essence. Annual goals are preceded by a business plan each time, enabling a real assessment of the overall result of a given work (point 2).

The environment towards the analysis of activity, industry, and corporation was indicated through the analysis of opportunities and the analysis of competition and competitors in a stronger executive value (point 3). The control and evaluation of effectiveness should be implemented, according to the authors, at the stage of strategic analysis and when choosing a specific strategy for the company's operations. Implementation of the strategy would also involve verification of the idea (Figure 4.5).

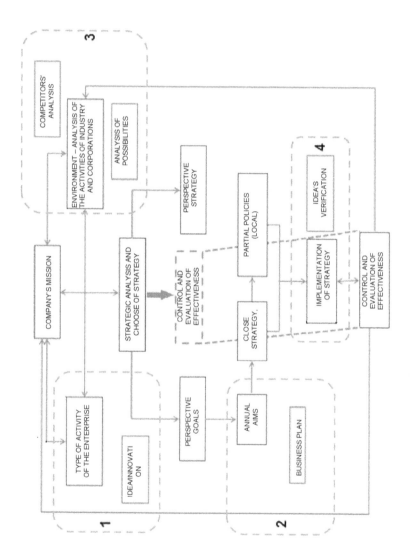

FIGURE 4.4

Scheme of the strategic management model with the changes introduced, taking into account management in SMEs in the province of Kuyavia-Pomerania.

Source: Own elaboration based on Stabryła, 1995, p. 34.

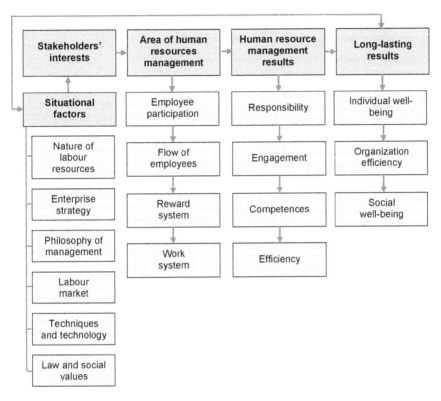

FIGURE 4.5

Diagram of the human resource management model.

Source: Own elaboration based on Bąk-Grabowska, 2011, pp. 43–46.

As indicated by the analysis of Figure 4.5, in the human resources management model (HRM), compared to the model of personnel management, more attention is paid to the issues of strategy and the way in which human resources affect the achievement of organizational goals. The diagram shows that the company cares about meeting the needs of "internal stakeholders" as well as it desires to ensure that human resources are developed in order to meet future challenges of the organization. Thus, the managers try to take action to ensure the use of human energy that determines the effective work of the team. The HRM model emphasizes the importance of flexibility and the ability to react quickly and adapt to changes in the company's environment.

The implementation of the human resource management model in project management ensures the appropriate level of line and managerial staff, determining the quality of the company's operations and the quality of the product or service, which translates into an increase in the competitive advantage of the organization on the market. The HRM model uses an economic approach consisting in maximizing effects while minimizing costs, but employee morale is one of the most important issues of the company's operations.

HRM adopts a systemic approach to business analysis and management, utilizing human resource planning, recruitment and selection, assessment, training and development, and a remuneration system. It should be emphasized that these systems should correlate with each other and be integrated. According to E. McKenna and N. Beech, this is how the function of the HRM model helps the organization to achieve greater efficiency and profitability (McKenna & Beech, 1999, p. 25).

The next stage under consideration in this chapter is the analysis of the general model of EU project management in small and medium enterprises, which is shown in Figure 4.6.

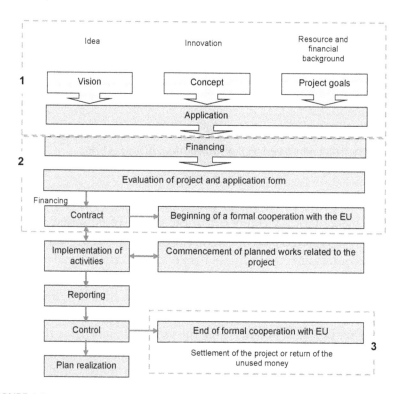

FIGURE 4.6

General outline of the EU project management model in SMEs.

Source: Prusak, Strojny & Baran, 2015, p. 96.

On the basis of the aforementioned model, an attempt was made to indicate differences in relation to project management in SMEs in Poland. The updated model is shown in Figure 4.7.

When discussing Figure 4.7, it should be noted that some of the elements have been implemented, but at this stage of developing the scheme, the nomenclature of all processes and components was not specified. In addition, the authors were not sure whether a given action had been fully implemented in this scope. Without a precise nomenclature, it is impossible to define and analyse the course of the process. The elements subject to the phenomenon of unspecified nomenclature include idea, innovation and resource, and financial background, which should be in fact determined at the stage of submitting the application (first item).

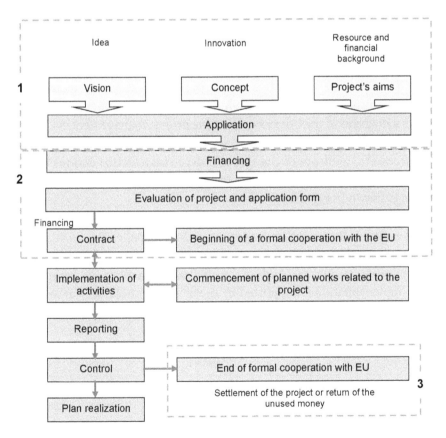

FIGURE 4.7

The EU project management model relating to – project management in SMEs.

Source: Own elaboration based on Prusak, Strojny & Baran, 2015, p. 96.

The analysis of the second area indicate that financing in EU projects takes place only after the project and its application have been assessed. The third area (point 3), which takes place after the end of formal cooperation with the EU, consists in the settlement of the project, which in such a situation results in the return of the unused part of the financial resources or the advance payment collected inconsistently with the eligible costs or the presentation of a reset settlement.

The scrutinized data show that the projects managed in a traditional way are implemented according to a detailed plan, i.e. a schedule of activities. This document includes a detailed estimation of the costs of activities, prepared before the implementation of each project.

Apart from minor modifications during the project realization (resulting, for example, from shifting some activities over time or from ongoing risk analysis), the project's goal is achieved by precise execution of the plan, i.e. implementation of the mission and method clearly defined at the beginning of the activities. The goal is defined by specific, measurable, and time-defined indicators and sources of their verification. As part of traditional project management, two models of the project management cycle are distinguished, i.e. linear and gradual (Wysocki, 2013, p. 104). Figure 4.8 shows a diagram of the linear model of the project management cycle.

The model in Figure 4.8 was modified, indicating the elements in which it is necessary to introduce changes in order to take further actions in the field of an effective model approach to project management. The modified model is shown in Figure 4.9.

According to us, additional elements should be included in the basic linear model of the project management cycle, i.e. application form, innovation, motivation, human resource management, project evaluation, and its application evaluation. Adding the application element, the legitimacy of its implementation is supported by the fact of the necessary awareness

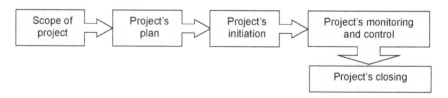

FIGURE 4.8

The linear model of the project management cycle.

Source: Own elaboration based on Wysocki, 2013, p. 18.

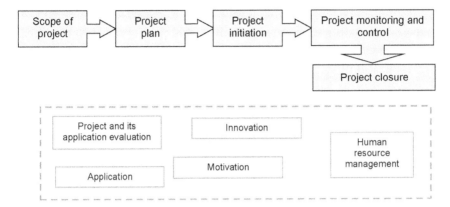

FIGURE 4.9
Linear model of the project management cycle, including our own changes.

Source: Own elaboration based on Wysocki, 2013, p. 18.

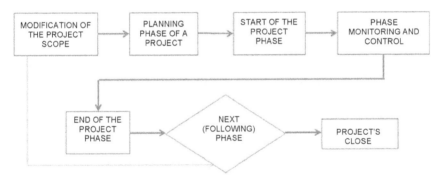

FIGURE 4.10
The gradual model of the project management cycle.

Source: Own elaboration based on Wysocki, 2013, p. 19.

of taking the necessary actions that determine the commencement of a given project. According to us, the lack of any of the listed added elements affects the scoring of the application, i.e. they can create relative chances for success in project management.

The second of the mentioned models of the project management cycle is, as mentioned, the gradual (phased) model, the diagram of which is shown in Figure 4.10.

In the model presented in Figure 4.10, changes and updates were introduced as well. These additions concern the yellow triangle marked, and the phrase "settlement of the application".

It is emphasized that the initial visualization treated all the elements as properly correlating with each other and not requiring changes. However, it was decided to take into account elements such as evaluation of project and application form, idea and innovation, application, motivation, and HRM, as well as settlement of the application and project evaluation together with the application.

In addition, according to us, for more effective project management, the planning of the project phase should be switched with the modification of the project scope. All these changes are shown in the diagram of the step-by-step management model in Figure 4.11.

It should be noted that in all the aforementioned models, it is not possible to start a new stage of the project if the previous one has not been completed. Additionally, the chronology and systematization of activities do not allow for their re-execution, repetition, or any improvements. Sequential ordering aims to realize achievements identified at the start of the project.

As indicated by the analysis of the literature on the subject and selected models, the usage of traditional management allows us to obtain the best results in the case of projects in which

- goals are clearly defined (according to the SMART criteria – specific, measurable, translatable into actions, realistic, captured in time);
- there are a small number of changes to the scope of the project and these are anticipated in advance;
- routine and repetitive activities are used (e.g. annual or quarterly cycles); and
- it is possible to use proven templates (due to careful planning before the start of the project and the low probability of unforeseen risk).

The considerations made so far have allowed for a summary of the advantages and disadvantages of introducing a traditional model of project management in Polish enterprises, which is shown in Figure 4.12.

The traditional model of project management assumes acting according to a detailed plan. On the contrary, the agile management, points to developing an action plan after the completion of each project cycle. The end of a given cycle is identical with the project team's analysis of achievements regarding accomplishments and failures, and the further plan. Therefore, the project goal is achieved in incremental steps. Agile-managed projects are thus not implemented according to a precise, rigid and unchangeable plan. Therefore, the project goal is achieved in incremental steps. Agile-managed projects are thus not implemented according to a precise, rigid,

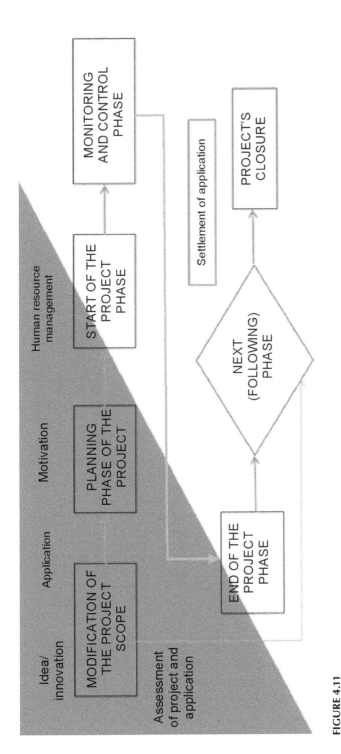

FIGURE 4.11

The gradual model of the project management cycle, considering proprietary changes.

Source: Own elaboration based on Wysocki, 2013 p. 19.

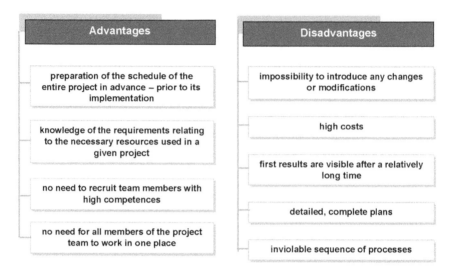

FIGURE 4.12

Summary of advantages and disadvantages of introducing a traditional project management model in a small or medium enterprise.

Source: Own elaboration.

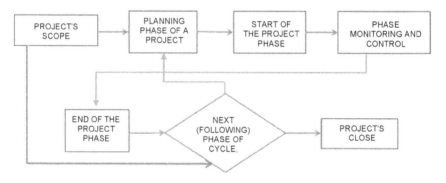

FIGURE 4.13

Scheme of the adaptive model of the project management cycle.

Source: Own elaboration based on Wysocki, 2013, p. 14.

and unchangeable plan. As a part of agile project management, the adaptive model of the project management cycle is most often used – it is presented in Figure 4.13.

Similarly as before, we decided to distinguish elements that, according to us, should be implemented for the greater project performance. These elements are marked in Figure 4.14 using a triangle and the label "settlement of the application".

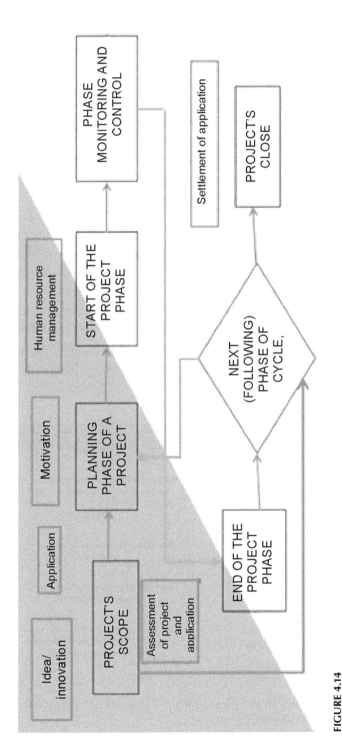

FIGURE 4.14

Scheme of the contemporary adaptive model of the project management cycle.

Source: Own elaboration based on Wysocki, 2013 p. 14.

Analyzing the adaptive model, it is obvious that more elements are to be implemented due to the fact that the adaptive model was created for the implementation of complex projects characterized by a greater degree of uncertainty, in which there is no possibility of full decomposition of requirements. As emphasized by A. Kiełbus, this is determined by the fact that not in all cases the exact needs of project recipients and possible solutions leading to the achievement of goals are known.[2]

Adaptive models are most often used in cases where the initial version of the solution is known, but some features, functionalities, or assumptions are not specified. For this reason, the next stages of the project are planned in a way that allows the implementation of the missing elements of the solution.

Bearing in mind the previous considerations, the advantages and disadvantages of introducing an adaptive model of project management in Polish enterprises were compared, which is shown in Figure 4.15.

In the next stage, projects managed in an extreme manner were analysed, which are developed on the basis of assumptions (hypotheses) regarding the future goals of the project and the ways to achieve them. The project's realization cycle, in this case, is therefore based on the

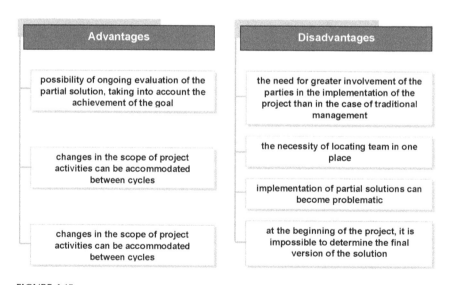

FIGURE 4.15
Summary of advantages and disadvantages of introducing an adaptive project management model in a small and medium-sized enterprises.

Source: Own elaboration based on Wysocki, 2013 p. 23.

reasonability of predetermined assumptions. The end of a given phase of the project determines the drawing of conclusions from the previous activities by the project team and the definition of the goals of the next phase, which are usually more precise than the initial hypotheses (Wysocki, 2013, 477). Figure 4.16 shows an extreme model of the project management cycle.

As shown in Figure 4.16, in extreme management, the current phase is implemented on the basis of conclusions from the previous phases, thus leading to obtaining information aimed at directing the project team to the most effective and efficient achievement of the goal and solution in the next phase.

It needs to be noted, that an extreme model of the project management cycle is used within the scope of extreme management. One of the advantages of this method is the possibility of leaving several solutions until almost the last moment of the implementation of a given stage of the project and a wider spectrum of partial solutions. When discussing the disadvantages of this method, the following were distinguished: confusion in relation to the source of the search for the solution and no guarantee of the effectiveness of the action taken (Baran, M. Kłos, Metody zarządzania projektami unijnymi realizowanymi przez uczelnie wyższe. Przedsiębiorczość i Zarządzanie, 14(11), 2013, pp. 11–12). Therefore, it was decided not to propose changes to this model schema, thus recognizing that its form currently presented in the literature may refer to the entire phase, which makes it fully justified.

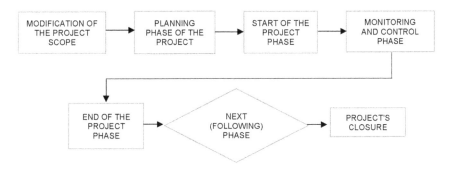

FIGURE 4.16

Scheme of the extreme model of the project management cycle.

Source: Personal studies based on Wysocki, 2013 p. 31.

4.4 IDENTIFICATION OF THE ELEMENTS OF AN EFFECTIVE EU PROJECT MANAGEMENT MODEL IN SMALL AND MEDIUM-SIZED ENTERPRISES

When dealing with projects co-financed with the EU's funds, it is emphasized that they have become a stable element determining economic and social development in Poland. So currently, there is a need to know issues related to EU project management and funds which, according to development trends, will be implemented in the need for functioning of initiators, beneficiaries, as well as contractors of subsequent projects on behalf of the EU. The variety of programmes and European projects determines, however, the problem of choosing the right planning method and implementation of these projects, i.e. the methodology of management of EU projects and funds (Tkaczyński, Willa & Świstak, 2008, pp. 14–17).

EU funds are primarily financial resources used in order to support and transform the economies of the EU Member States, modernize them, and influence the competitiveness of the international market.

The resources in the budget of the EU come from the following three main sources:

- customs duties levied on goods imported from countries that are not members of the EU (the so-called traditional own resources of the Union);
- VAT revenues – a specific percentage paid by the state to the EU on the funds originating from VAT;
- resources dependent on the national income of each member state – each European country pays 0.73% of its gross national product (GNP) to the EU budget, which is currently the largest source of EU funds.

Bukowski, Saj, and Pelle indicate that the basic instrument in striving to achieve EU's policy coherence is the European regional policy, most often expressed by the degree of differentiation in the level of GDP per capita, unemployment, and quality of life (Bukowski, Saj & Pelle, 2008, pp. 13–28).

Therefore, it becomes important to introduce modern standards for managing projects and EU funds in order to define documentation, work breakdown structure, risk management and manage the project budget in the most standardized way, as possible. Researchers believe that the implementation of corporate solutions of European enterprises in the field of project and EU fund management standards is possible in every enterprise and organization (Sierak & Górniak, 2011).

Considering that SMEs play an important role as an element of the development potential of regions, the local and regional market is their basic source of supply, e.g. in labour resources and materials, and, most importantly, it is also the basic sales area for their goods or services. The importance of the SME sector in the light of the national economy is determined by the ability of these enterprises to be flexible and understand so that they can react very quickly to market needs. They are also characterized by the ability to create new jobs while maintaining relatively low costs of jobs and the ease of adapting to the place, time as well as resources. When talking about the impact of SMEs on the development of the economy, attention should be paid to the necessity of their openness to technical and organizational progress, which is intensified in large enterprises as the implementation of project management methods. M. Borowiec-Gabryś emphasizes that this method should therefore also support the activities of SMEs (Borowiec-Gabryś, 2020, pp. 261–273).

The main objective of the implementation of projects supported, organized, or promoted by the EU is to increase innovation, efficiency, and effectiveness in the operation of SMEs (Borowiecki, Kusio & Siuta-Tokarska, 2019, pp. 65–71). As mentioned at the beginning of the chapter already, EU projects are complicated, which determines the involvement of many entities – both directly interested (enterprises – clients) and those not having tangential connections (local community, local government). The essence of the implementation and realization of EU projects is their financing – the EU most often invests the largest part of the costs related to the realization of a specific project. It follows that financing, resource as well as technological analysis of the company are a necessary and integral element of the model of EU project management. Figure 4.17 presents a universal model of EU project management in SMEs (Brzozowska, 2013, pp. 67–78).

The diagram of the general model of EU project management in SMEs in Figure 4.17 includes six basic elements resulting from establishing cooperation with the EU, as well as two auxiliary elements aimed at organizing processes within the enterprise.

As the analysis of Figure 4.17 shows, it is important to develop a vision, prevailing concept and goals of the project. The culmination of this stage is to define and communicate the proposed final goals of the project to the

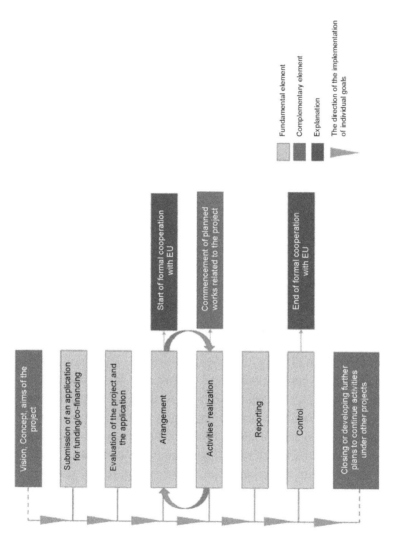

FIGURE 4.17

Scheme of the general model of EU project management in SMEs.

Source: Own elaboration.

stakeholders. Although these activities are not mandatory in terms of obtaining EU support or recommendations, according to us they significantly facilitate the specification of mandatory elements, i.e. the plan, budget and outcomes. What is more, during the implementation of the project at this stage, especially with regard to SMEs, the processes and forms of communication with the environment should be systematized (Szlachta, 1997, p. 105).

According to the presented scheme, the second stage of project implementation and management is submitting an application for co-financing or financing. At this time, all processes for formalization of the planned activities in the project begin. For SMEs, this element is a challenge, as it requires meeting numerous requirements, which is the responsibility of a small group of people, mostly three. For sake of comparison, in large enterprises the formalization and analysis of procedures related to granting financing is dealt by a few to a dozen people (Szlachta, 1997, pp. 107–108).

The third stage consists in evaluating the project and the application form. On the basis of the submitted documents, the Department of European Funds assesses whether the documentation is consistent, complete, and substantive in terms of the budget and the technology used in the project. Positive evaluation, without indicating corrections, allows us to move to the next stage. In the situation of identifying areas requiring correction or issuing a negative opinion on the submitted project, the project manager is obliged to carry out re-analysis. Failure to remedy the deficiencies or inconsistencies results in a total refusal to establish cooperation with the EU.

The nature of the project, the dynamism of the work, the realization time, and the adopted methodology of performance determine the commencement of the implementation stage. According to the literature on the subject, a good practice is the previous conclusion of an agreement by the company with the EU due to the EU's formal acceptance of the project and declaration of participation in the project. In the area of implementation of project activities, the company starts implementing previously planned solutions. R. Kasprzak emphasizes that interference and making corrections in the previously approved action plan are allowed, but they must not affect the main idea of the project, and any change in the budget management must be approved by the EU in advance (Kasprzak, 2009).

The completion of activities obliges the project leaders to prepare a report on the implementation of the project. This document should contain information on the achieved goals, social changes, and the course of each process as a part of the undertaken activities. This should be supported by financial data, photos, reports, and other documents proving that the undertaking has been carried out. Reporting marks the transition to the last stage of formal cooperation with the EU – i.e. control. Its purpose is to check the real achievements of the company, resulting from the organization of the project, and to determine the degree of implementation of the activities included in the initial project plans.

Depending on the nature of the project (strategic or tactical), the company may close it or take steps to continue work on the further development of the undertaking. Researchers emphasize that SMEs, which undertake activities related to strategic goals and mission, most often continue the implementation of the project (taking into account subsequent goals, but related to those that were the subject of the previous project) (Gorzelak & Jałowiecki, 2001, pp. 58–59).

Analyses of the EU projects show that they can be perceived as large-scale events that require managers not only to thoroughly understand the project management area but also to understand human resources as well as financial management. Managers are obliged to cooperate effectively with partners, as well as to behave and react appropriately in any crisis situation. Among the actions that the company's personnel should undertake before applying for grants for EU projects, the following can be distinguished: development of a reliable, specific management plan for future projects; understanding the principles of conducting activities in the field of EU law; and familiarization with the detailed conditions regarding the undertaken activity in the context of EU law, getting to know specific conditions regarding the assumptions of the project or the organization of documentation and accounting in the project.

In order to talk about an effective advanced project management plan, those responsible for its implementation should take into account all the factors mentioned earlier, especially in terms of personnel management, finances, and cooperation with partners. Unfortunately, entrepreneurs benefitting from EU projects are not always fully aware of this. They do not understand the scale of future activities. As the project's analysis shows, in many cases, even the most qualified project team may not be able to cope with complex tasks. Failure can be seen in the lack of appropriate tools or insufficient qualifications of employees involved in a given project. Therefore, the project coordinator should then ensure cooperation with entities that will commission specific tasks within the project, but this should be planned in advance, before submitting an application for EU funding. It is permissible to sign cooperation agreements with partners who implement EU projects in order to regulate the rights and obligations of both parties.

An important issue in managing an EU project is budget. The substantive preparation of estimated project-related expenses is the responsibility of the project coordinator, but the company's accountant is a person obliged to accept their compliance with the budget and regulations. The literature on the subject states that the larger the budget of a given EU project, the more important it is to employ a qualified accountant to take care of it. The project implementation plan should also include the budget and resources for remuneration for its participants.

Risk management is an important element of project management in the activity of both the project designer and the implementer. As part of this process, problems related to risk accompanying each project are solved in a methodical manner. They should be developed taking into account both the individual areas of the company's activity within the project and as an entire integrity (Skorupka, Kuchta & Górski, 2012). Proper risk management is tantamount to its identification and taking action to eliminate it or limit its negative effects. In the aid projects of the EU (Olejniczak & Olejniczak, 2004), regardless of the standardized risk, there is a specific risk – relates only to these projects (Sąsara, https://www.taskbeat. pl/2013/01/jak-zarzadzac-projektami-unijnymi/, reading: 11.07.2021).

The essence of the proper management of the EU project is the competent performance of activities, taking into account the correlation of entities and responsibilities related to the delegation of powers.

Relationships and division of tasks should be based on specific and transparent rules, taking into account both the capabilities of the team of employees and contractors. A favourable division of tasks also takes into account the needs of personal and professional development of all people included in the project, which should be manifested, among others, in the selection of employees in such a way that they could improve their skills and acquire new competences by implementing a given project, which in turn determines personal satisfaction.

Responsibility and competences are correctly understood as the awareness of responsibility for the work performed by people who undertake it. Awareness of the consequences of individual activities and of creation is best realized through mutual support of employees/people involved in the project, smooth exchange of information, and, on the part of supervisors, through motivation and noticing effort, especially individual initiative.

Influencing expectations seems to be the area of activities that is the most complicated in the whole management process. It consists of noticing, reconciling, and stimulating the expectations of both the environment and the individualized motivation to work of people involved in the implementation of a given undertaking. The calculations of both participants and contractors are helpful in taking appropriate actions in this matter. As J. Bizon-Górecka treats, creating a team is a challenge, but it also allows the development of personal and social competences of the project manager, i.e. the ability to listen and communicate with others and to solve problems together (Bizon-Górecka, 2009, pp. 21–25).

As mentioned earlier, EU co-financed projects constitute an important element supporting economic and social development in Europe. What is more, knowledge related to the management of EU projects and funds becomes almost obligatory in the business sphere.

Funds for the implementation of EU projects come from all EU countries – they are worked out by all EU citizens (Figure 4.18). This determines the assessment of implemented projects by local and regional environments, as well as by citizens of other member states. When talking about European projects, the following features can be distinguished:

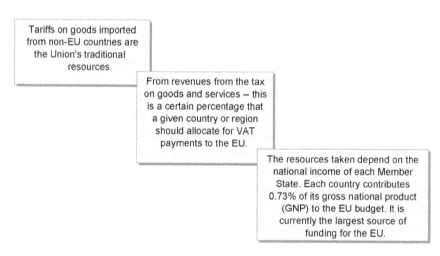

FIGURE 4.18
Funds in the budget from EU sources.

Source: Own elaboration based on GUS (Central Statistical Office) and Eurostat, 2019.

- they involve significant human resources;
- provide participants with detailed and competent methodological assistance;
- the origin, material, or social status of project participants is irrelevant;
- the education and professional experience of both the beneficiaries and those implementing project activities do not affect the possibility of undertaking the project; and
- they can be carried out in groups or separately.

Groups of projects create programmes understood as groups of interrelated projects implemented in a coordinated way in order to achieve a common goal, which is also impossible to be implemented by specific projects separately. Therefore, programmes are a superior category over projects.

The purpose of the appropriate and reliable organization of work under a given programme is the introduction of correct mechanisms for managing projects and EU funds. As is shown by the literature on the subject, the nowadays knowledge of the mechanisms of the functioning of the EU (and especially EU procedures) is rudimentary, which makes it difficult to fully use the aid funds.

Summing up so far considerations, it can be stated that skilful management of projects and EU funds opens the prospect of achieving many benefits, ad exemplum, higher production efficiency, acquisition of newer technologies, better organization of work, which determines greater competitiveness of the company on the market and increases its financial income (Wyrozębski, 2011, pp. 71–73).

When considering a modern approach to European project management, attention should be paid to the project according to the PRINCE2 and PMBoK methodologies. As part of the former, an organization is established (for a specific time) in order to produce unique, but predefined, results in a set time using predefined resources (Axelos, 2019). According to PMBoK, a project is understood as a temporary activity undertaken in order to create a unique product, provide an innovative service or achieve an unconventional result.

In one of the previous subsections, the types of projects were described due to non-identical differentiating criteria. At this point, however, it should be emphasized that EU projects, depending on the scope and type of undertakings, are usually divided into projects: research, technical, production, and of management systems. Their short description is presented in Figure 4.19.

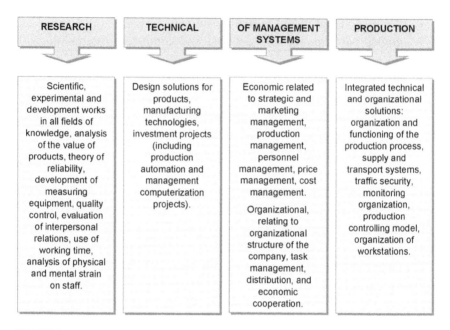

FIGURE 4.19

Classification of EU projects according to the type of undertaking undertaken.

Source: Own elaboration based on Stabryła, 2006.

Currently, SMEs constitute the backbone of economic development, employing approximately 67% of all people working in the EU. The literature on the subject treats that they are of key importance, not only to the aforementioned economic growth but also to innovation, job creation, and social inclusion in the EU. This becomes the determinant of decision-makers looking for effective supporting tools and activities to accelerate the growth of SMEs in their regions.

It is visible in a significant change of priorities – from programmes based on subsidies to those individualized, directed at the demand for small and medium enterprises. This opens up development opportunities for coaching programmes, which are now becoming one of the most promising types of support for innovation. Public intervention, understood as a coaching programme dedicated to SMEs, is justified by limiting the enterprises of this sector to only their own sphere of influence and the lack of interest by entities managing entities in external aid – especially when making strategic decisions.

Some SMEs have already used advisory services offered by private consulting companies. It should be noted that the quality offered by advisers is significantly different from each other, which led to the conclusion that companies sometimes spend time and money on services that have no relative impact on their operations or cause negative effects through, inter alia, incorrect advice. The value of business coaching by the owners of the organizations translates into their search for a high-class coach, but it often turns out that such units require too much financial commitment. According to A. Stabryła, a number of European regions are therefore considering the possibility of introducing an effective coaching programme for SMEs or would like to improve their existing programmes (Stabryła, 2006). These trends are visible in several European regions through SME instrument coaching services, where the smE-MPOWER methodology has been adopted and is applied. In this context, the main goal of the design options document is to improve the quality of coaching services provided to SMEs by exploring the possibilities of successfully implementing SME-MPOWER in many regions.

The purpose of implementing the aforementioned activities is to help agencies develop and implement a regional coaching programme, which is the result of the implementation of the "Peer-BIT" project, implemented by five European regions: South Moravia, Lithuania, Upper Austria, Western Switzerland, and Saxony-Anhalt (Zwikael, 2009, pp. 94–103).

SMEs and start-ups (see Chapter 3), stimulate innovation in the European economy. However, it is noticeable that only a part of their potential is used, which is determined by soft factors limiting them in the areas of, e.g., strategy, market, or organization. It is therefore legitimate to supplement currently present innovation systems with a component based on current needs and demand. For many years, SMEs have been focused on soft factors, with a small European project consortium initially pursuing this vision while developing a coaching framework for partnership building and strategic collaboration. Only later did they become the focal point of the West Switzerland innovation platform (platin), from where its success spread to the Czech South Moravia region and to other initiatives. As indicated by M. Trocki et al., with the introduction of the smE-MPOWER coaching system by the European Commission for the SME instrument programme in 2018, it became inevitable to develop a scalable and professional solution (Trocki, Grucza & Ogonek, 2019, pp. 14–15).

Currently, the coaching platform dedicated to SMEs is one of the most modern solutions in coaching. In agreement with the European Commission, this platform will be made available to regional and national training initiatives for SMEs, as well as for research and innovation programmes implemented by small and medium enterprises. It is emphasized that the basic ethical principles of SME-MPOWER guarantee a common philosophy of coaching tools, trainers' profiles, and WEB platform software codes, which determines relatively cheap access to SME assets. In addition, it gives entities the opportunity to adapt a coaching programme to their specific strategy of supporting business innovation. SME-MPOWER will thus expand its influence on the international community, which is to result in the involvement of new partners in specific support for SMEs, determining their further success. J. Wójcik emphasizes that positive feedback from SMEs on the implementation of these solutions, both at the EU and regional levels, is a highly credible and promising option (Wójcik, 2019, pp. 33–34).

When treating EU business projects as multifaceted undertakings, their essence which is action, is emphasized. The goal of their implementation is to achieve parameters such as time, scope, cost, and quality at the previously assumed level. Ergo, the key is to introduce precisely standardized project management methods. As has been emphasized in the considerations so far, the management of EU projects and funds in modern Europe has gained special importance, especially in the face of intensive socio-economic development. Currently, it is an extensive and complete field of knowledge, characterized by, inter alia, methods proven in practice and an effective education system.

4.5 VERIFICATION OF THE EFFECTIVENESS OF THE EU PROJECT MANAGEMENT MODEL IN ENTERPRISES

The subject of carried out research were enterprises from the SME sector in which the impact of EU funds on management was demonstrated. The main goal of the research was to identify an effective model of management of SME enterprises implementing EU projects, which are the determinants of accelerating the growth of European enterprises' development.

In order to achieve the indicated objective of the study, the management areas subject to the greatest changes in small and medium enterprises in Poland implementing EU projects were identified. The development of Polish enterprises was assessed by analysing the value of EU funds in relation to their own funds.

Scientific research begins with the formulation of the research objective understood as this which orients our cognitive endeavours – "scientific cognition of the empirically existing social reality, a description of a phenomenon (e.g. social innovation), an institution (school, educational care facility) or unit (gifted student)" (Dudkiewicz, 1996, p. 15). When formulating the problem of research, we should first realize what range of phenomena we would like to make a statement about, and only then: what – in connection with the research objective formulated in this way – the scope of reality we want and are able to cover with our research. The aim of the research should define the researched population, and not vice versa. "Any action, including scientific research, without specifying the purpose it is to serve, should be considered in terms of irrational" (Nowak, 2007, p. 45).

The following theoretical objectives have been specified:

- systematization of knowledge on enterprise management and the selection of EU project management models that are relatively least complicated to implement in SMEs in Poland;
- identification of key factors in the development of models of SME management in Poland in the coming years;
- identifying organizational factors and aspects affecting effective project management in SMEs; and
- verification of hypotheses.

At the stage of the main research, in order to collect the necessary measurable data for the research, it was decided to use the interview. It is a technique of obtaining information based on direct communication between the researcher and the respondents (Martyniak, 2000, p. 253). It consists in answering the questions asked by means of direct (personal or telephone) contact between the examined person and the interviewer (Żurawik, 1996, p. 110). "It consists in asking the respondent a certain number of questions aimed at solving the research problem" (Pabian & Gworys, 2008, p. 31).

A questionnaire form (i.e. a set of questions written in a certain way on pieces of paper or other medium in order to evoke the desired answers) (Kaczmarczyk, 2014, p. 136), concerning employees' opinions on factors affecting their motivation to work was considered an adequate research tool. The questionnaire is an operationalization of a specific research issue, which means that the problem formulated in theoretical terms has been translated into the language of the questionnaire and addressed to a specific group of respondents. From the point of view of the content of the questionnaire, it consists of three parts: the appeal, a set of questions, and the metrics which include questions about the respondents of research (Pocztowski, 2000, p. 28).

"Using a questionnaire, it is assumed that the object of study can give us directly the value of the property under study" (Ackoff, 1969, p. 264). As the researchers emphasize, "[T]he basic function of the questionnaire is measurement. The measurement takes place here by instrument interference with in the consciousness of the person being measured" (Kaczmarczyk, 2014, p. 136).

For this reason, the questionnaire is considered an invasive tool that can easily lead the respondent out of their comfort zone, resulting in, for example, reluctance to give answers or a tendency to answer incompletely or incorrectly. In order to counteract such effects, the questionnaire should be well thought out in advance and carefully prepared by going through the gradual stages of construction:

- formulation of an initial list of questions,
- formulation of initial variants of answers to questions,
- preliminary check of the form through scientific consultations and literature studies,
- design of a sample questionnaire that needs to be validated by initial measurement and modification of the questionnaire items through logical analysis, and
- construction of the final version of the questionnaire.

Among the listed stages of the sequence of actions, it is of key importance to carry out a trial measurement, which determines the final modification of the questionnaire positions. It is the final phase of preparation of the tool applicable to the main study. The result of the test of the tool and additional scientific consultations was the development of the final version of the questionnaire. In accordance with the rules for the preparation of questionnaire forms (Maszke, 2008, p. 232), care was taken to make it as concise as possible. As noted by K. Śmiatacz, an extensive tool can tire the respondents. When asked, they usually become weary over time, which usually has a negative impact on the reliability of their answers (Śmiatacz, 2012, p. 127).

The questions contained in the questionnaire covered all issues and hypotheses related to the purpose of the research. In accordance with the rules for the preparation of survey forms, the questionnaire was enriched with an introductory sentence. Due to C. Frankfort-Nachmias, it allows us to explain the purpose of the survey to the respondents, convincing them to answer and convincing them that all information obtained from them will remain confidential (Frankfort-Nachmias & Nachmias, 2001, p. 115). The next step was to categorize the issues, prioritize them in a strictly defined order, and limit the content of the questions asked.

The specified goals and research hypotheses were implemented and verified during empirical research with the usage of the selected research method – i.e. the diagnostic survey method. On the basis of theoretical knowledge of the issues under study and the key determinants of effective management and implementation of projects in SMEs (i.e. organization of teamwork, appropriate management, communication), a questionnaire was created. It consisted of two parts. The first of them contained 47 detailed questions relating to the realization of project management processes in SMEs. The second one, known as the metric (a set of closed questions about the respondent, and sometimes also about the economic unit about which he answers), dealt with the level of education, work seniority, age, and gender of the respondents. When constructing the questions, the following recommendations were taken into account (Frankfort-Nachmias & Nachmias, 2001, p. 115; Lutyński, 2000, pp. 150–175):

- the number of questions should not be too long, as the respondents usually begin to show weariness over time, which negatively affects the reliability of their answers;
- none of the questions should be formulated in such a way that it is impossible to give a reliable answer;
- questions cannot be ambiguous;
- should take a closed form;
- should be relatively simple, i.e. the usage of specialized, technical vocabulary, ambiguous phrases, and terms that may be difficult and incomprehensible to respondents should be avoided as far as possible;
- each of the questions should be formulated on the basis of knowledge of the issues it concerns; and
- questions must be formulated in such a way as to enable objective, verifiable and comparable data to be obtained.

There was also information that the conclusions of the analysis will be used for scientific purposes only. Nothing more than summary information, specifying general patterns for the entire industry, can be disclosed in scientific publications or used as teaching material.

The questionnaire survey was conducted among 348 employees at managerial (including enterprise owners) and operational levels in SME enterprises in Poland, implementing EU projects. The method of statistical analysis was chosen to develop the results of the research conducted among them – measures of descriptive statistics (in the basic data presentation) and mathematical statistics.

The ordered research material was subjected to the following stages of analysis:

1. Verification of null hypotheses – test of the randomness of the sample
2. Relationship between variables using the chi-square test of independence
3. The strength of the relationship between the variables using the non-parametric Kruskal-Wallis test

The empirical research covered both quantitative research using aggregated data and the general characteristics of the respondents.

The respondents were randomly selected from among all SME enterprises, which determined the sample of relevant data subjected to statistical analyses. The descriptive statistics indicate that the standard error is 1.12336 of the lower bound of 18.7105 and the upper bound of 23.1357 and the 5% trimmed mean of 18.4415 with a median of 18 and a variance of 311.697 with a skewness of 3.404 and a kurtosis of 15.095, where, based on the collected raw and calculation data, it was indicated that the number of surveyed respondents, 348, is sufficient.

It should be added that before undertaking the appropriate research on selected people from the group described in the aforementioned categories, a prior study was conducted in order to verify the design of the research tool (in the literature on the basics of conducting social research; it is emphasized that the pilot study will be methodologically appropriate if it is carried out on a set of people with the same attributes as the representatives of the main study sample) (Fowler, 2002, p. 112).

Taking such actions was justified by the awareness that the key factors for evaluating high standards of research include both theoretical validity (defining to what extent the used measurement tool measures the researched relationship, i.e. whether it is properly correlated with the theories and concepts being used) (Bingham & Felbinger, 2002, pp. 37–38) and reliability, understood as measurement precision, i.e. determining to what extent the observations and results obtained using a specific tool can be repeatable and accurate (Rossi, Freeman & Lipsey, 1999, pp. 447–448).

The recommended tests for the research tool are the so-called pilot studies, also referred to as pre-tests or, for example, reconnaissance research.[3] Researchers emphasize that their use is a good practice in the conditions of undertaking a specific research effort: "the general rule in quantitative research, i.e. questionnaires, […] is to precede the main research with some form of preliminary research" (Sztabiński & Sztabiński, 2004, 2005, p. 55).

One of their basic functions is to improve the effectiveness of the main research by confirming the usefulness of the already prepared research tool (questionnaire) to be used in a specific environment and to assess the validity of the selection of methods (Nowak, 2007, p. 59). In other words, the pilot is used to assess (based on the response of the respondent) whether the questionnaire questions are

- understandable for the respondents (are they properly formulated?);
- not irritable, which may negatively affect the value or possibility of obtaining information;
- unambiguous; and
- have a complete set of answer variants.

In addition, on its basis, it is possible to assess the general perception of the interview and individual questions by the respondent (interesting, difficult, etc.). The interviewers also assess the completeness and accuracy of the provisions presented in the manual, the method of adopted interview arrangement, etc., and in the case of using additional research tools – e.g. tests for respondents or questionnaires completed by them themselves – the place of their use in the interview and the adopted method of encouraging the respondents to complete (Sztabiński & Sztabiński, 2004, p. 57).

The researchers add that the reliability of the tool can also be assessed as a pre-test. This category relates to the amount of error associated with a given measurement tool, i.e. the error arises randomly in successive measurements made with the same instrument (Bryda, Jelonek & Worek, 2010, p. 66). Conclusions from the pilot study are the basis for developing the final version of the research tool (Glińska, Florek & Kowalewska, 2009, pp. 63–64).

The research carried out as a part of this book made it possible to understand the specificity of the perception of EU project management processes and models that determine enterprise management in small and medium entities in the example of Poland. In the empirical part, a statistical analysis was carried out, and the obtained information was used to develop a proprietary project management model and to define recommendations.

In SMEs in Poland, the effectiveness of the innovation system is based on undertaking innovative activities by a given entity. The human resources of each small and medium enterprise determine the direction of its activity. It is emphasized that the experience of human capital is realized in decisions made by employees. Thus, their skills and competences determine their attitude towards innovation. As desirable features for the introduction of innovative processes in an entity, competences in the broad sense largo were specified, i.e. knowledge, skills, and abilities of each person involved in a given project. The factors of the innovation system in enterprises in Poland linked in this way are presented in Figure 4.20.

It seems natural that the innovative system in an enterprise is determined by the key principles, such as, searching for innovative solutions, creating an information base on innovations, setting directions for innovative activity, creating appropriate criteria and structures for it, activating the entrepreneurship of employees, and including them in the process

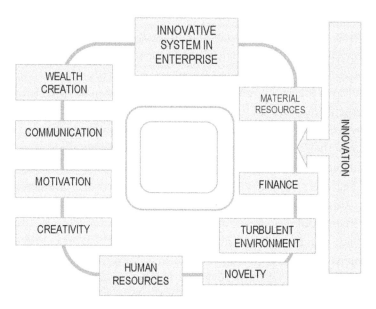

FIGURE 4.20
Factors of the innovative system in an enterprise.

Source: Own elaboration.

of change. The innovation model is therefore considered on the resource level, focusing at the same time on the aspects of motivating and implementing innovation with all its conditions.

On the basis of the conducted research and the obtained results, the determinants that shape the choice of the management model in Polish small and medium enterprises were specified. The implementation of these activities is shown in Figure 4.21.

In Figure 4.21, it was decided to graphically indicate the correlation of the specified determinants with the EU project cycle management process discussed earlier, the factors of the innovative system used in enterprises, and the model of strategic management used by SMEs in Poland.

On the basis of the previous considerations and analyses of the results of our research, an original model of EU project management in small and medium enterprises was developed, which is presented in Figure 4.22.

The proprietary EU project management model presented in Figure 4.22 includes an innovative approach to projects' implementation in SMEs. This was identified due to the implementation of determinants that affect the choice of the enterprise management model and linking them with the models modified in the previous sections, models of project cycle management, and strategic management of SMEs while taking into account the innovative factors of the enterprises. The need to implement determinants shaping the management of small and medium enterprises to other areas of management processes is also emphasized.

The offered framework of the EU project management in SMEs in Poland is characterized by flexibility and openness to changes, as well as current needs. An appropriate system of strategic management and factors of innovation management determines access to full and current information on the EU project being realized. The role of the management staff is the basis for the effectiveness of the previous model. It significantly changes the current approach to project management, directing the correct course of the EU project management process to achieve organizational, financial, and technical success. The need to make decisions regarding the pursuit of innovation at every stage of the entire process and its individual elements is also emphasized.

As we indicate, all the components of EU project management in SMEs correlate with each other, thus, they are necessary for the proper realization of European projects by the entities selected in the study.

In the developed model, a new concept of "model parachute" was offered, which embraces the assessment (darker arrows) of the effects resulting

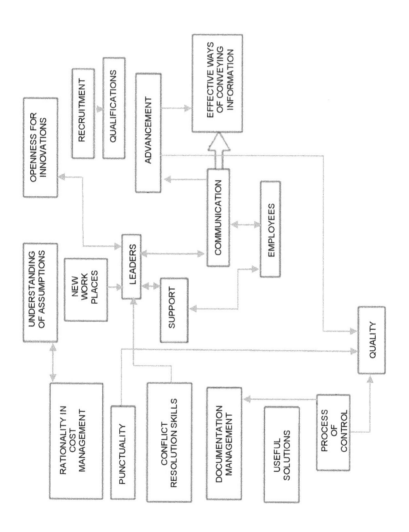

FIGURE 4.21

Determinants shaping management of small and medium enterprises.

Source: Own elaboration based on data collected during empirical research.

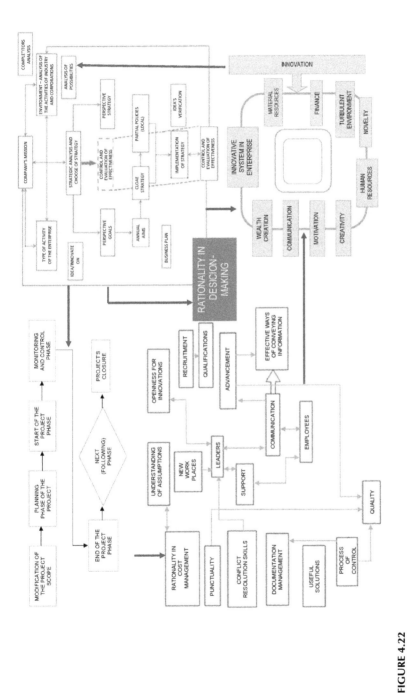

FIGURE 4.22

The model of EU project management in SMEs in Poland.

Source: Original study based on theoretical findings and own research results.

from the action and the implementation of the adopted assumptions, which must be brought back to the initial state by proceeding in accordance with the directional (arrows) and essential (visible circles) elements with the necessary (correct, rational) adaptation of the elements of model layout (frames). This "necessity" of exceptional precision requires (dashed frames) proper preparation for the implementation of a model that is a solution to a given assumption. As it is shown by theoretical considerations, as well as the analysis of the results of our, empirical research, the management of EU projects in SMEs is a complex process. Economic practice assumes that organizations which decide to implement a given EU project more often decide to later apply in the next competitions and show interest in implementing further European projects.

Based on the analysis of the results of the conducted empirical research in the field of EU project management by SMEs in the example of Poland, the following conclusions were drawn:

1. Activities requiring improvement and streamlining of project management processes:
   - functions of management, among them planning, organizing, controlling;
   - proper organizational design;
   - promoting creativity;
   - diversified, multicultural project teams;
   - the process of improving teams' competences, implementation of training projects that improve the project management process;
   - implementation of IT systems supporting project management;
   - recruit to project teams people with appropriate competences in this area;
   - team competences in terms of time management skills;
   - team competences in the field of communication, teamwork, cooperation, and conflict resolution (financial, interpersonal, resource);
   - planning skills necessary to implement resources;
   - process of implemented projects' control;
   - procedures and techniques for organizing and implementing projects; and
   - realization of the project that meets instrumental, structural, subjective, and teleological standards.

2. Activities in the scope of the process that do not require improvement and support (according to respondents):
   - rational actions are taken in order to solve specific problems;
   - defining the scope of implemented projects;
   - appointing employees responsible for project realization;
   - management of a project team;
   - risk management; dynamic capability development, organizational resilience, and responsiveness to crises;
   - rational project management towards adapting to the dynamic environment;
   - project teams are open to development in terms of knowledge and communication;
   - project teams are innovative;
   - have the awareness and vision of creating new jobs and the usefulness of solutions resulting from implemented projects; and
   - the documentation management process in terms of its storage, readability, and archiving is efficiently implemented.

The carried out research helped to identify and verify the scale of problems and risks of actions taken by SMEs, and the results obtained confirm the main hypothesis. It is emphasized, however, that the proposed proprietary model is not an ideal one and it does not constitute a final solution for project management by SMEs. However, it may be the right starting point for further studies and research, to which the authors decided to devote a separate work. Further in-depth analysis of the proposed solutions is recommended, especially with regard to the SME sector in Europe.

NOTES

1 The analysis of data from literature sources is often referred to in methodology as desk research. Such secondary research boils down to reaching the best sources using the library work technique. The choice of the method was mainly dictated by the desire to fulfil the so-called continuity of knowledge principles. According to it, the necessary starting point of the scientific efforts should be the consideration of the already existing state of knowledge. Should be this way, no matter of whether the final result of scientific effort is to be the development of knowledge within the framework of theoretical explanations present in the literature (or a step, discontinuous change in describing reality, only), In other words, before undertaking one's own studies, one should familiarize oneself with the results achieved by other researchers who have previously dealt with the subject under consideration. Such a procedure allows one

not only to learn the previous findings but also, by means of replication, enables their additional dissemination, as well as the disclosure of possible inconsistencies and cognitive gaps that justify the need to continue the considerations or undertake new research. The researchers are of the opinion that "all scientific articles, promotional papers, monographs or applications for funding for research from available sources should [...] refer to the existing state of knowledge" (see more: Schroeder, 1997, p. 18; Czakon 2016, p. 119).

2 A. Kiełbus, Spojrzenie na zarządzanie projektami informatycznymi. *Mechanika. Czasopismo Techniczne, 7*(108), 2011, pp. 216–217.

3 The terminology used to describe them varies; the review was prepared by K. Lutyńska (compare Lutyńska, 1975).

Conclusion

The implementation of projects should not be treated by SMEs as a goal itself. On the contrary, they should consider projects as an instrument for achieving the overarching goals of survival and development. Projects should be seen in terms of a complex set of measures undertaken in order to achieve the company's strategic intents, such as improving the efficiency of management, building a strong competitive position, obtaining economic benefits, expanding competitive capabilities.

In general, the goal of the company should be defined as the objectively and subjectively defined future, desired state or result of the company's operation, "possible and expected to be achieved in the period covered by the short-term or long-term action plan" (Peszko, 1997, p. 41). It means that the goal means an event and/or a state of affairs to be achieved by the enterprise in a conscious manner and in accordance with the adopted development path (Koźmiński, 2013, p. 42).

In entities conducting business activity based on registration in the business activity register, non-identical types of goals can be indicated and distinguished on the basis of the level of management at which they are arranged. The first of them are strategic goals set by the top management of the organization (Griffin, 1996, p. 214).

Most often, they are part of the strategy of the entire organization. In this context, they are paramount, focusing on doing the right things (Mikołajczyk, 2008, p. 192). Goals set at lower levels are focused on how to operationalize the activities that are necessary to achieve the overarching goals.

Goals that are understood as sets of specific intentions, therefore, have a hierarchical structure (Krupski, 2004, p. 17). As indicated earlier, the starting point for dividing them by importance is the level of management at which they are formulated.[1] However, further on, also within the goals set at individual levels, the more important and less important ones can be distinguished. The gradation of goals at individual levels may differ between companies from countries with different cultures (Filipiak, 1996, p. 42).

DOI: 10.1201/9781003309901-5

For example, the hierarchy of strategic goals of US companies is different than European ones. For the former, the most important goal is to return the invested capital. Then there are the profits for the shareholders and the achievement of a significant market share. For companies from the old continent, the most important strategic goals are the same, but the market share is considered more important than for American companies. In addition, companies from the European cultural circle do not attach so much importance to generating profits for investors. Internationalization is more important to them (Wasilewski, 1998, pp. 89–91).

The described state of affairs results, among others, from the fact that one of the basic characteristics distinguishing representatives of one culture from others is the values professed by its representatives (Moran, Harris & Moran, 2007, pp. 7–9). The conviction about what is most important (both in private life and within the organizational reality) is the basis for setting the goals to be achieved by a personal or institutional unit (more on the impact of cultural differences on the implementation of projects, the authors wrote in one of the book's chapters).

It should be emphasized that the fulfilment of a specific hierarchy of goals, both by American and European companies, will eventually lead to obtaining financial resources. In this context, profit, understood in terms of earning more than the cost of capital, should be considered in the category of one of the superior values for all units constituting a set of entities operating on the market. P. J. Szczepankowski is right when emphasizing that entrepreneurship is a simple reaction to supply and demand, and making a profit is not only the main goal for most firms but also the main motive for them to undertake various activities, e.g. of a project nature (Szczepankowski, 2000, pp. 111–113).

However, the implementation of a specific set of intermediate goals encounters more and more difficulties in practice, e.g. organizational, financial, or managerial. Therefore, enterprises are forced to replace sets of specific objectives with one basic objective to which long-term activity should be subordinated. As it was said earlier, the goal that integrates the basic areas of the company's operation and sets the direction of its activity in the long term is profit. This fact is confirmed by researchers, who say, "[T]he main goal of any enterprise is to achieve profit and multiply capital" (Szatkowski, 2016, p. 24). H. Zadora adds that this objective is of fundamental importance for any type of enterprise distinguished on the basis of its size: "the larger the enterprise, the greater its capital needs" (Zadora, 2011, p. 61).

FIGURE 5.1
Illustrating the relationship between projects, partial goals set by the company, and its profit.

Source: Own elaboration.

As it was mentioned, the implementation of hierarchically arranged intermediate goals serves as a consequence to multiply one's own financial resources (Figure 5.1). Among the goals, the implementation of which allows a business to earn a profit, one can mention, according to researchers (Jasiński, 1997, p. 20), the following:

- Gaining an overwhelming competitive position
- Reduction of operating and production costs, including:
  - Reducing the share of personnel costs
  - Reduction of energy consumption
  - Reduction of shortages
  - Reduction of material consumption
  - Reduction of design costs
- Meeting the needs of buyers, also by expanding the range of products
- Increasing productivity
- Opening new sales markets:
  - National
  - Foreign
- Improvement of working conditions
- Obtaining better results from activities and operations
- Increasing market share
- Improvement of the company's image
- Many others

Nowadays, the implementation of goals resulting in the achievement of superior value (in the form of achieving profits) is often carried out through project activities. The main motive for taking it is, therefore, usually the desire to achieve benefits for oneself. Small and medium-sized companies operating on a commercial basis undertake work on projects primarily because they consider the introduction of improvements and new solutions, thanks to them, as a means to achieve specific benefits (achieving intermediate goals), which may later translate into the level of profits.

However, it should be here emphasized that in the light of the assumptions underlying the social economy theory, which emphasizes such values as ethics or greater social solidarity, the approach subordinating goals to economic success should be considered ambivalent. "However, it is difficult to deny the right of the owner of the enterprise (capital provider) that the main goal of his activity is to maximize profits" (Szatkowski, 2016, p. 24). After all, it is generally accepted that public and non-profit organizations are responsible for achieving non-profit goals. Financed from such sources as, for example, the state budget, they can focus on the implementation of their tasks without the need for an entrepreneurial search for opportunities to earn money.

Still, enterprises, including small and medium-sized ones, should undertake only such projects, the implementation of which will not involve any damage to the natural or socio-cultural environment. This follows from the rules of the so-called sustainable development (development that can be maintained in the long term), which has been steadily gaining in importance for many years.

Currently, the concept of sustainable development is polysemantic and is sometimes understood differently depending on the represented scientific discipline. Different interpretations concern different aspects. According to researchers, this term means (Mika, 2015, p. 11):

- from the point of view of geographical space (territorial systems) – maintaining proper relations between the economic, natural, and social subsystems, which determine the implementation of socially desirable functions in development, as long as it happens within the limits of acceptable changes;
- in terms of ecological economy – maintaining the access of the next generations to environmental values and the socio-cultural environment, as well as striving for inter- and intra-generational justice in access to goods; and
- in analyses in the field of mainstream economics and spatial management – sustaining growth factors.

What is common in thinking about sustainability is expressed in the pursuit of balancing three spheres: the natural environment, the economy, and the social system. The complexity of the processes that make up the functioning of modern communities requires coherent action taking into account social, ecological, and economic conditions, leading to sustainable development. This balance is seen "as a specific system that requires the harmonious integration and functioning of all three spheres, since the elimination of one of them prevents the functioning of the other two" (Huczek, 2012, p. 20).

Sustainable development therefore assumes the need to combine actions aimed at achieving a balance between the implementation of economic (e.g. ensuring jobs) and social aims (e.g. preserving the cultural heritage of a specific region, promoting local products, limiting meat consumption for plant-based diet) and maintaining the natural environment unchanged in the way of, e.g.,

- reducing greenhouse gas emissions;
- promoting renewable energy sources;
- protecting ecosystems;
- reducing plastic waste;
- reducing appropriate antibiotics, pesticides, fertilizers, and heavy metals;
- preventing food waste;
- developing green infrastructure and better spatial planning; and
- many others.

This is to be done by taking responsible and well-thought-out projects in various areas of human activity related to improving the quality of life of citizens and protecting the earth. As noted by W. Toczyski, these activities are to meet the needs of contemporary people, without depriving future generations of the ability to meet their own needs (Toczyski, 2004, p. 15).

A concept related to sustainability and a specific contribution of the business sphere to the implementation of the postulates of sustainable economic development is the concept of corporate (enterprises') social responsibility (Bilińska-Reformat, 2013, p. 73). According to her, being responsible means for enterprises to invest in human resources, relations with the environment, and environmental protection, as well as informing about these activities, which contributes to the increase in the competitiveness of the enterprise and the creation of conditions for sustainable social and economic development.

It is sometimes interpreted and defined in various ways, although most of the terms present in the literature are of a substitutive nature. J. F. Stoner and his team define it as voluntary actions taken by a company to have a positive impact on the society in which it operates. According to K. Davis and R. Blomstron, corporate social responsibility (CSR) should be treated as an obligation for the management of enterprises to choose and take such decisions and actions that contribute to both the care of one's own interest (multiplying profit) and the protection and multiplication of social welfare (Kowalczewski, 2008, p. 322).

A. Verbeke is satisfied with the statement that a socially responsible business is one that feels social, i.e. imposes voluntary obligations on itself, the fulfilment of which is to help people in the environment (Verbeke, 2013, p. 383). The authors of the International Business Leaders Forum say that "CSR means transparent business practices based on ethical values and respect for employees, societies and the environment, and supporting the sustainable success of the company" (Rudnicka, 2012, pp. 40–41).

What is common in thinking about CSR, is that it is considered possible to maintain a balance between material (economic), natural, and social goals. In other words, CSR is a kind of specific management philosophy that takes into account ethical, social, and ecological aspects both in economic activity and in relations with the environment. Activities of this nature are voluntary and go beyond legal requirements; however, the organization attaches great importance to responsible and ethical conduct with respect to the natural environment. It is important that its activities become an integral part of corporate management and its daily practice.

The new concept is somewhat in opposition to the traditional model of management, solely subordinated to making a profit, the beginnings of which some researchers see in the works of Adam Smith already.[2] CSR is strongly focused on actions towards internal and external stakeholders. It is also conditioned by the requirements of the implementation of activities stemming from the principles of sustainable development. Hence, the Nobel Prize winner in economics, Milton Friedman, described CSR as, a fundamentally subversive doctrine (Moon, 2014, p. 1).

According to CSR, SMEs cannot be guided only by the economic profit and loss account in their operations. This tool must still be in use because without the achievement of the goals of multiplying a firm's assets, there can be no question of survival in today's highly competitive market. At the same time, however, sufficiently wealthy firms must undertake projects related to the preservation of the natural environment, as well as projects focused on the protection of the interests of the society, whose members include potential recipients of the products firm manufacture.

It would be wrong to think that today's small and medium-sized companies can only focus on creating new solutions that in the future will directly translate into the level of their profits. Demanding business conditions do not exempt representatives of the business sphere from undertaking projects aimed at preparing (and subsequently implementing) new solutions that may contribute to the development of the quality of social life in the environment in which companies operate. The desirability of such activity results from two basic facts:

- The need for a wise and humane sense of co-responsibility for the realities and living conditions in a particular community. It should be an unforced element of the management practice of every entity that is familiar with the principles of business ethics.
- The need to take preventive measures. Globalization processes and competitive struggle lead firms to such actions that may seem pejorative in social perception. People often forget that commercial entities make a specific contribution to the development of local communities, providing jobs, wages, and benefits as well as tax revenues. Researchers note that by contrast, people are often inclined to believe that firms use their size and power for anti-social behaviour.[3] Meanwhile, running a business in a socially responsible manner makes it possible to gain the trust of the community's inhabitants and to win the favour of local government authorities, on whom decisions directly related to the company and its activities often depend.

Outlays incurred on social projects should not be treated as a cost (as in the case, for example, of funds spent on improving the quality of manufactured products or the level of service) but rather considered in terms of investments.

This is due to the fact that although the outlays incurred to support social or environmental projects do not bring direct and quick financial benefits, at the same time, they improve the quality of life in the company's surroundings. The company itself benefits from this. The development of any enterprise depends on the health and stability of the community in which it operates and on the well-being of the members of the community. The company is part of its environment. There are certain interactions between it and the representatives of the community. A healthy society in which a company operates is conducive to its own development.

NOTES

1 The number and even the type of management levels may vary among research-ers, although most studies distinguish the following levels: strategic, tactical, and operational. According to S. P. Robbins and D. A. DeCenzo, the criterion for their separation is the non-identical proportions of time needed to perform individual managerial functions (for example, research results show that at the lowest level, as much as 51% of the activity time is spent on conducting, while at the highest level, only 22% – at the expense of planning and organizing) and the resulting information needs (smaller or greater) of decision-makers at a certain level (compare Robbins, DeCenzo, 2002, pp. 36–37; Unold, 2009, p. 57; Walas-Trębacz, 2010, p. 63).

2 Scottish philosopher and economist born in 1723. Widely regarded as one of the fathers of the classical trend in economics. More on this topic can be found in Berry, Paganelli, and Smith (2013).

3 M. Rybak, *Etyka menedżera. Społeczna odpowiedzialność przedsiębiorstwa*, Wydawnic two Naukowe PWN, Warszawa, 2007, p. 15.

References

Abdel-Hamid H., The economics of software quality assurance, [in:] *A. Simulation-Based, Case Study*, MIS Quarterly, 12(3), 1988, p. 395.

Aboramadan M., Albashiti B., Alharazin H., Zaidoune S., Organizational culture, innovation and performance: a study from a non-western context, *Journal of Management Development*, 39(4), 2020, pp. 437–451.

Abt S., *Logistyka w teorii i praktyce. Wydawnictwo Akademii Ekonomicznej w Poznaniu*, Poznań, 2001, p. 131.

Ackoff R., *Decyzje optymalne w badaniach stosowanych*, PWE, Warszawa 1969, p. 264.

Adamczak A., Gędłek M., *Wynalazki w działalności małych i średnich przedsiębiorstw*, Krajowa Izba Gospodarcza, Warszawa, 2009, p. 5.

Adamowicz M., *Zintegrowany i zrównoważony rozwój wsi i rolnictwa a wspólna polityka rolna. Problemy rolnictwa światowego*. T. XI, Wyd. SGGW, Warszawa 2004, pp. 237–239.

Adamowicz M., *Teoretyczne uwarunkowania rozwoju rolnictwa z uwzględnieniem procesów globalizacji i międzynarodowej integracji*. Roczniki Nauk Rolniczych, seria G, t. 94, Warszawa 2008, pp. 49–64.

Anning-Dorson T., Boadi Nyamekye M., Engagement capability, innovation intensity and firm performance. *Journal of African Business*, 21(4), 2020.

Astrachan J., Shaker M. C., Family businesses' cto the U.S. Economy: a closer look. *Family Business Review*, 16(3), 2003, pp. 212–215.

Axelos. Prince2-skuteczne zarządzanie projektami. TSO 2019.

Bahadur M., Project definition, lifecycle and role of project managers. https://www.researchgate.net/publication/340544935_Project_definition_Lifecycle_and_role_of_Project_Managers (reading: 15.05.2022).

Bąk M., Eksport oparty na własności intelektualnej – wyzwaniem dla polskich przedsiębiorstw XXI wieku, [in:] M. Bąk, P. Kulawczuk (eds.), *Poradnik eksportera i IP dla MSP*, Krajowa Izba Gospodarcza, Warszawa 2010, p. 10.

Bąk-Grabowska D., Elastyczny model zatrudnienia w świetle koncepcji zarządzania zasobami ludzkimi. *Prace Naukowe Uniwersytetu Ekonomicznego we Wrocławiu*, 162, 2011, pp. 43–46.

Baran M., Kłos M., Metody zarządzania projektami unijnymi realizowanymi przez uczelnie wyższe. *Przedsiębiorczość i Zarządzanie*, 14(11), 2013, pp. 11–12.

Barnes M., Innovation – why project management is essential to successful businesses. *International Journal of Project Management*, 9(4), 1991, pp. 207–209.

Bartol K. M., Martin D. C., *Management*. McGraw-Hill, New York 1992, p. 44.

Bartosik-Purgat M., *Otoczenie kulturowe w biznesie międzynarodowym*. PWE, Warszawa 2006, p. 30.

Baruk J., Organizacyjne uwarunkowania działalności innowacyjnej przedsiębiorstwa, [in:] M. Brzeziński (ed.), *Zarządzanie innowacjami technicznymi i organizacyjnymi*, Difin, Warszawa 2001, p. 76.

Batt R., Doellgast V., *Groups, Teams, and the Division of Labor: Interdisciplinary Perspectives on the Organization of Work, [in:] The Oxford Handbook of Work and Organization*, Oxford University Press, New York 2005, p. 139.

Behan A., Pojęcie i prawnokarna ochrona programu komputerowego, *Czasopismo prawa karnego i nauk penalnych* z. 1, 2018, p. 47.

Berkowitz E., Kerin R., Hartley S., Rudelius W., *Marketing*. Fourth Edition. IRWIN, Boston, New York 1994, p. 127.

Berry C. J., Paganelli M. P., Smith C., *The Oxford Handbook of Adam Smith*, Oxford University Press, Oxford 2013.

Bhattacharyya S. S., Thakre S., Coronavirus pandemic and economic lockdown; study of strategic initiatives and tactical responses of firms. *International Journal of Organizational Analysis*, 29(5), 2021, p. 1240.

Białoń L., *Zarządzanie działalnością innowacyjną*, Placet, Warszawa 2010, p. 95.

Biernat-Jarka A., Zarządzanie projektem logistycznym w przedsiębiorstwie. *Logistyka*, Nr 4, 2014, pp. 3495–3497.

Bilińska-Reformat K., Wykorzystanie koncepcji CSR w działalności sieci handlu detalicznego, *Handel Wewnętrzny*, t. 3, nr 5–6, 2013, p. 73.

Bilton C., Cummings S., *Creative Strategy. Reconnecting Business and Innovation*. John Wiley and Sons, Chichester 2010.

Bingham R. D., C. L. Felbinger, *Evaluation in Practice. A Methodological Approach*, Seven Bridges Press, New York 2002, pp. 37–38.

Bizon-Górecka J., W poszukiwaniu modelu zarządzania organizacją przez projekty. *Przegląd Organizacji*, 2, 2009, pp. 21–25.

Blank S., Dorf B., *Podręcznik startupu. Budowa wielkiej firmy krok po kroku*, Helion, Gliwice 2012.

Błaszczyk T., Trzaskalik T., Wielokryterialne planowanie projektów. *Decyzje*, 7, 2007, pp. 64–67.

Block V., Philosophy on innovation: a research agenda. *Philosophy of Management*, 17(1), 2018, pp. 1–5.

Bogan C. E., *Benchmarking jako klucz do najlepszych praktyk*, Helion, Gliwice 2006, p. 221.

Bonikowska M., *Podręcznik zarządzania projektami miękkimi w kontekście Europejskiego Funduszu Społecznego*. Ministerstwo Rozwoju Regionalnego. Warszawa 2006, p. 52.

Boone L. E., Kurtz D. L., *Management*, McGraw-Hill, New York 1992, p. 6.

Borowiec-Gabryś M., Projekty turystyczne współfinansowane ze środków Unii Europejskiej w województwie małopolskim. *Przedsiębiorczość – Edukacja*, 16(2), 2020, pp. 261–273.

Borowiecki R., Jaki A. (ed.), *Global and Regional Challenges of the 21st Century*. Economy Studies from Economics and Management. Katedra Ekonomiki i Organizacji Przedsiębiorstw, Kraków 2011, p. 24.

Borowiecki R., Kusio T., Siuta-Tokarska B., The role of a manager in managing intellectual capital in the context of innovative projects in an enterprise. *Organization and Management*, 1(184), 2019, pp. 65–71.

Borowiecki R., Rojek T., Współcześni inicjatorzy przełomów w zarządzaniu. *Przegląd Organizacji*, 3, 2011, p. 25.

Borowiecki R., Siuta-Tokarska B., Konkurencyjność przedsiębiorstw sektora MSP w Polsce w świetle samooceny ich właścicieli i menedżerów. *Przegląd Organizacji*, 10, 2016, pp. 4–7.

Bracht U., Geckler D., Motschmann T., Projektsimulation als Instrument zur änderungsrobusten Konfiguration von Planungsprojekten, *Projektmanagement aktuell*, October(4), 2009, p. 19.

Braha S., The etymology of words. https://www.researchgate.net/publication/333772536_The_Etymology_of_Words_Contents (reading: 15.05.2022, p. 2).

Brilman J., *Nowoczesne koncepcje i metody zarządzania*, PWE, Warszawa 2002, p. 95.

Browaeys M. J., Price R., *Understanding Cross-Cultural Management*, Prentice Hall. London-New York-Boston-San Francisco-Toronto-Sydney-Singapore-Hong Kong-Tokyo-Seoul-Taipei-New Delhi-Cape Town- Madrid-Mexico City-Amsterdam-Munich-Paris-Milan 2008, pp. 10, 21–25, 39.

Bryda G., M. Jelonek, B. Worek, Jak skonstruować dobre narzędzie do ewaluacji jakości zajęć? Refleksje praktyczne, [in:] W. Przybylski, S. Rudnicki, A. Szwed (ed.), *Ewaluacja jakości dydaktyki w szkolnictwie wyższym. Metody, narzędzia, dobre praktyki*, Wyższa Szkoła Europejska, Kraków 2010, p. s. 66.

Brzeziński S., *Zarządzanie przedsiębiorstwami społecznie odpowiedzialnymi a globalne procesy integracyjne*. PWE. Warszawa 2016, s. 16.

Brzozowska A., Bubel D., Pabian A., Implementation of technical and information systems in environmental management. *Procedia - Social and Behavioral Sciences*, 213, 2015, pp. 992–999, https://doi.org/10.1016/j.sbspro.2015.11.516

Brzozowska K., *Zaangażowanie środków Unii Europejskiej w finansowanie projektów PPP w Polsce. Zeszyty Naukowe Uniwersytetu Szczecińskiego*. Ekonomiczne Problemy Usług, 108, 2013, pp. 67–78.

Budnikowski A., *Międzynarodowe stosunki gospodarcze*. Polskie Wydawnictwo Ekonomiczne, Warszawa 2006a, p. 434.

Budnikowski A., *Międzynarodowe stosunki gospodarcze*. PWE, Warszawa 2006b, pp. 434–444.

Bukłaha E., Wybrane aspekty controllingu projektów w świetle badań empirycznych. *Studia i Prace Kolegium Zarządzania i Finansów SGH w Warszawie*, (159), 2018, p. 182.

Bukowski M., Saj W. M., Pelle D., *Wpływ funduszy unijnych na gospodarkę Polski w latach 2004-2020*. Ministerstwo Rozwoju Regionalnego. Departament Koordynacji Polityki Strukturalnej, Warszawa 2008, pp. 13–28.

Cabała P., *Metody doskonalenia procesów zarządzania projektami w organizacji*, Difin, Warszawa 2016, pp. 34–35.

Campbell D., Hamill J., Purdie T., Stonehouse G., *Globalizacja. Strategia i zarządzanie*. Ferberg, Warszawa 2001, p. 25.

Caproni P. J., Arias M. E., Managerial skills training from a critical perspective. *Journal of Management Education*, 21(3), 1997, p. 293.

Chell E., *Entrepreneurship: Globalization, Innovation and Development*. Thomson Learning, London 2001.

Christensen C. M., Raynor M. E., *Innowacje, napęd wzrostu*, Studio Emka, Warszawa 2008, pp. 17–18.

Chudziński P., Cyfert S., Dyduch W., Zastempowski M. Projekt Sur(vir)val: czynniki przetrwania przedsiębiorstw w warunkach koronakryzysu. *e-mentor*, 5(87), 2020, 34–44. https://doi.org/10.15219/em87.1491

Chudziński P., Dyduch W., Cyfert S., Leadership decisions for company SurVIRval: evidence from organizations in Poland during the first Covid-19 lockdown. *Journal of Organizational Change Management*, 35(8), 2002, pp. 79–102.

Clough B., Microcars, [in:] M. Tovey (ed.), *Design for Transport: A User Centred Approach to Vehicle Design and Travel*, Routledge, Taylor & Francis, London, New York 2016, p. 225.

Cooper L. G., Managing the dynamics of project and changes at flour, [taken from:] J. M. Lyneis, D. N. Fort, *System Dynamics Applied to Project Management, System Dynamics Review*, 23(2–3), 2007, p. 157.

Cox D. M. T., *Project Management Skills for Instructional Designers*. iUniverse, New York, Bloomington 2009, p. 5.

Cron D. et al., Organisationale Kompetenz – Eine neue Perspektive für Projektarbeit. *Projektmanagement aktuell*, 7, 2010, p. 15.

Czakon W. (ed.), *Podstawy metodologii badań w naukach o zarządzaniu*, Wydawnictwo Nieoczywiste – GAB Media, Piaseczno 2016, p. 119.

Czakon W., Komańda M. (eds.), *Interdyscyplinarność w naukach o zarządzaniu*, Wydawnictwo Uniwersytetu Ekonomicznego w Katowicach, Katowice 2011, p. 19.

Czekaj J., Benchmarking – metoda racjonalizacji organizacji. *Ekonomika i Organizacja Przedsiębiorstwa*, 9, 1995, p. 5–7.

Czyżewski A., Grzelak A., Rolnictwo w Polsce na tle sytuacji ogólnoekonomicznej kraju w okresie kryzysu 2007–2009, [in:] *Roczniki Nauk Rolniczych. Annals of Agricultural Science*. Series G - Economy, Vol. 98, No. 3, Wieś Jutra Sp. z o.o., Warszawa 2011, p. 21.

Dadel M., *Jak stworzyć dobry projekt*. Polsko- Amerykańska Fundacja Wolności. Warszawa 2007, pp. 10–11.

Daft R., Marcic D., *Management. The New Workplace*. South-Western Cengage Learning. New York 2013.

Danielak W., Mierzwa D., Bartczak K. *Małe i średnie przedsiębiorstwa w Polsce. Szanse i zagrożenia*. EXANTE. Wrocław 2017, pp. 7, 60.

Davis A., *Public Relations*, PWE, Warszawa 2007, p. 83.

de Melo G., Etymological wordnet. Tracing the history of words. "Proceedings of the Ninth International Conference on Language Resources and Evaluation (LREC'14)", [in:] Nicoletta Calzolari, Khalid Choukri, Thierry Declerck, Hrafn Loftsson, Bente Maegaard, Joseph Mariani, Asuncion Moreno, Jan Odijk, Stelios Piperidis eds.), *European Language Resources Association (ELRA)*, European Language Resources Association (ELRA), Reykjavik 2014, p. 1148.

De Wit B., Meyer R., *Synteza strategii*. PWE, Warszawa 2007, p. 11.

De Wit B., Meyer R., *Strategy. Process, Content, Context*. Thomson Publishing, London, 2010.

Dekier Ł., Grycuk A., *Programy sugestii pracowniczych – doświadczenia polskich przedsiębiorstw*, Stowarzyszenie Lean Management, Wrocław 2014, p. 4.

DeSanctis G., Glass J. T., Ensing I. M.: Organizational designs for R&D. *Academy of Management Executive*, 16(3), 2002, pp. 55–66.

Domiter A., Marciszewska A., *Zarządzanie projektami unijnymi*. Teoria i praktyka, Wydawnictwo Difin, Warszawa 2013, p. 36, 42.

Donelley R., The family business. *Harvard Business Review*, 42(4), 1964, p. 93.

Donnelly J. H., Gibson J. L., Ivancevich J. M., *Fundamentals of Management*. IRWIN. Homewood, Boston 1992, p. 102.

Drab-Kurowska A., Sokół A., *Małe i średnie przedsiębiorstwa wobec wyzwań rozwoju technologii XXI wieku*. Wydawnictwo CeDeWu, Warszawa 2010, p. 14.

Drobiak A., *Podstawy oceny efektywności projektów publicznych*. Wydawnictwo Akademii Ekonomicznej Katowicach, Katowice 2008, p. 14.

Drucker P. F., *Innowacje i przedsiębiorczość. Praktyka i zasady*. PWE. Warszawa 1992, p. 44.

Drucker P. F., *Natchnienie i fart, czyli innowacja i przedsiębiorczość*, Studio Emka, Warszawa 2004, pp. 32–40.

Dudkiewicz W., *Praca magisterska przewodnik metodyczny*, Strzelec, Kielce 1996, p. 15.

Duncan N., Capturing flexibility of information technology infrastructure: a study of resource characteristics and their measure. *Journal of Management Information Systems*, 12, 1995, p. 37.

Duncan W. R., *Guide to the Project Management Body of Knowledge*. PMI Standards Committee, PMI Publishing Division, Upper Darby, 1996, p. 11.

Duszyński J., Afelt A., Ochab-Marcinek A., Owczuk R., Pyrć K., Rosińska M., Rychard A., Smiatacz T., *Zrozumieć COVID-19. Opracowanie zespołu ds. covid-19 przy prezesie polskiej akademii nauk*. Polska Akademia Nauk. Warszawa 2020, p. 7.

Dyduch W., Strategic processes and mechanisms of value creation and value capture: some insights from business organisations in Poland, [in:] *Effective Implementation of Transformation Strategies*, Palgrave Macmillan, Singapore 2022, pp. 289–316.

Dyduch W., Organizational design supporting innovativeness. *Przegląd Organizacji* (2), 2019.

Dyduch W., Bratnicka-Myśliwiec K., Hybrydyzacja przedsiębiorstw w kontekście nowych modeli pracy. *Studia i Prace Kolegium Zarzadzania SGH*, 184, 2022, pp. 35–37.

Dyduch W., Chudziński P., Cyfert S., Zastempowski M., Dynamic capabilities, value creation and value capture: evidence from SMEs under Covid-19 lockdown in Poland. *PLoS ONE*, 16(6), 2021, e0252423. https://doi.org/10.1371/journal.pone.0252423

Dziadek K., Audyt projektów współfinansowanych ze środków funduszy unijnych. Zeszyty Naukowe Uniwersytetu Szczecińskiego. *Finanse, Rynki Finansowe, Ubezpieczenia*, 30, 2010, pp. 254–255.

EU portal. https://ec.europa.eu/regional_policy/en/policy/themes/ict/; https://ec.europa.eu/info/strategy/priorities-2019-2024/europe-fit-digital-age_en (reading: 15.08.2022).

Falkowski A., Tyszka T., *Psychologia zachowań konsumenckich*, GWP, Warszawa 2001, p. 86.

Filipiak M., *Socjologia kultury. Zarys zagadnień*, Wydawnictwo Uniwersytetu im. M. Curie-Skłodowskiej, Lublin 1996, p. 42.

Firlej K. A., Finansowanie działalności badawczo-rozwojowej w świetle założeń strategii "Europa 2020", [in:] P. Antonowicz, P. Galiński, P. Pisarewicz (ed.), *Perspektywa ekonomiczna, finansowa i prawna kreowania wartości w gospodarce*, Wydawnictwo Uniwersytetu Gdańskiego, Gdańsk 2020, pp. 75–76.

Fischer T., *Managing Value Capture*. Gabler Verlag-Springer, Monachium 2011.

Fisher Y. The sense of self-efficacy of aspiring principals: Exploration in a dynamic concept. *Social Psychology of Education*, 14(1), 2011.

Flaszewska S., Zakrzewska-Bielawska A., Organizacja z perspektywy zasobów – ewolucja w podejściu zasobowym, [in:] Adamik A. (ed.), *Nauka o organizacji. Ujęcie dynamiczne*, Wolters Kluwer, Warszawa 2013, p. 223.

Fowler F. J., *Survey Research Methods*, Sage Publications, New York 2002, p. 112.

Frankfort-Nachmias C., Nachmias D., *Metody badawcze w naukach społecznych*. Wydawnictwo Zysk i S-ka. Warszawa 2001, p. 115.

Frishkoff P. A., Understanding Family Business: What is a Family Business?: frishkoffbus.orst.edu. (reading: 12.11.2022).

Fudaliński J., *Analizy sektorowe w strategicznym zarządzaniu przedsiębiorstwem*, Wydawnictwo Antykwa, Kraków 2002, p. 200.

Gabler Wirtschaftslexikon, Stichwort: Komplexität, online abrufbar unter. http://wirtschaft slexikon.gabler.de/Archiv/5074/komplexitaet-v6.htmp; G. Patzak, Messung der Komplexität von Projekt, Projektmanagement aktuell 2009, p. 42.

Gajewski S., *Zachowanie się konsumenta a współczesny marketing*. Wydawnictwo Uniwersytetu Łódzkiego Łódź 2007, p. 100.

Galanti G. A., An introduction to cultural differences. *Western Journal of Medicine*, 172(5), 2020, p. 335.

Gartner Glossary. https://www.gartner.com/en/information-technology/glossary/it-infrastructure

Gesteland R. R. *Różnice kulturowe a zachowania w biznesie*. PWN. Warszawa 2000, pp. 16–17, 58.

Gierszewska G., Romanowska M., *Analiza strategiczna przedsiębiorstwa*. PWE. Warszawa 2009, p. 23, 24.

Gieryszewska G., Wawrzyniak B., *Globalizacja. Wyzwanie dla zarządzania strategicznego*. Wydawnictwo Poltex, Warszawa 2001, p. 19.

Gillespie K., Jeannet J. P., Hennessey H. D., *Global Marketing*. Houghton Mifflin Company. Boston-New York 2007, pp. 72, 77.

Glapiński A., Schumpeterowska teoria przedsiębiorcy, czyli skąd się bierze pies. *Konsumpcja i Rozwój*, nr 1, 2012, pp. 3–5.

Glinka B., Gudkova S., *Przedsiębiorczość*, Wolters Kluwer, Warszawa 2011, p. 88.

Glińska E., Florek M., A. Kowalewska, *Wizerunek miasta. Od koncepcji do wdrożenia*, Wolters Kluwer, Kraków 2009, pp. 63–64.

Głód G., Głód W., Barriers to the development of family businesses. *Research on Enterprise in Modern Economy - Theory and Practice* (4), 2017, p. 40.

Główny Urząd Statystyczny, *Działalność badawcza i rozwojowa w Polsce w 2017 r*, GUS, Warszawa 2018, p. 15.

Godin B., *Innovation. The history of a category. Project on the Intellectual History of Innovation*, Canadian Science and Innovation Indicators Consortium, Montreal 2008, p. 5.

Gorzelak G., Jałowiecki B., Strategie rozwoju regionalnego województw: próba oceny. *Studia regionalne i lokalne*, 1(5), 2001, pp. 58–59.

Grabowska M., Planowanie projektów, [in:] J. Rzępała, M. Pieńkos, T. Leśniowski (eds.), *Zarządzanie projektem badawczym*. Oficyna Drukarska - Jacek Chmielewski, Kraków 2015, pp. 25–26.

Green S. D., Sergeeva N. (2019). Value creation in projects: Towards a narrative perspective. *International Journal of Project Management*, 37(5), pp. 636–651. https://doi.org/10.1016/j.ijproman.2018.12.004

Gretsch O., Salzmann E., Kock A., University-industry collaboration and front-end success: The moderating effects of innovativeness and parallel cross-firm collaboration. *R&D Management*, 49(5), 2019.

Griffin R. W., *Podstawy zarządzania organizacjami*, Wydawnictwo Naukowe PWN, Warszawa 1996, pp. 43, 214.

Griffin R. W., *Fundamentals of Management*. Houghton Mifflin Company, Boston, New York 2002, p. 7.

Griffin R. W., *Fundamentals of Management*. Houghton Mifflin Company, New York, Boston 2008, p. 6.

GUS, *Działalność innowacyjna przedsiębiorstw w Polsce w latach 2016–2018*, GUS, Warszawa 2019.

Guzek M., *Międzynarodowe stosunki gospodarcze*, Wyd. Wyższej Szkoły Biznesu, Poznań 2001, p. 18.

Haffer J., *Skuteczność zarządzania projektami w przedsiębiorstwach działających w Polsce*. Towarzystwo Naukowe Organizacji i Kierownictwa, Toruń 2009, p. 30.

Hall H., *Marketing w szkolnictwie*, Oficyna a Wolters Kluwer Business, Kraków 2007, p. 64.

Hampden-Turner Ch., Trompenaars A., *Siedem kultur kapitalizmu*, Oficyna Ekonomiczna, Kraków 2000, s. 11.

Harasim J., *Strategie marketingowe w osiąganiu przewagi konkurencyjnej w bankowości detalicznej*, Wydawnictwo Akademii Ekonomicznej w Katowicach, Katowice 2004, p. 47.

Harvard Business School, Strategy. *Create and Implement the Best Strategy for Your Business*, Harvard Business School Press 2005, p. XVI.

Harváth P., *Controlling*. München 2011.

Hashai N., Markovich S., Market entry by high technology startups: the effect of competition level and startup innovativeness. *Strategy Science*, 2(3), 2017, 141–160.

Herbolzheimer C., Lüthi B., Projektmanagement aktuell, 2008a, p. 14.

Herbolzheimer C., Lüthi B., Warum grosse IT-Projekte häufig scheitern – Erfolgsfaktoren zur Risikobeherrschung, Projektmanagement aktuell, 2008b.

Hillson D., *Managing Risk in Projects*. Routledge, Taylor&Francis Group, London, New York 2016.

Hitt M. A., Ireland R. D., Sirmon G., Trahms Ch. A., Strategic entrepreneurship: creating value for individuals, organizations and society. *Academy of Management Perspectives*, 25(2), 2011 May, pp. 57–75.

Hollander S., *The Sources of Increased Efficiency. A Study of DuPont Rayon Plants*, MIT Press, Cambridge 1965, p. XII–270.

Horst H. A., New media technologies in everyday life, [in] H. A. Horst, D. Miller (eds.), *Digital Anthropology*, Berg, London, England 2012, pp. 69–70.

https://archive.doingbusiness.org/en/rankings, accessed 16th November, 2022.

https://doi.org/10.1108/JMD-06-2019-0253

https://ec.europa.eu/futurium/en/eu-au-digital-economy-task-force/eu-digital-development-policy-0.html

https://www.javatpoint.com/software-definition (reading: 15.07.2022).

https://www.politykainsight.pl/multimedia/_resource/res/20105186, accessed 16th November, 2022.

Huczek M., Środowisko innowacyjne źródłem rozwoju regionu. *Zeszyty Naukowe Wyższej Szkoły Humanitas. Zarządzanie*, (2), 2012, p. 20.

INTOSAI Working Group on IT Audit. *Podręcznik kontroli systemów informatycznych dla najwyższych organów kontroli*. Departament Metodyki Kontroli i Rozwoju Zawodowego. Najwyższa Izba Kontroli. Warszawa 2016, p. 8.

Ivancevich J. M., Lorenzi P., Skinner S. J., Crosby P. B., *Management. Quality and Competitiveness*. IRWIN. Burr Ridge, Illinois, Boston, Massachusetts, Sydney 1994, p. 14.

Janasz W., Procesy innowacyjne w przedsiębiorstwie. Przedsiębiorstwo jako organizacja gospodarcza, [in:] S. Marek, M. Białasiewicz (ed.), *Podstawy nauki o organizacji*, PWE, Warszawa 2011, p. 269.

Janowicz J., Start-upy. Innowacyjne rozwiązania na trudne czasy, [in:] K. Pająk (ed.), *Innowacyjność wyzwaniem dla współczesnej gospodarki*, CeDeWu, Warszawa 2016, p. 175.

Jaruzalski T., *Efektywność i skuteczność wdrażania systemów IT w administracji publicznej. Wspomaganie procesów podejmowania decyzji*. Wydawnictwo CeDeWu. Warszawa 2009, p. 55.

Jasiński A. H., *Innowacje i polityka innowacyjna*, Wydawnictwo Uniwersytetu w Białymstoku, Białystok 1997, p. 20.

Jasiński A. H., *Innowacje i transfer techniki w procesie transformacji*. Difin, Warszawa 2006, pp. 12, 190.

Jaśniok M., *Strategie marketingowe na rynku politycznym*. Oficyna a Wolters Kluwer business, Kraków 2007, p. 33.

Jay A., *Machiavelli i zarządzanie*. PWE, Warszawa 1996, p. 225.

Jędrych E., Pietras P., Szczepański M., *Zarządzanie projektami*, Technical University of Łódź, Łódź 2012, pp. 116–117.

Jones M. T., *Artificial Intelligence. A Systems Approach*, Jones and Bartlett Publishers, Boston 2015.

Joseph H. A. M., Rodenberg R. M., *Competitive Intelligence and Senior Management*, Eburon Delft Academic Publishers, Amsterdam 2007, p. 234.

Kachniewska M., *Uwarunkowania konkurencyjności przedsiębiorstwa hotelowego*, Szkoła Główna Handlowa, Warszawa 2009, pp. 7, 12.

Kąciak E., *Teoria środków - celów w segmentacji rynku*. Studium metodologiczno-empiryczne, Wolters Kluwer, Warszawa 2011, p. 31.

Kaczmarczyk S., *Badania marketingowe. Podstawy metodyczne*, PWE, Warszawa 2014, s. 136.

Kalinowski T. B., *Innowacyjność przedsiębiorstw a systemy zarządzania jakością*, Wolters Kluwer, Warszawa 2010, p. 44.

Kałuża H., Firmy rodzinne w XXI wieku. Specyfika i sukcesja. *Zeszyty Naukowe Szkoły Głównej Gospodarstwa Wiejskiego w Warszawie Ekonomika i Organizacja Gospodarki Żywnościowej*, 75, 2009, pp. 52–55.

Kaplan R. S., Norton D. P., The balanced scorecard. Measures that drive performance. *Harvard Business Review*, 1, 1992, pp. 71–79.

Kaplan S., *The Invisible Advantage. How to Create a Culture of Innovation*, Greenleaf Book Group Press, Austin 2017, p. 20.

Kasperek M., *Planowanie i organizacja projektów logistycznych*. Wydawnictwo Akademii Ekonomicznej. Katowice 2006, pp. 10–12, 70–75, 121–122.

Kasprzak R., *Fundusze unijne: szansa na rozwój małych i średnich przedsiębiorstw*, Helion, Gliwice 2009.

Kerzner H., *Projektmanagment. Ein systemorientierter Ansatz zur Planung und Steuerung*, Mitp-Verlag, Bonn 2008, pp. 351–352.

Kiełbus A., Spojrzenie na zarządzanie projektami informatycznymi. Mechanika. *Czasopismo Techniczne*, 7(108), 2011, p. 216–217.

Kiełtyka L., *Komunikacja w zarządzaniu. Techniki, narzędzia i formy przekazu informacji*, Agencja Wydawnicza Placet. Warszawa 2002, pp. 371–372.

Kiełtyka L., Informatyczne przemiany zarządzania technologiami informacyjnymi w organizacjach. *Przegląd Organizacji*, 3, 2011, p. 27.

Kim E., Tang L., Bosselman R. Customer perceptions of innovativeness: an accelerator for value co-creation. *Journal of Hospitality & Tourism Research*, 43(6), 2019, 807–838.

Kirschbaum D. M., *Calculated Risk. Good Surprise, Bad Surprise: The Law of Unintended Consequences*. Community Risk Management and Insurance, Washington, DC 2000. www.pmi.org (reading: 25.07.2022 r.).

Klimczak B., *Globalizacja gospodarcza na przełomie tysiącleci. Globalizacja nr 28, Wrocławski Biuletyn Gospodarczy*, PTE Oddział we Wrocławiu, Wrocław 2002, pp. 39–47.

Knosala R., Deptuła A. M., *Ocena ryzyka*, PWE, Warszawa 2018, p. 26.

Kołodko G., *Wędrujący świat*. Prószyński i Spółka, Warszawa 2008, pp. 98–99.

Komisja Europejska. *Poradnik dla użytkowników dotyczący definicji MŚP. Rynek wewnętrzny, przemysł, przedsiębiorczość i MŚP*. Urząd Publikacji Unii Europejskiej. Luksemburg 2019, p. 4.

Konieczna-Domańska A., Turystyka jako sposób komercjalizacji kultury na przykładzie hoteli w obiektach zabytkowych. *Turystyka i rekreacja*, nr 16(2), 2015, p. 179.

Kopaliński W., *Słownik wyrazów obcych*, Wiedza Powszechna, Warszawa 1983.

Kopczewski M., *Alfabet zarządzania projektem*. HELION. Gliwice 2009, p. 25.

Korzeniowski L. F., *Menedżment. Podstawy zarządzania*. EAS. Kraków 2010, p. 236.

Kosińska E. (red.). *Marketing międzynarodowy. Zarys problematyki*. PWE, Warszawa 2008, p. 65.

Kotarbiński T., *Sprawność i błąd. Ogólne pojęcie planu*, PZWS, Warszawa 1966.

Kowalczewski W., *Zarządzanie organizacjami w teorii i praktyce*, Difin, Warszawa 2008, p. 322.

Kozak M., *Destination benchmarking. Concepts, practices and operations*, CABI Publishing, Oxon 2004, pp. 5–7.

Kozień E., Risk and its factors in project management. *Zeszyty Naukowe Uniwersytetu Ekonomicznego w Krakowie*, 766, 2007, p. 79.

Kozioł-Nadolna K., Modele zarządzania innowacjami w XXI wieku, [in:] Mikuła B. (ed.), *Historia i powstanie nauk o zarządzaniu*, Wydawnictwo Uniwersytetu Ekonomicznego w Krakowie, Kraków 2012, p. 298.

Koźmiński A. K., Organizacja, [in:] A. K. Koźmiński, W. Piotrowski (ed.), *Zarządzanie. Teoria i praktyka*, Wydawnictwo Naukowe PWN, Warszawa 2013, p. 42.

Koźmiński A. K., Piotrowski W., *Zarządzanie. Teoria i praktyka*, PWN. Warszawa 2013, p. 761.

Krakowska A., Specyfika projektów informatycznych, [in:] M. Sołtysik, M. Wesołowska (eds.), *Współczesne trendy w zarządzaniu projektami*. Mfiles.pl., Kraków 2016, p. 25.

Krawiec F., *Zarządzanie projektem innowacyjnym produktu i usługi*, Difin, Warszawa 2000, p. 152.

Krezymon M., Determinanty rozwoju przedsiębiorstw sektora MSP. *Współczesne Problemy Ekonomiczne*, 2, 2018, p. 23.

Krupski R., *Zarządzanie strategiczne. Koncepcje, metody*. Wydawnictwo Akademii Ekonomicznej we Wrocławiu, Wrocław 1998, pp. 14–15.

Krupski R., *Podstawy organizacji i zarządzania*, Wydawnictwo I-Bis, Wrocław 2004, p. 17.

Krynicki T. J., Kontekst i cele badania. [in:] A. Kowalewska, (ed.), *Firmy rodzinne w polskiej gospodarce. Szanse i wyzwania*, PARP, Warszawa 2009, p. 6.

Krzepicka A., Tarapata J., *Innowacje jako czynnik budowania wzrostu wartości przedsiębiorstwa*, Zeszyty Naukowe Wyższej Szkoły Humanitas, Zarządzanie 2012, no. 2, p. 75.

Kukułka A., M. Wirkus, Metody wielokryterialne wspomagania decyzji oraz ich zastosowanie w opracowaniu metody oceny nie potokowych procesów produkcyjnych, [in:] R. Knosala (ed.), *Innowacje w zarządzaniu i inżynierii produkcji*, Oficyna Wydawnicza Polskiego Towarzystwa Zarządzania Produkcją, Opole 2017, p. 613.

Kundu J., Project management software-an overview. *International Journal of Current Innovation Research*, 1(4), 2015, p. 91.

Laan S., IT Infrastructure architecture. Infrastructure building blocks and concepts. *Lulu. com* 2017, pp. 36–37.

Łada M., Budżetowanie projektów. *Przegląd organizacji* nr 3 (806), 2007, p. 37.

Łady M., Kozarkiewicz A., *Rachunkowość zarządcza i controlling projektów*, Wydawnictwo C.H. Beck, 2007.

Ładyka S., Pół wieku Unii Europejskiej i jej nowe wyzwania, [in:] E. Kawecka-Wyrzykowska (red.), *Unia Europejska w gospodarce światowej – nowe uwarunkowania*, SGH, Warszawa 2007, pp. 36–37.

Lamparska K., Innowacje otwarte a struktura sieciowa – ujęcie teoretyczne, [in:] R. Żuber (red.), *Zarządzanie innowacjami w przedsiębiorstwie. Wybrane aspekty*, Difin, Warszawa 2016, p. 42.

Lamy P., Europeanisons la mondialisation. *Le Monde*, 7(05), 2004, p. 15.

Leibold M., Probst G., Gibbert M., *Strategic Mangement in Knowledge Economy*. Wiley, Erlangen 2005, p. 15.

Leszczewska K., *Przedsiębiorstwa rodzinne. Specyfika modeli biznesu*. Difin. Warszawa 2016, p. 7.

Levitin A. J., *Business Bankruptcy. Financial Restructuring and Modern Commercial Markets*, Wolters Kluwer, New York 2016, p. 120.

Liberska B., Pojęcie i definicje globalizacji, [w] B. Liberska (red.), *Globalizacja. Mechanizmy i wyzwania*. WN PWN, Warszawa 2002, p. 20.

Lichtarski J. (ed.), *Podstawy nauki o przedsiębiorstwie*. Wydawnictwo Akademii Ekonomicznej we Wrocławiu, Wrocław 2007, p. 375.

Linton T., *The Cultural Background of Personality*, Appleton-Century-Crofts, New York 1945, p. 32.

Listwan T., *Encyklopedia zarządzania*, Difin, Warszawa 2004, p. 188.

Łoś-Nowak T., *Stosunki międzynarodowe. Teorie - systemy - uczestnicy*. Wyd. Uniwersytetu Wrocławskiego, Wrocław 2000, p. 112.

Łuczak T., Wybrane problemy klasyfikacyjne małych i średnich przedsiębiorstw prywatnych, *Gospodarka Narodowa*, (7), 1995, p. 7.

Luecke L., *Zarządzanie kreatywnością i innowacją*, MT Biznes, Czarnów 2005, p. 68.

Luger K., *Contributions to Economics*. Physica- Verlag. Heidelberg 2008, p. 25.

Lutyńska K., Pilotaż pogłębiony. Koncepcja, realizacja i analiza materiałów pilotażowych, [in:] Z. Gostkowski, J. Lutyński (ed.), *Analizy i próby technik badawczych w socjologii*, Ossolineum, Wrocław 1975.

Lutyński J., *Metody badań społecznych*. Łódzkie Towarzystwo Naukowe, Łódź 2000, pp. 150–175.

Maksymowicz A., Człowiek w społeczeństwie - kultura i kontrola społeczna, [in:] A. Augustynek, A. Maksymowicz (eds.), *Podstawy socjologii i psychologii*, Uczelniane Wydawnictwa Naukowo- Dydaktyczne. Kraków 2002, p. 29.

Marcinek K., *Finansowanie projektów inwestycyjnych na zasadach Project finanse*. Katowice 2006, p. 16.

Marcinkiewicz K., Paweł Nowak, Dominika Popielec, Magdalena Wilk, *Koronawirus wyzwaniem współczesnego społeczeństwa*. Polskie Towarzystwo Komunikacji Publicznej, Kraków- Wrocław 2020, p. 9.

Markowska M., Ocena zależności między rozwojem inteligentnym a odpornością na kryzys ekonomiczny w wymiarze regionalnym – przegląd badań. *Prace Naukowe Uniwersytetu Ekonomicznego we Wrocławiu*, nr 333, 2014, p. 23.

Martyniak Z. (ed.), *Zarządzanie informacją i komunikacją. Zagadnienia wybrane w świetle studiów i badań empirycznych*, Wydawnictwo Akademii Ekonomicznej w Krakowie, Kraków 2000, p. 253.

Martyniak Z., *Historia myśli organizatorskiej*, Wydawnictwo Akademii Ekonomicznej w Krakowie, Kraków 2002, s. 99.

Maszke A. W., *Metody i techniki badań pedagogicznych*, Wydawnictwo Uniwersytetu Rzeszowskiego, Rzeszów 2008, p. 232.

Matejun M., Wewnętrzne bariery rozwoju firm sektora MSP, [in:] Lachiewicz S. (ed.), *Zarządzanie rozwojem organizacji*, Tom II, Wydawnictwo Politechniki Łódzkiej, Łódź 2007, p. 122.

Maziarz P., Pierwszy komputer obchodził 75 urodziny. Benchmark.pl. https://www. benchmark.pl/aktualnosci/historia-rozwoju-komputerow-i-laptopow.html (reading: 29.08.2022 r.).

Mazurkiewicz P., *Europeizacja Europy, Wydawnictwo: Studium Generale Europa*, Uniwersytet Kardynała Stefana Wyszyńskiego, Warszawa 2001, p. 26.

McCarthy E. J., Perreault W. D., *Basic Marketing. A Global Managerial Approach*. IRWIN. Bur Ridge, Cape Town, Boston, Sydney 1993, p. 216.

McCartney S., *ENIAC. The Triumphs and Tragedies of the World's First Computer*. Walker & Co 1999.

McKenna E., Beech N., *Zarządzanie zasobami ludzkimi*, Wydawnictwo BERG, Warszawa 1999, p. 25.

McLeod A., *Blogi – od A do sławy i pieniędzy*, Złote Myśli, Gliwice 2006, p. 9.

Mika M., Turystyka zrównoważona – pytania o naukową użyteczność koncepcji. *Turyzm*, nr 25(1), 2015, p. 11.

Mikołajczyk J., *Ekonomika handlu*, WSiP, Warszawa 2008, p. 192.

Miłek J., Pojęcie analizy finansowej, [in:] Homo Creator. Red.: M. Miłek. *Wydawnictwo Stowarzyszenia Współpracy* Polska- Wschód. Kielce 2009, p. 62.

Ministerstwo Funduszy i Polityki Regionalnej, *Szczegółowy opis osi priorytetowych programu operacyjnego inteligentny rozwój 2014-2020*, MFiPR, Warszawa 2020, pp. 2–7.

Miron-Spektor E., Ingram A., Keller J., Smith W. K., & Lewis M. W., Microfoundations of organizational paradox: the problem is how we think about the problem. *Academy of Management Journal*, 61(1), 2018, pp. 26–45.

Misztal A., Otwarte innowacje w polskich przedsiębiorstwach – ewaluacja. *Zeszyty Naukowe Małopolskiej Wyższej Szkoły Ekonomicznej w Tarnowie*, 33(1), 2017, p. 27.

Modliński P., Analiza funkcjonalności oprogramowania wspierającego zarządzanie projektami w mśp. *Zeszyty Naukowe Uniwersytetu Szczecińskiego Studia Informatica*, nr 878(1), 2015, pp. 67–70.

Molendowski E., Polan W., *Dyplomacja gospodarcza. Rola i znaczenie w polityce zagranicznej państwa*. Oficyna Wydawnicza a Wolters Kluwer business. Kraków 2007, p. 87.

Moon J., *Corporate Social Responsibility. A Very Short Introduction*, Oxford University Press, Oxford 2014, p. 1.

Moran R. T., Harris P. R., Moran S. V., *Managing Cultural Differences. Global Leadership Strategies for the 21st Century*. Elsevier, Amsterdam, Boston, Heidelberg, London, New York, Oxford, Paris, San Diego, San Francisco, Singapore, Sydney, Tokyo 2007, pp. 7–13, 17.

Moroz M., The level of development of the digital economy in Poland and selected European countries: a comparative analysis. *Foundations of Management*, 9, 2017, p. 175.

Mroziewicz M., *Style kierowania i zarządzania*, Difin, Warszawa 2005, p. 110.

Mruk H., *Komunikowanie się w marketingu*, Polskie Towarzystwo Ekonomiczne, Warszawa 2004, p. 200.

Murray R., Caulier-Grice J., G. Mulgan, *The Open Book of Social Innovation*, The Young Foundation & NESTA, London 2010, p. 12.

Nadiv R., Home, work or both? The role of paradox mindset in a remote work environment during the COVID-19 pandemic. *International Journal of Manpower*, 5, 2021, p. 1183.

Neuhold E. J., Paul M., *Formal Description of Programming Concepts*. Springer-Verlag. Berlin, Heidelberg, New York, Paris, Tokyo, Hong Kong, Barcelona, Budapest 1992, p. 9.

Nowak S., *Metodologia badań społecznych*, Wydawnictwo Naukowe PWN, Warszawa 2007, pp. 45, 59.

Nowakowska E., Sulimiera-Michalak S., COVID-19 – choroba wywołana zakażeniem wirusem sars-cov-2 globalnym zagrożeniem dla zdrowia publicznego. *Postępy Mikrobiologii*, 53, 2020, p. 227.

Nowosielski S., Goals in scientific research management. methodological aspects. *Research Papers of Wrocław University of Economics*, 421, 2016, p. 470.

Oe H., The innovative organisation of Airbnb: Business model innovation and holacracy to enhance innovative business behaviour coping with the impact of the COVID-19. *International Journal of Business Innovation and Research*, 1(1), 2021, p. 85.

Ogolo J., Planning as a management function in business organisations. *African Business and Finance Journal. Siren Research Centre for African Universities Port Harcourt,* 4(3), 2011, p. 25.

Olejniczak A., Wpływ różnic kulturowych na rozwój organizacji. *Studia i prace wydziału nauk zarządzania,* (37), t.3, 2014, p. 117.

Olejniczak K., Olejniczak M., Ewaluacja projektów i programów finansowanych ze środków Unii Europejskiej. *Studia Europejskie,* 2, 2004, p. 57.

Oleksym T., Wyzwania ZZL związane z globalizacją i kryzysem, [in:] F. Bylok, L. Cichobłaziński (red.), *Problemy zarządzania zasobami ludzkimi w dobie globalizacji,* Wydawnictwo Politechniki Częstochowskiej, Częstochowa 2009, pp. 18–19.

Osterweil L. J., What is software, [in:] *The Essence of Software Engineering.* Red.: V. Gruhn, R. Striemer. Springer, Cham, Switzerland 2018, pp. 59–70.

Pabian, 2008b, pp. 77–78.

Pabian A., Kulturowe uwarunkowania tworzenia więzi z klientami na międzynarodowych rynkach instytucjonalnych. [in]: O. Witczak (ed.), *Budowanie związków z klientami na rynku business to business. Teoria i Praktyka,* CeDeWu Wydawnictwa Fachowe, Warszawa 2008, pp. 77–83.

Pabian A., Conducting personal sale's activities on b2b markets in conditions of coronavirus pandemic – selected aspects. *Zeszyty Naukowe Wyższej Szkoły Humanitas Zarządzanie,* 5, 2020, p. 212.

Pabian A., Gworys W., *Prace dyplomowe. Przygotowanie merytoryczne i redakcyjne.* WSHiT. Częstochowa 2008, p. 31.

Pabian A., Pabian B., Collaboration with foreigners in international employee teams from the perspective of the young generation. *European Research Studies Journal,* XXIV(4), 2021, p. 292.

Pakroo P. H., *Starting & Building a Nonprofit. A Practical Guide.* Nolo, Berkeley 2011, p. 37.

PARP (Polska Agencja Rozwoju Przedsiębiorczości). *Raport o stanie małych i średnich przedsiębiorstw w Polsce,* Grupa PFR, Warszawa 2021.

Patzak G., Projektmanagement aktuell 2009, p. 42.

Patzak G., Ratty G., *Projekt Management,* Linde International, Wien 2009, p. 219.

Pawlak M., *Zarządzanie projektami.* Wydawnictwo Naukowe PWN, Warszawa 2006, pp. 205–220.

Pease A., *Mowa Ciała. Jak odczytywać myśli innych ludzi z ich gestów.* Wydawnictwo Jedność. Kielce 2001, pp. 21–22;

Penc-Pietrzak I., *Strategie biznesu i marketingu,* WPSB, Kraków 1998, p. 17.

Perlow L., Repenning N., The Dynamics of Silencing Conflict, *Research in Organizational Behavior,* 29, 2009, p. 195.

Peszko A., *Podstawy zarządzania organizacjami,* Wydawnictwo AGH, Kraków 1997, p. 41.

Piasecki B., Rogut A., Smallbone D., *Wpływ integracji Polski z Unią Europejską na sektor MSP,* Polska Fundacja Promocji i Rozwoju Małych i Średnich Przedsiębiorstw, Warszawa 2000, p. 41–42.

Pietras P., Szmit M., *Zarządzanie projektami. Wybrane metody i techniki.* Oficyna Księgarsko-Wydawnicza Horyzont, Łódź 2003, pp. 7–8, 12, 15, 78.

Pinchot G., *Intrapreneuring.* Harper and Row, New York 1985.

Piwowarczyk J., *Rozważania o przejawach, rodzajach i konsekwencjach procesu globalizacji. Prace Naukowe KPAiM SGGW nr 33,* Wyd. SGGW, Warszawa 2004, pp. 155–166.

Pocztowski A., *Analiza zasobów ludzkich w organizacjach,* Wydawnictwo Akademii Ekonomicznej w Krakowie, Kraków 2000, s. 28.

Pojda M., Bukłaha E., Dlaczego projekty się nie udają?. https://gazeta.sgh.waw.pl/ekonomia-po-prostu/dlaczego-projekty-sie-nie-udaja (reading: 15.05.2022).

Poli K., What photo experts are saying about the disc, *Popular Photography*, 89(nr5), 1982, pp. 72, 182.

Pomykalski A., *Zarządzanie innowacjami. Globalizacja, konkurencja, technologia informacyjna*. Wydawnictwo Naukowe PWN, Warszawa 2001, p. 25.

Porter M. E., *Porter o konkurencji*, PWE, Warszawa 2001, p. 194.

Postawka M., Zarządzanie projektem innowacji, [in:] S. Łobejko (ed.), *Strategiczne podejście do innowacyjności w regionie*, Urząd Marszałkowski Województwa Mazowieckiego w Warszawie, Warszawa 2018, p. 5.

Pradies C., Aust I., Bednarek R., Brandl J., Carmine S., Cheal J., Cunha M. P., Gaim M., Keegan A., Lê J. K., Miron-Spektor E., Nielsen R. K., Pouthier V., Sharma G., Sparr J. L., Vince R., Keller J., The lived experience of paradox: how individuals navigate tensions during the pandemic crisis. *Journal of Management Inquiry*, 30(2), 2021, pp. 154–167.

Pretorius S., Steyn H., Bond-Barnard T. J., Leadership styles in projects: current trends and future opportunities. *South African Journal of Industrial Engineering*, 29(3), 2018, pp. 161–162.

Prusak J. Strojny M. Baran, Projekty badawcze w biznesie – analiza ryzyka na przykładzie planowania projektów współfinansowanych ze środków unijnych. *Przedsiębiorczość i Zarządzanie*, 16(12), part 2: Wybrane problemy zarządcze, rachunkowe i podatkowe w sektorze MSP, 2015, p. 96.

Prywata M., *Zarządzanie ryzykiem w małych projektach*. Polska Agencja Rozwoju Przedsiębiorczości (PARP), Warszawa 2010, p. 6.

Przychocka I., *Małe i średnie przedsiębiorstwa wobec wejścia Polski do Unii Europejskiej*, Wydawnictwo SIGMA SPJ, Warszawa 2012, pp. 13, 22–23.

Puranam P., Raveendran M., Knudsen T., Organization design: The epistemic interdependence perspective. *Academy of Management Review*, 37(3), 2012.

Puranam P., Singh H., Zollo M., Organizing for innovation: managing the coordina-tion-autonomy dilemma in technology acquisitions. *Academy of Management Journal*, 49(2), 2006, pp. 263–280.

Pszczołowski T., *Zasady sprawnego działania. Wstęp do prakseologii*, Wiedza Powszechna, Warszawa 1982.

Raport o stanie małych i średnich przedsiębiorstw w Polsce, PARP, Grupa PFR, Warszawa 2020, p. 8.

Robbins S. P., DeCenzo D. A., *Podstawy zarządzania*, PWE, Warszawa 2002, pp. 34, 36–37.

Rodney Turner J., *The Handbook of Project-Based Management, Improving the Process for Achieving*, McGraw-Hill Professional, New York, 1998.

Rogers E. M., *Diffusion of Innovations*, Free Press, New York 1995, p. 15.

Romanowska M., Determinanty innowacyjności polskich przedsiębiorstw. *Przegląd Organizacji*, (nr 2), 2016.

Rossi P. H., Freeman H. E., Lipsey M. W., *Evaluation. A Systematic Approach*, Sage Publications, London 1999, pp. 447–448.

Rudnicka A., *CSR – doskonalenie relacji społecznych w firmie*, Wolters Kluwer, Warszawa 2012, pp. 40–41.

Rump J., Schabel F., Wie Projektarbeit Unternehmen verändert. *Harvard Business Manager*, 2, 2010, p. 16.

Rutkowska A., Kulturowo-ekonomiczne aspekty komunikacji międzykulturowej. *Kultura i Wartości*, (25), 2018, p. 174.

Rybak M., *Etyka menedżera. Społeczna odpowiedzialność przedsiębiorstwa*, Wydawnictwo Naukowe PWN, Warszawa 2007, p. 15.

Rynarzewski T., Zielińska-Głębocka A., *Międzynarodowe stosunki gospodarcze*. WN PWN, Warszawa 2006, pp. 209–210.

Sadowska A., Czym są metodyki zarządzania projektami i którą wybrać dla Twojego projektu?. https://www.droptica.pl/blog/czym-sa-metodyki-zarzadzania-projektami-i-ktora-wybrac-dla-twojego-projektu/ (reading: 15.05.2022 r.).

Samset K., *Project Evaluation. Making Investments Succeed*. Tapir Academic Press, 2003.

Santon W. J., Etzel M. J., Walker B. J., *Fundamentals of Marketing*. McGraw-Hill. New York 1991, p. 118.

Sąsara W., Jak zarządzać projektami unijnymi?, 11 January 2013, https://www.taskbeat. pl/2013/01/jak-zarzadzac-projektami-unijnymi/ (dostęp 11.07.2021).

Sawhney M., Wolcott R. C., I. Arroniz, The 12 different ways for companies to innovate. *MIT Sloan Management Review*, 47(nr 3), 2006, pp. 74–81.

Schermerhorn J. R., *Introduction to Management*, International Edition, John Wiley & Sons, Hoboken, 2008, p. 16.

Schieman S., Badawy P. J. A., Milkie A. M., Bierman A., Work-life conflict during the COVID-19 pandemic. *Socius*, 7, 2021, pp. 7–12.

Schilke O, Hu S, Helfat C. E. Quo vadis, dynamic capabilities? A content-analytic review of the current state of knowledge and recommendations for future research. *Academy of Management Annals*, 12, 2018, 390–439.

Schroeder J., *Badania marketingowe rynków zagranicznych*, Wydawnictwo Akademii Ekonomicznej w Poznaniu, Poznań 1997, p. 18.

Serwis Rzeczpospolitej Polskiej, Ministerstwo Rozwoju, Strategia Europa 2020, https://www.gov.pl/web/rozwoj/strategia-europa-2020 (reading: 15.05.2022).

Shane S., *A General Theory of Entrepreneurship*. The Individual-Opportunity Nexus. Edward Elgar Publishing, Northampton 2003.

Siekierski J., Popławski Ł., *Globalisation Processes in Polish Agrobusiness. Economic Science for Rural Development*, nr 10. Jelgava Latvia University of Agriculture, Latvia 2006, pp. 123–129.

Sierak J., Górniak R., *Ocena efektywności i finansowanie projektów inwestycyjnych jednostek samorządu terytorialnego współfinansowanych funduszami Unii Europejskiej*, Oficyna Wydawnicza Szkoły Głównej Handlowej, Warszawa 2011.

Sikora J., Uziębło A., Innowacja w przedsiębiorstwie – próba zdefiniowania. *Zarządzanie i Finanse*, 2(2), 2013, p. 354.

Sikorski C., *Język konfliktu. Kultura komunikacji społecznej w organizacji*. Wydawnictwo C. H. Beck. Warszawa 2005, p. 47.

Skala A., *Digital Startups in Transition Economies Challenges for Management*, Entrepreneurship and Education, Palgrave Macmillan, Cham, Switzerland 2019, pp. 15–25.

Skidelsky R., Nikt nie wie co będzie dalej. EUROPA, Magazyn Idei. *Dziennika*, (251), 2009, pp. 2–3.

Skoneczna M., Fundusze unijne na rozwój start-upów, [in:] P. Antonowicz, P. Galiński, P. Pisarewicz (ed.), *Perspektywa ekonomiczna, finansowa i prawna kreowania wartości w gospodarce*, Wydawnictwo Uniwersytetu Gdańskiego, Gdańsk 2020, p. 283.

Skorupka D., Zarządzanie ryzykiem w przedsięwzięciach budowlanych. *Zeszyty Naukowe. Wyższa Szkoła Oficerska Wojsk Lądowych im. gen. T. Kościuszki*, 3(149), 2008, pp. 120–129;

Skorupka D., Kuchta D., Górski M., *Zarządzanie ryzykiem w projekcie*, Wyższa Szkoła Oficerska Wojsk Lądowych im. generała Tadeusza Kościuszki, Wrocław 2012.

Skowronek-Mielczarek A., *Małe i średnie przedsiębiorstwa*, Wyd. C.H. Beck, Warszawa, 2005, pp. 33–34.

Skowronek-Mielczarek A., Leszczyński Z., *Controlling - analiza i monitoring w zarządzaniu przedsiębiorstwem*. Wyd. Difin, Warszawa 2007, p. 183.

Sławińska M., Innowacje marketingowe w działalności przedsiębiorstw handlowych. *Annales Universitatis Mariae Curie-Skłodowska Lublin – Polonia*, XLIX, 2015, p. 158.

Śmiatacz K., *Badanie satysfakcji klientów na przykładzie rynku usług telefonii komórkowej w Polsce*, Wydawnictwa Uczelniane Uniwersytetu Techniczno-Przyrodniczego w Bydgoszczy, Bydgoszcz 2012, p. 127.

Smit P. J., de Cronje G. J., Vrba M. J., *Management Principles: A Contemporary Edition for Africa*, Juta & Company, Cape Town 2007, s. 33.

Smite D., Moe N. B., Klotins E., Gonzalez-Huerta J., From forced working-from-home to working-from-anywhere: two revolutions in telework, 2021. arXiv preprint arXiv:2101.08315.

Smura J., *Feedback jest kłopotliwy jak yeti*. https://konteksthr.pl/feedback-jest-klopotliwy-jak-yeti/ (reading: 05.12.2022).

Smyczek S., Kreowanie a dostarczanie wartości dla klienta poprzez sieci w sektorze usług. *Handel Wewnętrzny*, 2, 2009, pp. 96–97.

Snedaker S., Hoenig N., *How to Cheat at IT Project Management*, Elsevier Inc. New York 2005, pp. 163–165.

Sobocińska M., Badania marketingowe w dobie wirtualizacji życia społecznego. *Nauki o Zarządzaniu. Management Sciences*, 2(11), 2012, pp. 26–27.

Sokół A., Kulturowe uwarunkowania rozwoju wiedzy w regionach Polski. *Nierówności społeczne a wzrost gospodarczy*, (nr 20), 2011, p. 315.

Sokół-Szawłowska M., *Wpływ kwarantanny na zdrowie psychiczne podczas pandemi COVID-19*. Instytut Psychiatrii i Neurologii w Warszawie, Warszawa 2021, p. 57.

Solinska M., Iwaszczuk N., Rola małych i średnich przedsiębiorstw w gospodarce rynkowej. Львівськового державного університету внутрішніх справ, Науковій вісник, 2, 2008, p. 1.

Solomon M. R., Zachowania i zwyczaje konsumentów. Tłum A. Kasoń-Opitek, J. Sugiero, B. Sałbut. *Wydawnictwo*, HELION, Gliwice 2006, p. 545.

Sood A., Tellis G. J., Technological evolution and radical innovation. *Journal of Marketing*, 69(1), 2005, pp. 152–168.

Spałek S., Bodych M., *PMO: praktyka zarządzania projektami i portfelem projektów w organizacji*, Helion, Gliwice 2012, pp. 42–43.

Spang K., Özcan S., GPM – studie 2008/2009 zum stand und trend des projektmanagement, http://www.gpmipma; Standish Group International CHAOS Rising: D. Yeo, Critical failure factors in information system projekt. *International Journal of Projekt Management*, 20, 2002, p. 241.

Spychalski G., Procesy Globalizacji w kształtowaniu rozwoju obszarów wiejskich. *Roczniki Naukowe Stowarzyszenia Ekonomistów Rolnictwa i Agrobiznesu*, t. XI, z. 4, 2009, s. 319.

Stabryła A., *Podstawy zarządzania firmą*, Wydawnictwo Naukowe PWN, Warszawa–Kraków 1995, p. 34.

Stabryła A., *Zarządzanie projektami ekonomicznymi i organizacyjnymi*, Wydawnictwo Naukowe PWN, Warszawa 2006, p. 31, 34, 110.

Stabryła A., Koncepcja zarządzania wiedzą i rozwojem przedsiębiorstwa. *Zeszyty Naukowe Małopolskiej Wyższej Szkoły Ekonomicznej w Tarnowie*, 26(1), 2015, pp. 169–178.

Statistics Poland. https://stat.gov.pl/en/topics/economic-activities-finances/activity-of-enterprises-activity-of-companies/registrations-and-bankruptcies-of-enterprises-in-the-second-quarter-of-2022,21,14.html; accessed 16th November, 2022.

Stauffer D., Personal innovativeness as a predictor of entrepreneurial value creation. *International Journal of Innovation Science*, 8(1), 2016, pp. 4–26.

Stauffer D. A., Evaluating mindset as a means of measuring personal innovativeness. *International Journal of Innovation Science*, 7(4), 2015a, pp. 233–248.

Stauffer D. A., Valuable novelty: a proposed general theory of innovation and innovativeness. *International Journal of Innovation Science*, 7(3), 2015b, pp. 169–182.

Sterman J. D., Business Dynamics, K. G. Cooper, *Naval Ship Production – a Claim Settled and a Framework Built, Interfaces*, 10(6), 1980, p. 20.

Sterman J. D., *Business Dynamics: Systems Thiking and Modeling for a Complex World*. McGraw-Hill Education, Boston 2000.

Sterman J. D., Does, formal system dynamics training improve people's understanding of accumulation? *System Dynamics Review*, 2010, p. 316.

Stoner J. A. F., Freeman R. E., Gilbert D. R., *Kierowanie. Polskie Wydawnictwo Ekonomiczne*. Warszawa 2001, pp. 79–81, 136–141, 186.

Strategic Objectives. Mc-Graw Hill Professional, New York 1998.

Strużyna J., Rozwój zarządzania zasobami ludzkimi. [in:] J. Pyka (ed.), *Nowoczesność przemysłu i usług*. Wyd. TNOiK, Katowice 2010, p. 409.

Sutherland J., Canwell D., *Klucz do zarządzania strategicznego. Najważniejsze teorie, pojęcia, postaci*. PWN, Warszawa 2007, pp. 143–147.

Swedberg R., *Joseph A. Schumpeter. His Life and Work*, Polity Press, Cambridge, Malden 1993.

Szaflarski K., I. Markiewicz-Halemba, Innowacyjność a specjalizacje eksportowe polskich przedsiębiorstw w fazie wychodzenia z kryzysu, [in:] S. Wydymus, M. Maciejewski (eds.), *Tradycyjne i nowe kierunki rozwoju handlu międzynarodowego*, Wydawnictwo CeDeWu, Warszawa 2014, p. 237.

Szatkowski K., *Zarządzanie innowacjami i transferem technologii*, Wydawnictwo Naukowe PWN, Warszawa 2016, pp. 24, 94–114;

Szczepankowski P. J., *Fuzje i przejęcia. Techniki oceny opłacalności i sposoby finansowania*, Wydawnictwo Naukowe PWN, Warszawa 2000, pp. 111–113.

Szlachta J., *Programowanie rozwoju regionalnego w Unii Europejskiej*, Wydawnictwo Naukowe PWN, Warszawa 1997, p. 105.

Sztabiński P. B., Sztabiński F., Jak połączyć pilotaż z badaniem próbnym? Przykład europejskiego sondażu społecznego 2004. *Ask: Research and Methods*, (14), 2005, pp. 55, 57.

Sztucki T., *Encyklopedia Marketing. Definicje, Zasady, Metody*. Placet, Warszawa 1998, pp. 58, 202.

Szumilak J. (ed.), *Rola handlu w tworzeniu wartości dla nabywcy*, Fundacja Uniwersytetu Ekonomicznego w Krakowie, Kraków 2007, pp. 26, 27.

Szymańska A., Innowacyjność produktowa przedsiębiorstw produkcyjnych a preferencje konsumentów. *Prace Komisji Geografii Przemysłu Polskiego Towarzystwa Geograficznego*, (20), 2012, p. 147.

Szymonik A., Nowak I., *Współczesna logistyka*, Difin, Warszawa 2018, p. 187.

Szymura-Tyc M., *Zarządzanie przez wartość dla klienta*. Budowa wartości firmy, http://www.zti.com.pl/instytut/pp/referaty/ref4_full.html (reading: 12.10.2022).

Talbot M., *Make Your Mission Statement Work*, How to Books, Ltd. Oxford 2003, p. 15.

Tarczyński W., Mojsiewicz M., *Zarządzanie ryzykiem. Podstawowe zagadnienia*, PWE, Warszawa 2001, p. 11.

Tarnawa A., Zbierowski P., Nieć M., Zakrzewski R., Skowrońska A., Kosińska A. (2022). GEM Polska 2022. Raport z badania przedsiębiorczości. PARP.

Terziovski M., Innovation practice and its performance implications in small and medium enterprises (SMEs) in the manufacturing sector: a resource-based view. *Strategic Management Journal*, 31(8), 2010, pp. 892–902.

Tidd J., Bessant J., *Zarządzanie innowacjami. Integracja zmian technologicznych, rynkowych i organizacyjnych*. Wydawnictwo Wolters Kluwer, Warszawa 2013, pp. 55, 687, 694

Tkaczyk T. (red.), *Problem dostosowania polskich przedsiębiorstw do standardów europejskich*. Wyd. SGGW, Warszawa 2005, pp. 12–13.

Tkaczyński J. W., Świstak M., Sztorc E., *Projekty europejskie. Praktyczne aspekty pozyskiwania i rozliczania dotacji unijnych*, Wydawnictwo C.H. Beck, Warszawa 2011, p. 21.

Tkaczyński J. W., Willa R., Świstak M., *Fundusze Unii Europejskiej 2007–2013. Cele – Działania – Środki*. Wydawnictwo UJ, Kraków 2008, pp. 14–17.

Toczyski W., *Monitoring rozwoju zrównoważonego*, Wydawnictwo Uniwersytetu Gdańskiego, Gdańsk 2004, p. 15.

Tranfield D., Denyer D., P. Smart, Towards a methodology for developing evidence-informed management knowledge by means of systematic review. *British Journal of Management*, (nr 14), 2003, pp. 207–220.

Trocki M., Podejście procesowe w zarządzaniu, in: *Wyzwania zarządcze w zmieniającym się otoczeniu*, Skowronek-Mielczarek A. (ed.). Oficyna wydawnicza SGH, Warszawa 2010.

Trocki M., *Organizacja projektowa. Podstawy, modele, rozwiązania*, PWE, Warszawa 2014.

Trocki M., Podstawy planowania przebiegu projektów, [in:] *Planowanie przebiegu projektów*. Trocki M., Wyrozębski P. (ed.). Oficyna wydawnicza szkoła główna handlowa w warszawie, Warszawa 2015, p. 10.

Trocki M., Grucza B., Ogonek K., *Zarządzanie projektami*, PWE, Warszawa 2019, p. 14, 15.

Trocki T., Grucza B., Ogonek K., *Zarządzanie projektami*. PWE, Warszawa 2003, pp. 36–91.

Trocki M., Grucza B., *Zarządzanie projektem europejskim*. PWE, Warszawa 2007, p. 15.

Trocki M., Wyrozębski P., *Planowanie przebiegu projektów*. Oficyna wydawnicza szkoła główna handlowa w warszawie. Warszawa 2015.

Trzaskalik T., Wielokryterialne wspomaganie decyzji. Przegląd metod i zastosowań. *Zeszyty Naukowe Politechniki Śląskiej. Organizacja i Zarządzanie*, (z. 74), 2014, pp. 240–250.

Tushman M. Smith W. K., Chapman R., Westerman W. G., O'Reilly Ch. Organizational designs and innovation streams. *Industrial and Corporate Change*, 19(5), October 2010, pp.1331–1366.

Unold, *Systemy informacyjne marketingu*, Wydawnictwo Uniwersytetu Ekonomicznego we Wrocławiu, Wrocław 2009, p. 57.

Ustawa z dnia 30 maja 2008 r. o niektórych formach wspierania działalności innowacyjnej (Dz.U. 2008 nr 116 poz. 730).

Verbake A., *International Business Strategy*. Cambridge University Press. Cambridge, New York, Melbourne, Madrid, Cape Town, Singapore, Sao Paulo, Delhi 2009, pp. 435–445.

Verbeke A., *International Business Strategy*, Cambridge University Press, Cambridge,2013, p. 383.

Veryard R., *The Component-Based Business: Plug and Play*, Springer, London 2000, p. 2.

Wajda A., *Podstawy nauki o zarządzaniu organizacjami*. Difin, Warszawa 2003, p. 95.

Walas-Trębacz J., Wykorzystanie systemu monitoringu w przedsiębiorstwie, [in:] A. Stabryła (ed.), *Systemy controllingu, monitoringu i audytu w przedsiębiorstwie*, Wydawnictwo Mfiles.pl., Kraków 2010, p. 63.

Walaszczyk L., *Social Innovation Based Model for the Analysis of Enterprise Operations.* *Łukasiewicz Research Network*, Institute for Sustainable Technologies, Radom 2020, p. 56.

Wanicki P., Źródła finansowania projektów innowacyjnych. *Studia Ekonomiczne. Zeszyty Naukowe Uniwersytetu Ekonomicznego w Katowicach*, 341, 2017, p. 359.

Ward M., *Pięćdziesiąt najważniejszych problemów zarządzania*, Wydawnictwo Profesjonalnej Szkoły Biznesu, Kraków 1997, p. 86.

Wasilewski L., *Europejski kontekst zarządzania jakością*, Instytut Organizacji i Zarządzania w Przemyśle Orgmasz, Warszawa 1998, pp. 89–91.

Wasiluk A., Innowacyjność współczesnych przedsiębiorstw, [in:] W. Kowalczewski (ed.), *Zarządzanie współczesnym przedsiębiorstwem, Wydawnictwo Akademickie Dialog*, Wydawnictwo Akademickie Dialog, Warszawa 2002, p. 335.

Wasiluk A., Źródła i cele innowacji wprowadzanych w przedsiębiorstwach. *Zeszyty Naukowe Politechniki Białostockiej. Ekonomia i Zarządzanie*, z. 8, 2003, p. 337.

Waszkiewicz J., *Jak Polak z Polakiem. Szkice o kulturze negocjowania*. Wydawnictwo Naukowe PWN. Warszawa 1997, p. 26.

Watson G. H., *Strategic Benchmarking Reloaded with Six Sigma*, John Wiley & Sons, Inc., New Jersey 2007, p. 5.

Wawrzyniak A., Kuczborska K., Lipińska-Opałka A., Będzichowska A., Kalicki B., The 2019 novel coronavirus (2019-nCoV) – transmission, symptoms and treatment. *Pediatr Med Rodz*, 20, 2019, p. 1.

Webber R. A., *Zasady zarządzania organizacjami*. PWE, Warszawa 1996, p. 245.

Weick K.: *Substitutes for Strategy. W: The Competitive Challenge Red. J.* Teece, MA, Ballinger, Cambridge 1987.

Westland J., *Global Innovation Management. A Strategic Approach*, Pelgrave, New York 2008, p. 8.

Whittaker S., *Information Management and Computer Security* 1999a, p. 3.

Whittaker S., *What Went Wrong? Unsuccessful Information Technology Projects*, Information Management and Computer Security 1999b, p. 23.

Wiankowski S., *Dostosowanie sfery badawczo-rozwojowej w Polsce do funkcjonowania w europejskiej przestrzeni badawczej*, Instytut Organizacji i Zarządzania w Przemyśle Orgmasz, Warszawa 2005, p. 213.

Wierzbicki K., *Zarządzanie firmą u progu XXI wieku*, Centrum Szkoleniowo-Wydawnicze Kwantum, Warszawa 1999, p. 16.

Williams T., *Modelling Complex Projects*, Wiley, London, UK, West Sussex 2002.

Winiarski B., *Asymetrie korzyści i zagrożeń w procesach globalizacji. Globalizacja gospodarcza na przełomie tysiącleci. Globalizacja nr 28*, Wrocławski Biuletyn Gospodarczy, PTE Oddział we Wrocławiu, Wrocław 2002, p. 23–32.

Winkler R., Chmielecki M., Komunikacja a dzielenie się wiedzą w projektowych zespołach międzykulturowych. *Zeszyty Naukowe Uniwersytetu Ekonomicznego w Krakowie*, 3(939), 2015, pp. 87–99.

Witek L., Adamczyk J. *Marketing międzynarodowy. Oficyna Wydawnicza Politechniki Rzeszowskiej. Oficyna*. Wydawnicza Politechniki Rzeszowskie, Rzeszów 2008, p. 135.

Witkowski J., Rodawski B., Pojęcie i typologia projektów logistycznych. *Gospodarka materiałowa i logistyka*, (Nr 3), 2007.

Wojciechowski Ł., Wojciechowski A., Kosmatka T., *Infrastruktura magazynowa i transportowa*, Wyższa Szkoła Logistyki, Poznań 2009, p. 15.

Wójcik J., *Wykorzystanie metody zarządzania projektami w małych i średnich przedsiębiorstwach*, Zeszyty Naukowe. Organizacja i Zarządzanie, Politechnika Śląska, 78, 2019, pp. 33–34.

Woźniak K., *System informacji menedżerskiej jako instrument zarządzania strategicznego w firmie, praca doktorska*, Akademia Ekonomiczna w Krakowie, Kraków 2005.

Wyroba A., Tkaczyk J., Zarządzanie innowacjami. *ABC Jakości. Badania. Certyfikacja. Notyfikacja. Quality Review*, 2, 2015, p. 5.

Wyrozębski P., *Metodyka PMI: Project Management Body of Knowledge, [w:] Metodyki zarządzania projektami*, Wydawnictwo Bizarre, Warszawa 2011, p. 71–73.

Wysocki R. K., *Efektywne zarządzanie projektami. Tradycyjne, zwinne, ekstremalne*, Helion, Gliwice 2013, pp. 18, 104, 477.

Yeo D., The value of management flexibility. *International Journal of Project Management*, 21(4), 2002, p. 241.

Zadora H., *Fuzje i przejęcia na rynku kapitałowym. Motywy, okoliczności i warunki oraz procedury, procesy i struktury*, Wydawnictwo Uniwersytetu Ekonomicznego w Katowicach, Katowice 2011, p. 61.

Zaorska A., *Integracja europejska w kontekście globalizacji*, Zeszyty Naukowe KGŚ SGH, Warszawa 2000, pp. 14–21.

Zieleniewski J., *Organizacja i zarządzanie*, Wydawnictwo Naukowe PWN, Warszawa 1960, p. 477.

Zieleniewski J., *Organizacja i zarządzanie*, PWN, Warszawa 1975, p. 226.

Zioło Z., Wpływ pandemii na zmiany zachowań podmiotów gospodarczych. *Prace Komisji Geografii Przemysłu Polskiego Towarzystwa Geograficznego*, 35(2), 2022, p. 20.

Żurawik B., *Zarządzanie marketingiem w przedsiębiorstwie*, PWE, Warszawa 1996, p. 110.

Zwikael O., The relative importance of the PMBOK® Guide's nine knowledge areas during project planning. *Project Management Journal*, 40(4), 2009, pp. 94–103.

Index